POLICY REFORM IN
AMERICAN AGRICULTURE

POLICY REFORM IN
AMERICAN
AGRICULTURE

Analysis and Prognosis

DAVID ORDEN

ROBERT PAARLBERG

TERRY ROE

THE UNIVERSITY OF CHICAGO PRESS

Chicago and London

David Orden is professor of agricultural and applied economics at Virginia Polytechnic Institute and State University. In 1998–99 he was a visiting professor in the Department of Economics and the Institute for International Studies at Stanford University.

Robert Paarlberg is professor of political science at Wellesley College and faculty associate at the Weatherhead Center for International Affairs at Harvard University. His recent books include *Leadership Abroad Begins at Home: U.S. Foreign Economic Policy After the Cold War* (1995) and *Countrysides at Risk: A Political Geography of Sustainable Agriculture* (1994).

Terry Roe is professor of applied economics and director of the Center for Political Economy at the University of Minnesota.

The University of Chicago Press, Chicago 60637
The University of Chicago Press, Ltd., London
© 1999 by The University of Chicago
All rights reserved. Published 1999

Printed in the United States of America
08 07 06 05 04 03 02 01 00 99   1 2 3 4 5

ISBN: 0-226-63264-4

Library of Congress Cataloging-in-Publication Data
Orden, David.
Policy reform in American agriculture : analysis and prognosis /
David Orden, Robert Paarlberg, Terry Roe.
         p.   cm.
Includes bibliographical references and index.
ISBN 0-226-63264-4 (cloth : alk. paper)
1. Agriculture and state—United States.   I. Paarlberg, Robert L.
II. Roe, Terry L.   III. Title.
HD1761.O67 1999
338.1′873—dc21   98-55710
                                                                              CIP

⊗ The paper used in this publication meets the minimum requirements
of the American National Standard for Information Sciences—Permanence of Paper
for Printed Library Materials, ANSI Z39.48-1992.

Contents

Tables

THIS BOOK EXPLORES alternative strategies for attaining policy reform in American agriculture. We trace the evolution of agriculture in the United States from the depression-era origins of modern policy, through the labor outmigration and growth of the 1950s and 1960s, into the tumultuous macroeconomic instability of the 1970s and 1980s, and finally to the emergence of a mostly competitive and wealthy commercial farm sector at the turn of the twenty-first century. Throughout our analysis, we concentrate on the main forces that have driven changes to agricultural policy. We demonstrate that many of the farm programs of the 1930s New Deal have undergone substantial reform, despite a firm grip on the policy process by farm lobbies and congressional agricultural committees. The most successful reforms have facilitated the structural transformation of agriculture and the more efficient operation of markets by "cashing out" programs that once restricted supplies and propped up commodity prices, turning these interventions toward less intrusive direct payments to farmers.

Changes to farm policy have also been driven by short-term market conditions, and by the evolving politics of legislative coalition building. We analyze the scope of past reform efforts, examine the modest contributions of international negotiations to domestic policy, and evaluate in detail the circumstances under which more substantive changes were made unilaterally by Congress in 1996. Throughout our discussion, we contrast the partially successful reform strategy of a cash out with alternatives that would either slowly diminish farm program entitlements or abruptly end interventions, with or without compensation. We assess future policy contingencies, emphasizing the uncertainty concerning whether further reforms will be pursued. While our tone is one of analysis more than advocacy, we argue that the partial reform of farm policy has not gone far enough to eliminate economic distortions and unnecessary program costs. We call for a strengthening and widening of recent farm policy changes in the years to come: the programs still dependent on market interventions should be cashed out, and all cashed-out programs, starting with those for which there were significant reforms in 1996, should be progressively eliminated.

Policy Reform in American Agriculture culminates from research undertaken from October 1994 to September 1996 with support of a grant from the Cooperative Research, Education and Extension Service (CRESS) of the United States Department of Agriculture. Our initial objective was to examine the interface of domestic policy and international trade agreements as determinants of the global competitiveness of U.S. agriculture. The November 1994 midterm election brought the first Republican-controlled Congress in forty years, and the looming farm bill debate was enveloped in a larger, and chiefly domestic, battle over the role and size of the federal government. When a market boom in 1995–96 then brought the highest farm commodity prices in twenty years, an economic twist was added to the new political circumstances. The Republican Congress took the opportunity presented by temporarily high prices to legislate some significant reforms, but other farm policies remained basically intact.

In response to these events, our work turned increasingly toward a qualitative analytical assessment of when agricultural policy can be reformed and how far such reforms can go. We were encouraged by experienced colleagues to develop this analysis in both a historical and a forward-looking perspective. The result over the next twenty-four months was a collaboration between David Orden and Robert Paarlberg to examine and describe the economic and political determinants of farm policy, resulting in *Policy Reform in American Agriculture*. We share senior authorship and have sought to present the best of our interdisciplinary synthesis. Throughout the manuscript drafting, Terry Roe served as valued reactor and reviewer. His contributions were particularly significant in the early phases of the project.

We are also indebted to many other farm policy participants and observers. Our fieldwork was aided in 1995 and 1996 by contacts in and out of government, on both sides of the political aisle. Among those who gave generously of their time, we would especially like to thank Wayne Boutwell, Keith Collins, Randy Jones, John Keeling, Bruce Knight, Bill O'Conner, J.B. Penn, Peter Vitaliano, and Pat Westhoff. We also benefited from comments at field meetings with farmers and from seminars at our institutions and the International Agricultural Trade Research Consortium. Constructive early suggestions were received from Sandra Batie, Harold Breimyer, Carol Brookins, Barbara Craig, Otto Doering, Christine Fastnow, Harold Guither, John Odell, Wayne Moyer, Phil

Paarlberg, Dan Pearson, Tim Peavey, Charles Riemenschneider, Lyle Schertz, John Stovall, Robert Thompson, Stefan Tangermann, and Luther Tweeten. Harry Ayer aided in publication of two early assessments of the farm bill developments.

Other colleagues assisted our inquiry at a later stage, when we began to sort out the implications of the new farm bill. We are particularly indebted to discussants at a May 1997 workshop at the National Center for Food and Agricultural Policy: John Campbell, Lynn Daft, Bruce Gardner, Dale Hathaway, D. Gale Johnson, and Ann Tutwiler. Helpful comments also were offered by Tim Josling, Anne Krueger, and Dan Sumner; in seminar discussions at the University of California, Davis, North Carolina State University, Stanford University, and Yale University; and at a session of the American Agricultural Economics Association. Written reviews were generously provided by Willard Cochrane and Vernon Ruttan of the University of Minnesota, by two anonymous reviewers for the University of Chicago Press, and at key junctures in the development of the manuscript by D. Gale Johnson, professor emeritus at the University of Chicago, and J. Paxton Marshall, professor emeritus at Virginia Polytechnic Institute and State University.

Finally, a few individuals shared their insights with us from the beginning to end of the project. To these friends we especially express our thanks: Howard Conley of the House Agriculture Committee, Joe Glauber of the Office of the Secretary of Agriculture, Jerry Hagstrom of the National Journal, Dale Hathaway of the National Center for Food and Agricultural Policy, David Hull of the Congressional Budget Office, and Don Paarlberg, professor emeritus at Purdue University. Kim Brauer, Jennifer Kittle, Rachel Miller, and Dot Wonorowski provided technical support at different stages of the work.

We believe that American agriculture is poised on the verge of another era of remarkable productivity growth and change. Our analysis demonstrates the economic promise of bringing this potential to fruition, along with the political contingencies that stand in the way of fully realizing its benefits. We thank the many individuals who have helped shape our assessments, and take final responsibility for the arguments we present and proposals we make for farm policy reform.

The Political Problem of Farm Policy Reform

FEDERAL GOVERNMENT POLICIES to subsidize farmers were initiated in the United States more than sixty years ago during the Great Depression, when world agricultural markets had collapsed and farmers were numerous and impoverished. Since that time, a process of modernization and restructuring has transformed American agriculture almost beyond recognition. Successive technological innovations have raised output levels and reduced per-unit production costs, and large parts of the farm sector have become engaged once again in commercial sales to world markets. Only a small fraction of the national labor force remains employed in agriculture, and those who own commercial farms are now generally wealthier than their fellow citizens who are not farmers.

As this transformation of agriculture proceeded, the federal farm programs of the New Deal era became increasingly obsolete. Support of farm prices did little to ease the outmigration of labor; supply controls damaged U.S. competitiveness; and as farmers became more prosperous, income transfers no longer benefited a disadvantaged segment of the national economy. Policy reforms along two dimensions became imperative. First, to permit an efficient expansion of markets, it was necessary to intervene less through price guarantees, acreage restrictions, export subsidies, and import barriers. Second, while removing market interventions, the cost of farm support programs to taxpayers somehow had to be constrained.

This book explores four alternative strategies for achieving these farm policy reform objectives. The strategies we consider differ by the speed of their implementation, and by the levels of compensation paid to past program beneficiaries. We evaluate the economic and political forces that have determined the success and failure of past reform efforts within this framework, and examine the uncertain prospects for adoption of further reform measures.

When the first Republican-controlled Congress in forty years wrote a new farm law in 1996—the Federal Agriculture Improvement and Reform (FAIR) Act—it was widely hailed as a substantial departure from the scope and costs of past farm programs. Our analysis and subsequent events suggest caution. The changes to farm policy made in 1996 were expensive, incomplete, and not necessarily permanent. The Republican members of Congress who authored the FAIR Act were not the most outspoken critics of farm support policies, but among their strongest traditional defenders. They were critical of some aspects of past program implementation, and they initiated market-liberalizing changes in several policy instruments. But Congress failed in 1996 to repeal legislation (the agricultural acts of 1938 and 1949) that continues to authorize intrusive government interventions. To avoid reversion to the terms of this antiquated legislation when the FAIR Act expires, Congress will have to write yet another farm bill, under conditions that may not be propitious for reform. Thus, the central policy reform problem in American agriculture endures: the problem of removing programs and entitlements that have lost their original justification.

Farm Policy Reform in Historical Context

Efforts to reform farm policy have been underway for a long time. In chapter 1, we examine the origins of this struggle, briefly describing the early evolution of agriculture as an export-oriented sector of the American economy, the collapse of farm exports and prices after the First World War, and the federal policy interventions to alleviate agriculture's desperate plight during the Great Depression. During this emergency, President Franklin D. Roosevelt's New Deal administration sponsored "temporary" remedial measures to control supplies and purchase surplus production of storable farm commodities. When the emergency ended, the New Deal farm programs proved not to be so temporary. Farm interest groups that had been strengthened by the operation of the new programs lobbied Congress effectively to extend supply controls and raise price levels. Problems then arose when the farm sector began to undergo rapid and dramatic transformation after the Second World War. Adoption of modern technologies caused production costs and farm commodity prices (adjusted for inflation) to move downward, where they butted against the legislated support levels. Consolidation brought increased productivity, and the number of independent farms plummeted in the 1950s and 1960s as millions of marginal farmers and farmworkers sought employment outside of agriculture. Price-support programs did little to cushion this difficult labor transition, because their benefits were capitalized into asset values with little effect on the incomes of farm labor or returns to farm capital.

In chapter 2, we turn from the economic dynamics of the structural transformation of agriculture to the politics of farm policy reform. We summarize relevant theories of interest-group behavior and political action that help explain why the New Deal–era farm programs have proved resistant to change and so difficult to remove. We then examine the significant efforts made to reduce the cost and intrusiveness of farm policies through unilateral postwar domestic legislation. Powerful farm lobby groups resisted the most radical efforts to eliminate price supports, production controls, and government-assisted crop storage and disposal programs, yet one crucially important change did take place. Starting in the 1960s, a gradual shift was made in some programs (particularly those for export crops): instead of seeking to boost market prices through production controls and government purchases, farm income began to be supported with direct cash payments. This was an incomplete version of reform, but it gave more latitude for markets to operate, and it was the only reform path that proved acceptable to the farm groups themselves.

The costs of farm policy were temporarily masked during the 1970s, when support levels fell behind inflation, and when markets tightened as crop exports soared. Expecting inflation to continue, Congress ratcheted nominal price-support levels upward; then when tight monetary policies were embraced in the 1980s, exports and market prices fell and farm program expenditures rose sharply, even with extensive supply controls reimposed. This prompted an important farm policy debate in 1985, but the outcome was only a partial reform victory. Price-support levels were lowered, offset by even larger direct cash payments. The intent was to revive overseas demand for U.S. farm products, but budget costs reached record levels.

In chapter 3, we examine an ambitious additional effort made between 1986 and 1993 to bring about greater farm policy reform through international negotiations in the trade policy forum provided by the Uruguay Round of the General Agreement on Tariffs and Trade (GATT). With market prices low and farm program costs high worldwide in 1986, this international negotiation strategy seemed compelling as an alternative to unilateral policy change. If several industrial nations could agree to reduce their domestic farm supports simultaneously, the adjustments borne by farmers giving up subsidies in any one country would be diminished, because subsidized production overseas would no longer depress world prices. Farm lobby objections to reform as "unilateral disarmament" might then be minimized.

The long international reform negotiation achieved only limited results. The seven years of multilateral talks (and related efforts to reach regional trade agreements) helped accelerate progress abroad, particularly in Europe, but added little or nothing to the pace of reform in the United States. During the Uruguay Round, U.S. farm lobbies found new ways to resist reforms. They continued to reject unilateral steps, and began arguing for more subsidies as "bargaining chips" to win a better multilateral deal. The international Agreement on Agriculture was finally reached in December 1993, committing GATT countries to an elaborate set of farm policy obligations. Yet, these obligations had already been watered down enough to ensure that most existing U.S. policies would be in compliance. Import restrictions were scarcely reduced and export subsidies were allowed to continue. Direct payments tied to participation in supply control programs were specifically exempted from disciplines in the final Agreement on Agriculture, and decisions about the level of income transfers to farmers were left strictly a matter for domestic policy.

The Unexpected 1996 Farm Bill

Those seeking reform of farm policy in the United States had reason to be frustrated at the end of the Uruguay Round. The restructuring and consolidation agriculture had undergone in the 1980s contributed to improved competitiveness, but the magnitude of farm program expenditures and supply controls generated deep reform pessimism. Congress had renewed farm programs with little change in 1990, while the international negotiations had simultaneously been deadlocked. Neither the percentage of net farm income derived from government payments nor the percentage of available crop acreage idled under government programs had declined since the 1950s (see table 1). Thus, when debate over the terms of a new farm bill got underway in 1995, with few constraints imposed by the Uruguay Round, experienced insiders expected that once again little substantive change would materialize from the domestic legislative process.

The 1996 FAIR Act confounded this common expectation. The first Republican-controlled Congress in four decades took the opportunity presented by temporarily high crop prices (the highest in twenty years) to legislate several significant changes in farm policy. For export crops, the FAIR Act (the so-called Freedom to Farm law) gave farmers increased planting flexibility and ended the authority for annual supply controls through 2002. The FAIR Act also capped price-support levels

Table 1.   Farm Program Interventions, 1956–1995

	Net Farm Income Derived from Government Payments (%)	Available Crop Acreage Idled under Government Programs(%)
1956–1959	7.2	8.6
1960–1969	20.2	21.9
1970–1979	9.5	8.3
1980–1989	29.9	15.2
1990–1995	21.4	23.1

Source: Data are derived from annual statistics presented in tables 8 and 9.

for export crops at low nominal rates, and turned the direct cash subsidies into fixed payments, scheduled in advance and "decoupled" to disassociate them from market prices or farmers' planting decisions. These changes in policy instruments were important, even radical. They potentially reduced the intrusion of farm programs in many commodity markets and sought to improve government budget certainty. Republican Senator Richard Lugar, chair of the Senate Committee on Agriculture, Forestry and Nutrition, asserted that the FAIR Act would "change agricultural policy more fundamentally than any law in sixty years" (Schmitt 1996, A1). When the Democratic president signed this new law, an April 5 *New York Times* headline read, "Clinton Signs Farm Bill Ending Subsidies."

In chapter 4, we explore the claims that the FAIR Act conclusively reformed farm policy or ended subsidies. We describe in some detail the political negotiations and market developments that led to the unexpected changes in 1996. Initially, farm lobby groups fought with some success to minimize the budget disciplines they feared under the new Republican Congress. Many of these lobby groups favored greater planting flexibility, but they resisted any move toward price-support caps or decoupled subsidy payments. Their resistance led some Republican members of the House Agriculture Committee to oppose the Freedom to Farm bill when it was first presented in 1995, defying the wishes of Republican leaders, who nonetheless inserted a payments decoupling proposal into partisan omnibus budget legislation. This first attempt to legislate new farm policy failed when the Democratic president vetoed the Republican budget, forcing Congress to start over again on farm policy renewal. By then, thanks to a continued sharp rise in commodity prices, more support had crystallized for the once-controversial payments decoupling, which was included in a farm bill passed early in 1996. Democrats who continued to criticize the bill were outnumbered, and the president signed the FAIR Act into law.

In chapter 5, we examine the political economy of the FAIR Act in greater depth. We argue that the coincidence of two independent political and economic events provides the most compelling explanation for its enactment, while other factors that might have favored reform played surprisingly small roles. Without the shift to Republican Party control of Congress after the November 1994 elections, and without the equally unexpected interlude of rising market prices, the most important reforms in the FAIR Act would not have been undertaken. Republican agriculturalists took the lead in seeking the elimination of unpaid annual "acreage reduction" supply controls. This was a change specifically favored by larger commercial farmers and agribusiness interests, and one that had not been made as long as the Democratic Party had controlled Congress. It then took high prices and the prospect of a cash payments windfall to inspire the switch to decoupling. Neither the elimination of acreage reduction programs nor decoupling of payments from planting decisions and prices had a dramatic effect on production in the short run, because high farm prices would have resulted in few supply controls (or other production distortions for export crops), even under the previously existing programs. Still, an important experiment with new policy instruments had been launched. Democrats confronting such high prices might have opted to ratchet up the more traditional price and income supports, rather than seek decoupled payments or an end to supply control authority.

Contingent Future Policy

Even when it was adopted, there were reasons to be skeptical that the 1996 FAIR Act had permanently reformed farm policy. From the start it was expensive, yielding an immediate payments windfall to export crop producers. While authority for unpaid annual supply controls was revoked, the authority for *paid* idling of a large amount of cropland (one-tenth of the U.S. total) through a multiyear "conservation reserve" remained in place. Various market-intrusive import restrictions were also retained (for dairy products, sugar, and peanuts), export subsidies were reauthorized, and the 1938 and 1949 legislation threatened renewal of intrusive government supply controls and price supports. Then, when market prices fell in 1998, Congress and the president approved still more supplemental payments to farmers, doubling the cost of farm programs at a time when the FAIR Act was supposed to keep those costs fixed.

Might the 1996 FAIR Act evolve from this costly and limited move toward planting flexibility and decoupled cash payments for export crops into a more complete version of policy reform? In chapter 6, we delineate the forces that will drive future farm policy and describe the circumstances in which reforms might be advanced. Under one set of circumstances (perhaps not likely, but at least possible), Congress might decide to move even further in a reform direction after the FAIR Act. If farm commodity prices in the marketplace rebound, and if Republicans retain control of Congress, farm lobby advocates could have trouble in 2002 arguing for another expensive extension of direct cash subsidies to export crop producers. If these subsidies are disciplined or ended, then interventions that have proven more resistant (sugar import restrictions, or wheat export subsidies, for example) might also succumb to reform. At this point, the limited reforms achieved by the FAIR Act would become more complete and more convincing.

Under less favorable circumstances, some of the FAIR Act results could be reversed by 2002 and further reform progress could become impossible. In at least one future scenario (again possible, though perhaps not likely), if farm commodity prices are low, the FAIR Act could be replaced with legislation that not only maintains direct subsidies to farmers, but does so once again through market-distorting interventions. Some influential congressional Democrats never accepted the decoupled payments approach, and the president vowed to somehow restore a "safety net" of support policies coupled to the market even as he signed the FAIR Act into law. Thus if Democrats regain control of Congress and market prices are low, key aspects of the FAIR Act could be overturned. Under these circumstances, decoupling would come to be portrayed as an expensive experiment that gave farmers a quick windfall but then malfunctioned and harmed agriculture, discrediting the reform idea.

Alternative Reform Strategies

Our analysis of the political problem of policy reform in American agriculture reflects upon the broader question of how public policies conferring benefits on specific constituencies can be constrained or eliminated once the original justification for those benefits has weakened or disappeared. Dismantling past policies that are no longer needed, and are no longer working properly, is a formidable task in the face of organized interests prepared to defend them, but strategies are available to weaken or remove such programs.

Compensation	Speed of Implementation	
	Slow	Fast
Yes	Cash out	Buyout
No	Squeeze out	Cutout

Figure 1.   Alternative Reform Strategies

In the abstract, four alternative strategies are available to advocates of policy reform in agriculture (see figure 1). Farm program interventions can either be dismantled slowly or quickly, and either with or without compensation. A slow, compensated transformation of programs we call a *cash out*. A quicker, compensated termination we call a *buyout*. A slow, uncompensated diminution is a *squeeze out*, while a quick, uncompensated elimination is a *cutout*.

If the reform goal is to reduce budget costs as well as market distortions, the cash-out and buyout approaches might seem the least attractive. The cash-out option in particular may lead only to a slow reduction in market interventions, perhaps with no end to cash compensations. This least attractive strategy, however, is the only one that has proven politically attainable and durable since the 1960s.

Cash Out

A cash out is only a partial approach to reform because it leaves market intervention policies in place for some time and imposes a potentially open-ended burden on taxpayers, all the while allowing farm lobby groups and their supporters in Congress and at the U.S. Department of Agriculture (USDA) to retain dominance over the policy process. The cash-out strategy gives markets more room to operate, and has been particularly favored by export-oriented farmers and agribusinesses as a way to attain sales abroad without sacrificing government support for farmers at home. An early proposal to cash out farm price guarantees was made by the secretary of agriculture in 1949, under the Brannan Plan. This early proposal was rejected by Congress, in part because of extensive reliance on supply controls as it moved toward cash payments. Not until the 1960s, when it became clear that high price-support levels were hurting U.S. farm exports, did a belated shift begin toward letting market prices fall and instead using cash payments to support farm income. This cash out has provided only a partial solution to the larger policy reform problem, but it may eventually serve as a foundation for more ambitious and less expensive squeeze-out measures. The gains from pursuing a cash out in the meantime are fewer market distortions, fewer production restraints, and more competitive export pricing.

Buyout

This approach would bring a quick end to farm support programs, with political resistance from farmers overcome through an up-front windfall of temporary compensatory payments. A short-run increase in subsidy payments might be a cost-effective way to proceed (if linked to an ironclad guarantee of permanent program demise), and might be justified as compensation for any drop in farm asset values associated with an end to farm subsidies. This reform strategy is not easily accomplished in farm legislation, where no Congress has ever considered itself bound by the decisions of a predecessor. Buyouts have been attempted in the past, most notably in the 1985 farm bill debate when Senators Rudy Boschwitz and David Boren offered a proposal to drop traditional farm supports and replace them with a generous but temporary stream of decoupled transition payments. This buyout, which we examine closely for some of its similarities to the FAIR Act, failed to catch hold in 1985: it was rejected simultaneously by budget officials, who thought it was too expensive, and by farmers, who thought it was not generous enough. The substantial cash payments made to farmers under the 1996 FAIR Act were occasionally represented at the time as a buyout, but they bought little assurance of final program termination.

Squeeze Out

A slow squeeze-out strategy would reduce the market-distorting effects of farm programs without cash compensation. If the costs of program participation increase over time while the growth of benefits is constrained, farmers might be induced to quit the programs voluntarily, thus avoiding a difficult final legislative confrontation. This strategy can be pursued explicitly, through a legislated or administered withdrawal of market interventions or cash payments, or it can be pursued tacitly, by fixing benefits in nominal terms, then allowing inflation to erode their real value. A slow squeeze out also can be accomplished by targeting benefits only to certain categories of farmers, or by tying those benefits to a progressively more onerous set of performance requirements, such as stringent environmental regulations.

It may seem surprising with such a variety of options available that little reform has been attained through squeeze outs. Attempts made to lower farm support prices during the 1950s had the intent of a squeeze out, but farm production costs were falling so rapidly that program participation remained attractive to most farmers. An implicit squeeze out seemed underway in the inflationary 1970s, but farm program defenders were able to ratchet intervention up to levels that proved costly when inflation itself was later squeezed out of the economy. The squeeze-out approach was unattractive in the past partly because of the reliance of commodity-support programs on production controls; in order for these controls to be effective, rates of participation in the programs had to be kept high. This constraint was lifted under the FAIR Act, because payments were decoupled from production. If Congress in 2002 extends the decoupled payments initiated in 1996 but mandates a progressively lower level of cash compensation, then advances to the reform process under the FAIR Act might evolve into a more far-reaching squeeze out.

Cutout

The abrupt cutout strategy would produce a quick and explicit end to farm support programs, without cash compensation. Among other things, under this approach the permanent legislation for these programs would have to be repealed. This approach, which would leave markets free to function and taxpayers free from the burden of paying cash subsidies to farmers, has been favored by the most radical farm program critics. Virtual cutouts were proposed several times by Republican presidents in the 1970s and 1980s, but in each case a bipartisan coalition of agriculturalists in Congress rejected the administration's plan immediately, then wrote their own farm bills to keep existing support levels mostly intact. Farmers are likely to view any sharp termination of cash payments as an unacceptable cutout, despite any windfall of decoupled payments they earlier received when market prices were high. Whether political prospects for a cutout have nevertheless been improved by operation of the FAIR Act is an important question we address in chapter 6.

While the FAIR Act might evolve under the right circumstances into a slow squeeze out, a permanent buyout, or even a cutout, it is not evident that Congress was following any of these strategies coherently in 1996. Clearly it did not achieve a cutout, because the FAIR Act left permanent legislation in place and provided generous cash subsidies to farmers in the short run. Just as clearly Congress was not advancing a squeeze out with the FAIR Act, because the generous new decoupled payments it authorized were much greater than expected, and so unencumbered by regulations and easy for farmers to obtain that voluntary program participation increased as a result. The FAIR Act also failed to ensure a buyout of farm programs, because it maintained permanent legislation and a baseline for continued farm program spending.

The reform path Congress took in the 1996 act was, in fact, the familiar one of a heavily compensated cash out of farm programs, with all the benefits and risks that the cash-out strategy has historically entailed. Under the FAIR Act, a market-oriented cash out was advanced for export crops, with payments more fully decoupled than ever before—but with high budget costs. The farm subsidy budget baseline was extended and provision of additional subsidies (as in 1998) never was precluded. Inconsistencies persist, with policies for import-competing commodities still market distorting; for these commodities, not even a cash out was secured under the FAIR Act. If the farm lobby remains powerful, and the agriculture committees in Congress retain control of the policy process, there are ready venues under the FAIR Act either for traditional program defense or for the design of new support programs to benefit another generation of organized farm lobby constituents.

In the chapters that follow we document these assertions and examine future farm policy contingencies in depth and detail. Our analytic tone remains more positive than normative. The message of our analysis is that a political battle to eliminate market interventions and terminate farm subsidies still remains to be fought. In a concluding chapter, we draw several inferences from the farm policy reform history we examine, and we consider how reform might best proceed after the FAIR Act, with the goal of bringing policy more in line with the evolving realities of the farm sector. We suggest a strategy of extending the cash-out approach to the import-competing commodity programs that have so far eluded reform, and we describe ways to shift from a modest cash out to a more ambitious squeeze out that could end some outdated and costly farm sector interventions. Even in our final chapter, we are reform-minded analysts and observers more than advocates. The recent political economy of American farm policy provides us with plenty of action to observe and explain.

Chapter One

New Deal Policies and a Changing Farm Sector

FARM COMMODITY-SUPPORT PROGRAMS were first enacted in the United States in 1933 as one part of President Franklin D. Roosevelt's New Deal. A collapse of world farm commodity markets after the First World War had ended an export-sustained nineteenth-century expansion of American agriculture; this was followed by a devastating economy-wide financial crisis during the Great Depression. A government response to this damaging crisis had some justification, and the New Deal programs for agriculture produced some positive effects at the time. Yet these new farm programs did not expire when the crisis ended. The New Deal interventions created institutional mechanisms through which farm lobby groups continued to influence national policy, and the farm support programs established in the 1930s became consolidated by the end of the Second World War.

As politically powerful farm groups and farm state members of Congress were defending and perpetuating the New Deal programs, the structure and financial condition of U.S. agriculture began to undergo what would become a remarkable transformation. By the early 1950s, levels of farm outputs were increasing rapidly as a result of technological innovations. Supply growth in excess of increases in demand caused prices of farm products to fall relative to prices of other goods and services. An enormous labor adjustment out of agriculture took place as low-cost mechanical, chemical, and biological inputs were brought into the production process, as rural education and infrastructure improved, and as the nonfarm economy grew. This brought a transformation from labor-intensive to technology- and capital-intensive agriculture unimaginable at the turn of the century, or even in the 1930s. As one result, the majority of those who remain on farms seventy years later are no longer economically disadvantaged. The wages, incomes, and wealth of farmers have all gone up, despite declining farm commodity prices.

The markets growing most rapidly for American farm products also became global once again rather than domestic. Starting in the 1960s, and strengthening substantially in the early 1970s, this reemergence of commercial world markets was advantageous for agriculture but forced American farmers to compete directly with farmers from other exporting nations. A growing dependence on international markets turned the New Deal–era practice of controlling supply to boost crop prices with supply controls into a liability that impaired U.S. agriculture's global competitiveness.

As the technological and economic transformation of agriculture progressed, the "temporary" farm policies improvised in the 1930s thus became unsuited for the farm sector that emerged. Supply-control and price- and income-support programs did not have much long-term effect on the earnings of farm labor, or on the rate of return to farm capital, but continuation of these programs was costly to taxpayers and consumers, and the benefits of the policies were concentrated in the asset values of a decreasing number of increasingly wealthy farm owners. Still, the traditional programs were hard to change. In this chapter, we examine the origins of New Deal–era farm programs, describe the transformation that has since occurred in agriculture, and show that the farm commodity-support programs have lost their original rationale.

The Political Origins of Farm Programs

Agriculture has traditionally been an export-oriented sector of the American economy. The original colonies were founded as a source of agricultural products and raw materials, and farms accounted for more than three-fourths of the total value of U.S. exports into the nineteenth century, with tobacco and then cotton the quintessential export crops. More than 75 percent of the tobacco produced was shipped abroad in this early period, and more than 80 percent of cotton output was exported in the 1830s. By the time of the American Civil War, cotton alone accounted for more than 50 percent of total U.S. export value (Lipsey 1994).

During the second half of the nineteenth century, westward expansion tripled the farming area of the United States. A sharp decline in farm prices after the Civil War, a movement into marginal farming areas in the newly settled lands, and a general price-level deflation in the latter part of the century created hardships for farmers. Industrial development progressed rapidly during this period, and agriculture's relative importance in the national economy declined. Productivity growth in U.S. agriculture lagged behind manufacturing in the 1800s, and a growing population of urban workers and immigrants increased domestic demand for farm products. Nonetheless, the expansion of cultivated land area might have driven real farm prices downward, or

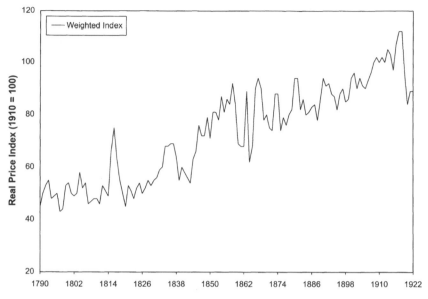

Figure 2.   Real Prices of Farm Products, 1790–1922
Source: Alvin H. Hansen, "The Effects of Price Fluctuations on Agriculture," *Journal of Political Economy* 33 (1925): 196–216.

falling real prices might have curtailed the extension of farming acreage, had it not been for the strength of foreign demand. Growing European demand, aided by declining freight rates that lowered effective prices abroad, helped sustain an upward trend (subject to substantial cyclical variations) in prices of farm goods relative to prices of nonfarm goods and services, as shown in figure 2. Foreign markets absorbed one-third of the increase in total agricultural output, and almost one-half of the increase for wheat was sold overseas. Agriculture continued to account for almost 50 percent of the total value of exports from the United States in 1900. These exports provided much of the revenue needed to service an international debt (estimated at nearly 20 percent of annual national output by 1897) that had accumulated as capital inflows had financed growth of the nation.

Nineteenth-century agricultural policy essentially embraced a laissez-faire approach toward the functioning of farm markets. Even so, numerous government measures aided development of agricultural production or helped facilitate distribution. Canal and railroad transportation infrastructures were subsidized. National policies to provide new settlers with access to land culminated in the Homestead Act of

1862; the U.S. Department of Agriculture and the system of Land-Grant colleges were founded in that year as well. The Land-Grant college system was strengthened by federal funding of agricultural experiment stations in 1887. But calls for even modest interventions in agricultural markets, such as special authority for farm cooperatives or farm credit assistance, were rejected. The more radical proposals of the 1890s Populist Party also fell short of enactment.[1]

First World War Boom and Collapse

Due to a slowdown in expanding farmed acreage, the early 1900s were a relatively prosperous period for existing farm owners in the United States. The onset of the First World War brought a further farm export boom, real growth, and inflation. Net farm income doubled in nominal terms to $8.9 billion between 1914 and 1918, as prices received by farmers for crops rose 102 percent and for livestock 79 percent.[2] Farmers responded by taking on debt to expand their production capacity. The boom extended past the 1918 armistice, through 1919, and into 1920, as the nominal value of agricultural exports soared to $3.8 billion, almost four times (in real terms, more than twice) its prewar level. Agricultural leaders feared a postwar collapse of prices, as had followed the Civil War, but hoped it could be "restricted to a short period or avoided altogether" (Fain 1920, 8). They erroneously speculated that in the long run food was "almost certain to call forth a larger share of workers' incomes" (Warren 1919, 14). This speculation drew more from their memories of nineteenth-century events than from an accurate understanding of the economic realities of the twentieth century.

A postwar collapse came late in 1920, primarily due to a drop in foreign demand. Crop prices fell 40 percent between spring planting and fall harvest, and farm export values and net income were halved in this single year. Over the next decade, exports to Europe remained limited by a depressed economy, German war reparation payments, generally high postwar foreign debts, and some recovery of European domestic

---

1. Benedict (1953) offers a definitive reference on the early history of American agriculture and agricultural policy. Cochrane (1993) provides a general narrative description of the forces influencing agricultural development since the colonial period.

2. Historical data series of the USDA provide a rich factual basis for describing the evolution of American agriculture since the First World War. These series provide detailed statistics on many facets of production, prices, investment, input utilization, trade, and other economic aspects of the farm sector. We draw extensively on the USDA data in this and subsequent chapters.

Table 2.   Balance of U.S. Agricultural and Merchandise Trade (in Billions of Dollars), 1901–1949

	Agriculture	Merchandise		Agriculture	Merchandise
1901	.53	.67	1926	−.64	.39
1902	.42	.48	1927	−.37	.68
1903	.39	.39	1928	−.38	1.04
1904	.36	.47	1929	−.33	.84
1905	.22	.40	1930	−.40	.78
1906	.38	.52	1931	−.12	.33
1907	.37	.45	1932	−.08	.29
1908	.44	.67	1933	−.02	.23
1909	.21	.35	1934	−.05	.48
1910	.08	.19	1935	−.27	.24
1911	.26	.52	1936	−.38	.03
1912	.17	.55	1937	−.81	.27
1913	.21	.65	1938	−.26	1.13
1914	.12	.47	1939	−.32	.86
1915	.48	1.09	1940	−.50	1.40
1916	.17	3.09	1941	−1.12	1.80
1917	.37	3.28	1942	−.47	5.32
1918	.46	3.12	1943	.16	9.58
1919	1.65	4.02	1944	.53	10.33
1920	.17	2.95	1945	.46	5.65
1921	.55	1.98	1946	.98	4.80
1922	.55	.72	1947	.91	8.67
1923	−.28	.36	1948	.64	5.53
1924	−.01	.98	1949	.83	5.43
1925	.22	.68			

Note: Positive balances indicate a trade surplus, negative balances indicate a trade deficit.
Source: U.S. Department of Commerce, *Historical Statistics of the United States from Colonial Times to 1970* (Washington, D.C.: U.S. Government Printing Office, 1975).

farm output. The U.S. agricultural trade balance slipped into deficit for the first time in 1923 (see table 2). Farm prices and income remained low in the United States and debts became unserviceable, even though the rest of the economy rebounded from a brief recession and prospered throughout the 1920s.

The relatively depressed conditions in agriculture after the First World War came at a time when farmers in the United States were not a particularly well-organized or powerful constituency inside the political system.[3] Right up to the time of the 1929 stock market crash, agricul-

---

3. See Benedict (1953) and Cochrane (1993). Finegold (1982) and Alexander and Libecap (1998) also discuss the origins of farm programs. Hansen (1991) provides a thorough chronology of the congressional access and influence of farm lobby groups from 1919 through 1981.

ture experienced difficulty advancing its interests within the national public policy arena, especially relative to the interests of industry. Many poor and small farms were failing in the 1920s, yet price-boosting farm programs or income support programs were not enacted.

The dominant industrial interests sought to avoid schemes that would raise the prices paid by farm-product processors, or increase the urban cost of living, and hence drive up postwar wage demands. Industry benefited not only from low farm prices but also from generous trade protection policies, which were championed particularly by the Republican Party and which implicitly discriminated against export-oriented agriculture.[4] Farmers initially directed their ire at deflationary policies of the Federal Reserve Board established in 1913, blaming "tight money" for the collapse of farm prices, an argument made also by some prominent agricultural economists.[5]

Throughout this hard decade for agriculture of the 1920s, a so-called farm bloc in Congress sought macroeconomic and farm sector policies that would boost prices to levels that existed before the First World War. The farm bloc was supported by a newly formed national farm lobby organization, the American Farm Bureau Federation (AFBF, or Farm Bureau), which had a national membership of 450,000 families as early as 1922. Destined to become the largest farm membership organization, the Farm Bureau was strengthened by a close association at local and national levels with the Cooperative Extension Service established in 1914 by federal legislation to provide outreach education to farmers.

To obtain higher prices and incomes in the 1920s, farmers and their congressional representatives sought monetary reflation, extension of wartime export credit subsidies, improved domestic farm credit agencies, lower farm-to-market transportation costs, and strengthened

4. During the 1800s, tariffs were one of the principal government policies affecting agriculture. Average tariffs on dutiable imports exceeded 50 percent in the late 1820s, then fell below 20 percent by 1860. High tariffs during and after the Civil War provided protection to sugar and other import-competing agricultural products but negatively affected export-oriented commodities such as cotton, tobacco, wheat, and corn. Tariff levels fell again in the early 1900s; then the Fordney-McCumber tariff raised average protection to around 40 percent in 1921. This was followed by the Smoot-Hawley tariff in 1930, which pushed protection even higher. When the U.S. agricultural trade balance turned negative in the 1920s, some farm groups began demanding protection via high tariffs. See Benedict (1953) and Cochrane (1993) for discussions of these policies.

5. Orden (1990) reviews the arguments made about the collapse of agricultural prices and exports during the 1920s. George F. Warren (1928) of Cornell University was a leading proponent of the argument that the collapse of the money supply, not increased production, had depressed farm prices.

cooperative marketing. The farm bloc had some early legislative successes, and by the end of the decade the Republican administration and Congress had created the Federal Farm Board, authorized to lend $500 million to agricultural cooperatives for product merchandising and storage and processing facility construction. The Farm Board was limited to assisting voluntary efforts by farmers to improve marketing operations and the efficiency of their commercial activities. Its authority did not extend to any form of supply controls or guaranteed price supports.[6]

A prolonged battle to help farmers gain the trade protection then favored by the Republican Party was also fought by the farm bloc in the 1920s. Various "two-price" schemes (contained in the McNary-Haugen legislation) would have raised domestic farm prices to provide "parity" for agriculture with protected manufacturing, using export subsidies to dispose of farm output in excess of domestic consumption at whatever lower price levels the exports would attain on world markets. The farm bloc repeatedly failed to secure such a scheme to raise farm prices in the 1920s—three times it failed in Congress, and twice it was vetoed by a Republican president.

New Deal Policies

Farm commodity price-support programs were finally enacted in the early years of the Great Depression, after the election of a Democratic president and Congress, and after an economy-wide price collapse had deepened the crisis in the farm sector. After the stock market crash in October 1929, the contraction of the money supply was even more pronounced than in the previous decade and general deflation ensued, with farm prices falling most of all. The already low prices received by farmers fell by more than half again, while the prices farmers paid for nonfarm goods and services fell by only one-third. Net farm income for the entire nation dropped to $2 billion in 1932. Land prices, which peaked at $69 per acre in 1920 and dropped below $50 by 1930, now fell below $30. Agriculture, which still employed roughly one-quarter of the nation's workers, received only about 7 percent of the nation's much-reduced income. Farmers became desperate, and many turned to radical forms of direct economic and political action. They intercepted

6. The earlier legislation pursued successfully by the farm bloc included the Packers and Stockyard Act (1921), the Futures Trading Act (1921), the Capper-Volstead Cooperative Marketing Act (1922), and the Intermediate Credit Act (1923). None of this legislation authorized direct interventions to control commodity supplies or support market prices.

food shipments destined for urban areas, gathered as mobs to prevent farm foreclosure sales, and threatened those, including judges, who sought to take legal action against debtors.

Franklin D. Roosevelt assumed the presidency in 1933, following a sweeping nationwide electoral victory, with a commanding Democratic majority in both houses of Congress and a mandate to take decisive action. The workings of the "free market" had been so thoroughly discredited in public perception by three years of depression that Roosevelt pressed interventionist programs as a remedy. Roosevelt's recovery scheme for industry was the National Industrial Recovery Act (NIRA). His plans for agriculture were packaged together into the Agricultural Adjustment Act (AAA). Most of the original institutions and provisions of the NIRA were discarded within a few years, but those of the AAA were destined to last long beyond the emergency circumstances of their inception.

The radical plan of the NIRA was to establish "industry codes" to prop up prices and wages in part by restraining competition. It soon malfunctioned and collapsed under the weight of uninformed and incompetent government administration, plus intense opposition lobbying—first from big business and then from organized labor. By the time the Supreme Court declared the NIRA unconstitutional in 1935, the Roosevelt administration had already turned away from a centralized management approach in the industrial sector. Under the 1934 Reciprocal Trade Agreements Act, Roosevelt began to reverse the high tariff policies of the 1920s and to advocate free trade for industry.

The AAA was no less radical than the NIRA as an interventionist supply-control response to the emergency conditions of the depression, but both the real and the apparent performance of the AAA in the early 1930s built for it a stronger reputation and a more devoted and better organized constituency. When some supply management elements of the original AAA were also declared unconstitutional by the Supreme Court early in 1936, the political response was not to abandon the scheme, but to make whatever adjustments were necessary so that it could continue. A political alliance between farmers and the Progressive Era conservation movement (which had developed during the presidency of Theodore Roosevelt) supported land idling to control production when justified as resource conservation policy.[7] The AAA

---

7. See Cochrane 1993 for discussions of the Progressive Era conservation movement and other important agricultural legislation of that period, including the Reclamation Act

thus survived through Franklin Roosevelt's first term in office. When Roosevelt then swept to a second term later in 1936, carrying every single farm state with him in the process, a tradition of deep governmental involvement in the operations of farm markets became fully legitimized and more securely institutionalized.[8]

The original AAA was designed not by Congress or by farm organizations on the outside (the Farm Bureau had instead been championing the two-price plan) but rather by Roosevelt's "brain trust" inside the executive branch.[9] The starting point for these technocrats was an assumption that farm prices would not recover without production controls. Government constraints on domestic production or marketing designed to elevate agricultural prices had been recommended earlier by W. J. Spillman (1927) at USDA and John D. Black (1929) at Harvard University. This controversial proposition somewhat countered prevailing evidence that a financial and trade collapse, rather than a change in domestic supply conditions, had originally driven farm prices downward.[10] Nonetheless, supply controls, originally in the

---

(1902), the Food and Drug Act (1906), and, later, the establishment of Federal Land Banks (1916). Batie, Shabman, and Kramer (1985) also discuss the origins of the conservation movement and the New Deal–era alliance between farmers and conservationists.

8. In addition to the new AAA supply-control and price-support policies, other government programs to aid agriculture were strengthened or developed as part of the New Deal. These measures included enhanced credit institutions and assistance (the Farm Credit Act of 1933), subsidized crop insurance (included in 1938 agricultural legislation), and infrastructure investments under the Tennessee Valley Authority of 1933 and the Rural Electrification Act of 1936. Thus, a broad institutional infrastructure that had mostly been absent at the turn of the century was in place to implement government regulation and support activities for agriculture by the end of the New Deal. Benedict (1953) describes the origins of these policies. Rausser (1992) briefly discusses the political pressures to extend and expand this government regulation and assistance—and the reform challenges the resulting policies pose. A monograph series sponsored by the American Enterprise Institute addresses these challenges in detail for such agricultural policies as crop insurance, farm credit, environmental measures, food safety, and scientific research and development. See Sumner 1995 for summaries of these latter studies.

9. See Benedict 1953 for the origins and early history of the AAA, and Benedict and Hansen 1991 for further discussion of the early Farm Bureau price-support plans. The Farm Bureau quickly shifted its orientation toward the New Deal strategies, and its representatives were then instrumental in drafting and implementing the AAA.

10. Measures of farm output support the argument that the fall in farm prices, exports, and income originated mostly from changes in demand. An index of crop production averaged 67.1 from 1910 to 1919 and peaked at 76 in 1920. In response to the 1920 price collapse, the crop output index dropped to 65 in 1921, then recovered to an average of 71.7 during 1922–29 and an average of 71.0 during 1930–33. For livestock, the production index averaged 63.9 from 1910 to 1919, 70.1 in the 1920s, and 74.2 during 1930–33.

form of voluntary acreage reductions by farmers in return for cash "rental" payments by government, became the centerpiece of the original 1933 AAA.[11]

Because the AAA supply controls would require at least a season to take effect, Roosevelt's New Deal advisors believed that something more immediate was needed to bring financial relief to farmers. What they devised, in October 1933, was a system of "loaning" money to farmers who put crops in storage. Farmers could later pay back the loans with cash if prices rose enough to make the sale of their stored crops attractive. If prices did not rise, farmers could pay back the *nonrecourse* loans simply by forfeiting their crops—their collateral for the loans—to the government. The operation of this "commodity loan" program was entrusted to a new government agency, the Commodity Credit Corporation (CCC). The CCC, which was soon to emerge as the most important of all U.S. farm policy institutions, had its beginnings as just another one of the dozens of short-term emergency measures improvised by relatively autonomous executive branch officials during the early days of the New Deal.

In contrast to the NIRA, the emergency New Deal farm programs functioned tolerably well during Roosevelt's first term. The production control program proved only marginally effective in reducing output, but it did succeed in transferring—through the cash rental payments—much needed purchasing power to the farm sector.[12] These cash payments to farmers were essentially untargeted: the larger farms received the larger payments. But with incomes depressed on almost all farms, targeting of benefits was not a primary concern. If only the New Deal farm programs that were improvised in response to the economic emergency of the 1930s had been phased out once the emergency passed, there would be little reason to criticize them.

---

11. The AAA initially imposed supply controls on seven commodities: wheat, corn, cotton, rice, tobacco, hogs, and milk and milk products. Amendments to curtail supplies were added in 1934 for rye, flax, barley, grain sorghums, peanuts, sugar, and cattle, and in 1935 for potatoes. For other commodities (particularly many perishable goods), the AAA authorized marketing agreements to restrict the quantity and regulate the quality of products moving in interstate commerce. Section 22 of the AAA authorized quotas and tariffs on imports of agricultural commodities that threatened to interfere with the domestic supply-control programs.

12. Thirty-five million acres were taken out of production by the AAA in 1934, and payments to farmers between 1933 and 1936 totaled $1.1 billion.

Consolidation of the Farm Programs

Unfortunately, the farm programs of the early New Deal appeared to function so well and had such strong appeal to farm groups that some of their more dubious features were expanded and made permanent rather than reduced or eliminated. The most important of these features was the originally obscure commodity loan program of the CCC. This program exceeded all expectations in 1934, when prices were driven sharply upward by a severe drought that lasted through 1936. Farmers were able to sell their stored commodities at a profit and pay off their CCC loans with cash, so in its first year the CCC actually earned net revenue for the government. Secretary of Agriculture Henry A. Wallace immediately proposed an expansion of the program as a farm price stabilizing device, even describing it in Biblical terms as the nation's new "ever-normal granary" (Benedict 1953, 333).[13]

The CCC commodity loan programs began to malfunction when the power to set the "loan rates" at which crops could be forfeited to the government was taken over by Congress. These loan rates established a floor under market prices. When Congress legislated a renewal of the AAA in 1938, it mandated production controls and price-support loans for six crops (wheat, corn, cotton, rice, tobacco, and peanuts). The 1938 act also specified for the first time a precise parity formula for setting loan-rate levels. Under pressure from farm lobbies, Congress designed this formula to ensure that loan rates exceeded long-term commodity price trends. Farm program costs jumped to $763 million, more than double the average cost for the previous three years. In the hands of Congress, the commodity loan program had become a potentially expensive scheme for "stabilizing farm prices upward."[14] Specifically, the 1938 law made four policy instruments available to maintain price levels for the six "basic" storable crops: Payments could be made for shifting land into conservation uses; crop acreage allotments could be implemented to restrict production by farmers seeking to participate in the price-support programs; marketing quotas (enforced by penalties) could be imposed to restrict specific product sales if approved in a referendum by two-thirds of the growers; and, finally, the nonrecourse CCC loans themselves set the price floor.

13. The phrase "ever-normal granary" was first used by Wallace to describe the effects of government stockholding to stabilize commodity supplies and prices in June 1934.

14. This convenient phrase captures the dilemma of price stabilization programs subject to political pressure from lobbyists.

The farm lobbies that pressed Congress in the direction of supply controls and high price supports gained remarkable new political strength during the years of the depression, thanks partly to the intrusive operations of the AAA itself. To administer the AAA, the USDA was obliged in 1934 to establish more than 4,200 separate county-level production control committees. The Farm Bureau, which was already organized at the county level, found these new committees easy to dominate, and used them effectively as a setting in which to recruit and organize new dues-paying members. Between 1933 and 1940, Farm Bureau membership nearly tripled, even though the size of the total U.S. farm population was declining. A rival organization, the National Farmers Union (NFU), also grew in membership (see McConnell 1969, Finegold 1982, and Hansen 1991).[15]

Farm lobby power exercised primarily through Congress was thus able to convert the New Deal commodity loan program from a short-term stabilization device into a permanent farm subsidy mechanism. A degree of price-floor flexibility was retained in the 1938 farm law, but by this time Congress was granting most of the requests of price-support advocates. Loan rates were set higher and higher—initially at 70 percent of parity for corn and other basic crops in 1938 and 1939, and then at 85 percent of parity in 1941. By the onset of the Second World War, the Farm Bureau was not alone in calling for higher loan rates; the populist NFU was demanding 100 percent of parity. When market prices, boosted by wartime spending, made these high price supports temporarily affordable, Congress set the loan rates at 90 percent of parity. This would not be the last time farm groups would effectively use a temporary market price boom to ratchet up underlying support levels.

Despite the rising loan rates that Congress was busy legislating, little criticism of the commodity price-support programs was heard during the decade of the 1940s. At first, the wartime economic boom kept market prices well above the new loan rates. The war economy also helped move excess labor out of farming (the U.S. farm population declined from 30 million to 25 million).[16] This allowed an increase in farm size and put those who remained on the land in a much stronger financial condition. Bank deposits and currency holdings of farmers increased

15. The National Farmers Educational and Cooperative Union of America had been founded earlier in Texas in 1902.

16. Farm population characteristics are documented every ten years in the general census and every five years in a special census of agriculture.

fourfold during the war, mortgage debt declined, and farm real estate values increased by nearly 70 percent. Nor did the end of the Second World War bring a lapse back into depression, as some feared. Pent-up consumer demand for food exploded as wartime rationing controls were lifted, and generous government loans and grants to war-devastated nations in Europe (especially through the $12.3 billion Marshall Plan) boosted export demand. Thus for a time, high market prices masked the high commodity price supports still being legislated by Congress.

It was not until the mid-1950s, when farm prices fell at the end of the Korean War, that serious attention came to focus on the production distortions, and the taxpayer and consumer costs, associated with trying to maintain the intrusive commodity price supports originally established by the AAA in 1933. Yet, by the 1950s these price supports had become locked into the design of policy. A second generation of farmers was receiving the guarantees, and they had begun to view government support for agriculture as an enduring entitlement. They knew the rewards of the farm programs were being capitalized into property values and that those values might fall noticeably if the programs were ever terminated. The farm support programs came to be seen by farmers and farm lobby organizations not as dispensable subsidies but as part of an underlying social contract, almost the equivalent of a property right. Finding the political will to remove or change the terms of these programs was thus destined to prove difficult.

The Structural Transformation of Agriculture

Government farm commodity price-support programs had some justification during the depression years of the 1930s, when farmers were a relatively homogeneous, numerous, and conspicuously disadvantaged segment of the U.S. population. The economic health of many small rural communities was heavily dependent on the income of farmers in the 1930s; rural education and infrastructure lagged behind that of urban areas; and the domestic farm commodity markets that the government attempted to manage through supply-control and crop loan measures were temporarily closed off from global markets. All these fundamental structural characteristics would change in the years following the Second World War.

The changing circumstances of agriculture were easy for policy makers to miss initially, because a sharp drop in prices in the 1950s resembled the collapse after the First World War (see figure 3). That earlier

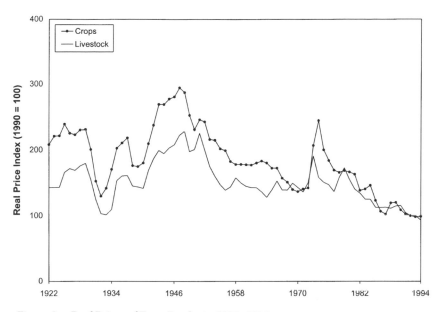

Figure 3.   Real Prices of Farm Products, 1922–1994
Source: Indices constructed from "Prices Received by Farmers" and "Gross National Product Deflator," *Economic Report of the President* (Washington, D.C.: U.S. Government Printing Office, 1996).

price collapse—caused almost entirely by a sudden collapse of demand—impoverished much of the farm population. Lower prices in the 1920s and 1930s had not reflected much real productivity growth within agriculture; farming was starting to become mechanized, but crop yields per acre planted had scarcely increased.[17] Meanwhile, because of high national unemployment, farmers had few alternative nonfarm opportunities through which to escape the low incomes they were earning.

In contrast, the downward trend in farm prices since the early 1950s has coincided with a long period of desirable growth in farm productivity and national economic expansion, rather than a renewed macroeconomic crisis or further collapse in export demand. As mechanical and

17. D. Gale Johnson (1997) emphasizes the recentness of the land productivity revolution. Significant agricultural scientific advancements began in the 1930s with the development of hybrid corn. This was followed over the next several decades with equally important improvements in the yields of grain sorghum, wheat, rice, and cotton. Overall, productivity growth in agriculture had lagged behind other sectors of the economy until about 1950.

biological capital and increasingly inexpensive purchased inputs have been substituted for labor and land in agricultural production, and as economies of scale have been achieved on larger farms, production costs have fallen. Although crop prices when adjusted for inflation have declined, the cost of producing those crops has fallen even faster, and the total volume of crops being sold has expanded. The trend decline of farm prices since 1950 thus reflects the success of the agricultural sector, not its failure or impoverishment. Nonfarm employment opportunities expanded in the national economy, and rising nonfarm wages eased the problem of labor adjustment accordingly. Many farmers and farmworkers left agriculture, either to retire or to seek more lucrative employment elsewhere. The productivity of those who remained to embrace the new production technologies and increase the size of their operations rose at a faster rate than in other sectors.

The success of this agricultural transformation in raising farm output and incomes in the United States since the Second World War does not imply that it was easily accomplished. Modernization required that individual farmers either "get big or get out."[18] Between the 1940s and the 1990s the number of independent farm operations fell from just over six million to around two million, and the number of farmworkers dropped even more sharply. In the 1950s and 1960s, farm labor use fell an average of more than 3 percent per year (see table 3 and figure 4). After 1970, labor use continued to decrease, from a much reduced base, at just under 2 percent per year. By the 1990s, less than 2 percent of the total U.S. labor force was employed on farms, down from 25 percent in the 1930s.

As the farm labor force diminished, the education and skill levels of remaining farmers and hired farmworkers improved, in large part as a result of public investments in rural education. The percentage of farm operators with a high school education or better rose from just 14.4 percent in 1949 to nearly 75 percent by the 1990s. The resulting improvements in skill levels were important to the efficiency of more technically advanced farm operations and to the well-being of the rural population.[19]

18. Above all others, this was the phrase that came to capture the challenge facing American farmers in the early postwar period.

19. The improved skill levels of the farm workforce reduced the estimated rate of decline of *quality-adjusted* labor in agriculture compared to the unadjusted rates (as shown in table 3).

Table 3.   Agricultural Output, Inputs, and Productivity, 1949–1991

	1949–59	1960–69	1970–79	1980–91	Overall (1949–91)
Output	1.93	1.37	2.54	0.67	1.58
Aggregate Inputs	0.05	−0.05	0.16	−0.79	−0.19
Labor					
Unadjusted	−3.76	−3.44	−1.82	−1.85	−2.68
Adjusted	−3.27	−2.87	−1.32	−1.51	−2.21
Land					
Unadjusted	−0.78	−0.50	−0.38	−0.27	−0.47
Adjusted	−0.58	−0.14	−0.09	−0.38	−0.30
Capital	1.38	0.68	−0.24	−1.19	0.10
Intermediate Inputs	3.83	2.88	1.81	−0.23	1.97
Productivity					
Labor	2.49	1.51	2.63	1.04	1.88
Multifactor	1.88	1.41	2.35	1.44	1.76

Source: Barbara J. Craig and Philip G. Pardey, "Productivity Measurement in the Presence of Quality Change," *American Journal of Agricultural Economics* 78, no. 5 (December 1996): 1349–54; and personal correspondence

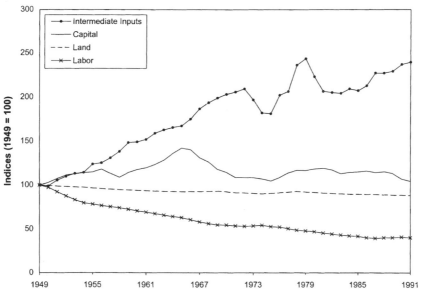

Figure 4.   Agricultural Input Usage, 1949–1991
Source: Barbara J. Craig and Philip G. Pardey, "Productivity Measurement in the Presence of Quality Change," *American Journal of Agricultural Economics* 78, no. 5 (December 1996): 1349–54; and personal correspondence.

The net outmigration of farm labor in the last half of the twentieth century was made possible in part by increased investments by farmers in tractors, machinery, buildings, land improvements, and biological capital (livestock breeding herds). The use of purchased intermediate inputs—especially improved seeds, chemical fertilizers, pesticides, and herbicides—has increased even more than capital investments (again, see table 3 and figure 4). Most good farmland has remained in production—the total acreage of available crop and pasture land remained essentially unchanged between the 1950s and the 1990s—while the new capital investments and purchased inputs have transformed production techniques. As basic research discoveries became embodied in commercial products, farm productivity and output soared. From 1949 through 1991, output grew an average of 1.58 percent per year (table 3), so total output volume in the 1990s was double that of the late 1940s, as shown in figure 5. The shift in input usage that occurred in conjunction with this output growth, and especially the productivity growth that accompanied investments and the use of purchased inputs, raised per worker labor productivity by some 400 percent from 1949 to

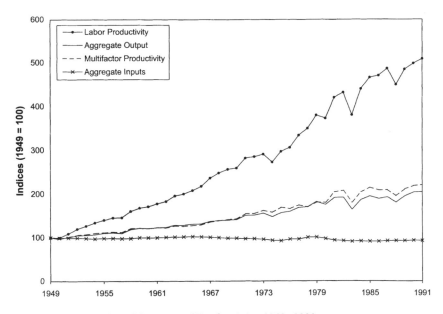

Figure 5.   Agricultural Output and Productivity, 1949–1991
Source: Barbara J. Craig and Philip G. Pardey, "Productivity Measurement in the Presence of Quality Change," *American Journal of Agricultural Economics* 78, no. 5 (December 1996): 1349–54; and personal correspondence.

1991 (figure 5). Yields per acre have risen equivalently.[20] This has made it possible for farm labor to earn much higher real wages despite declining farm commodity prices.

When the various resources used in production agriculture are all taken into account, total input use is estimated to have fallen by 0.19 percent annually since 1949 as substitutions for labor and land have occurred (table 3). Together with output growth, this implies that *multifactor* (or total) agricultural productivity has grown an average of 1.76 percent per year, more than doubling since the Second World War. Investments in publicly and privately funded agricultural research and development (R&D) have been important sources of the gains in productivity during the past five decades (see figure 6). Other sources of productivity growth have included public infrastructure investments, such as rural roads and extensions of electricity and communications systems, and the availability of new materials incorporating modern technologies. As with public education, public sector investments in research, development, and infrastructure have contributed to the process of agricultural modernization.

Total farm output has expanded at a faster rate than aggregate (domestic and international) demand for U.S. farm products throughout most of the period since the Second World War. This experience contrasts with the nineteenth century, when aggregate demand growth generally outpaced the expansion of supply. The U.S. population growth rate had declined by the 1950s, and although consumers' incomes increased with postwar prosperity, they spent a relatively small share of their income gains on food; higher incomes brought greater demand growth for nonagricultural goods and services. The long downward trend in farm prices relative to nonfarm prices shown in figure 3 has thus resulted from increased agricultural productivity since the Second World War, together with demand for agricultural products that grew more slowly and was relatively unresponsive (in terms of quantities purchased) to price changes.

A schematic representation of the crucial labor-adjustment process as agriculture modernizes within the context of the national economy is shown in figure 7.[21] The national economy is represented simply by two

20. For example, from 1940–49 to 1990–97, corn yields increased from 34 to 121 bushels per acre; wheat yields from 17.1 to 37.6 bushels per acre; and rice yields from 2,080 to 5,690 pounds per acre (Warren Jr. 1998).

21. Figure 7 is based on the specific-factors general equilibrium model developed by Jones (1971). Floyd (1965) uses similar concepts in a partial equilibrium framework to analyze the effects of alternative farm support programs.

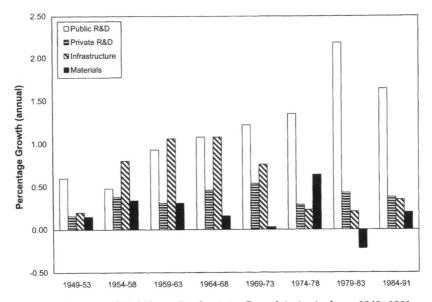

Figure 6.   Sources of Multifactor Productivity Growth in Agriculture, 1949–1991
Source: Munisamy Gopinath and Terry Roe, "Sources of Sectoral Growth in an Economy-Wide Context: The Case of U.S. Agriculture," *Journal of Production Analysis* 8 (1997): 293–310.

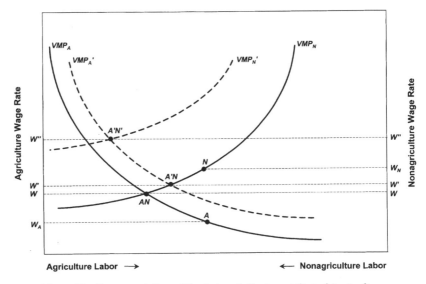

Figure 7.   Representation of the Labor Adjustment Out of Agriculture

sectors, agriculture (A) and nonagriculture (N). The national labor force is mobile between the two sectors, at least after a period of adjustment, but each sector is also assumed to use an immobile specific factor (such as land or capital). Labor use in agriculture is measured from the left end of the horizontal axis and labor use in nonagriculture is measured from the right end, with the width of the graph determined by the size of the total labor force. The value of the incremental (marginal) output from each additional unit of labor in a given sector (denoted VMP_A and VMP_N for agriculture and nonagriculture, respectively) is shown in the figure. This value is determined by multiplying the price of the product by the physical output of the additional labor unit; in competitive markets, the wage rate for labor is equal to its marginal value of output. Marginal physical products of labor decline as labor use increases but rise as labor quality improves or when there is an increase in the quantity or quality of the specific factor utilized in a sector.

The initial conditions that prevailed in the early 1930s, when the farm sector was depressed by a sharp drop in agricultural prices, are illustrated at the two points labeled A and N on the curves VMP_A and VMP_N in figure 7. With little short-run opportunity for movement of labor out of farming, the fixed labor on farms earned lower wages than nonfarm workers (W_A compared to W_N). If enough labor movement had occurred, a new equilibrium would have been established with less labor in agriculture and a common wage rate, W, at the point labeled AN. The depressed conditions of the 1930s, however, generated concerns that the returns of American farm labor might be fixed below nonfarm labor earnings.

An improvement in agricultural technology or an increase in the agricultural capital stock raises the productivity of farm labor and, at a constant agricultural price, shifts VMP_A upward. The increased supply available from the improvement in productivity also might lower the equilibrium agricultural price. A lower price reduces the gain in *value* of labor's agricultural output, shifting VMP_A back toward its original level. The relative strengths of these two offsetting effects determine the direction and magnitude of the final net shift. If the improved marginal physical product of agricultural labor raises its value despite a falling price, a shift from VMP_A to VMP_A' takes place, as shown in figure 7.

The effects on the labor market of the upward shift of VMP_A to VMP_A' are twofold. The increased value of output raises the wage rate in agriculture whether labor is temporarily immobile or not. If labor adjustments occur to equalize wages, a higher common equilibrium wage rate is established (W' corresponding to the point $A'N$) than without the improvement in agricultural labor productivity. More labor is retained in agriculture compared to nonagriculture.

Other changes also affect the agricultural labor markets as farming modernizes. Capital investments and productivity growth raised the marginal product of nonfarm labor as well as farm labor following the Second World War. With the demand for nonfarm goods and services more responsive to rising national income than the demand for agricultural products, the upward shift for the value of marginal output was greater for nonfarm labor than farm labor—even though labor productivity was rising faster in agriculture. The nonfarm growth causes the VMP_N curve in figure 7 to shift upward to VMP_N'. Farm labor could share in the real nonfarm wage growth, but only if movement of labor out of agriculture occurred. Long-run equilibrium with labor mobility shifts to the higher real wage W'', with labor use in agriculture reduced (at the point labeled $A'N'$).

When the technological transformation of American agriculture began in full force in the 1950s, the combination of low initial farm wages, falling farm prices, and relatively slow adjustment of the labor force were seen to define a unique "farm problem" (see Bruce Gardner 1991). Willard Cochrane, a prominent agricultural economist and eventual advisor to John F. Kennedy, characterized farmers as being on a technological "treadmill" (1958). In *Farm Prices, Myth and Reality,* Cochrane argues that as new production techniques developed, individual farmers had to adopt them earlier than most of their neighbors in order to stay competitive. This efficient behavior of individual farmers led to greater aggregate supply, which pushed down agricultural prices because of the smaller growth in aggregate demand. The lower prices then forced more farmers out of agriculture and required the ones who remained to adopt even more output-expanding modern technology. Despite their best efforts, Cochrane concludes, the internal dynamic of the technological treadmill made it impossible for enough labor adjustment to occur for farmers' earnings to keep pace with nonagriculture earnings.

While Cochrane accurately identifies one source of falling farm prices, his treadmill model fails to recognize the extent to which farm incomes could rise as labor adjustments took place and farmers left agriculture for higher nonfarm wages. The treadmill analysis was embraced by those who focused on the noneconomic difficulties that can accompany adjustments out of agriculture. When families leave

farming, their employment shift can also mean a painful change in identity, a rupture of social interactions, and a sale of the land and home-
steads that defined their heritage. But the lure to migrate is also unde-
niable, and, over time, the adjustments once identified by Cochrane as
so difficult were achieved.

The U.S. farm sector that has emerged from this important labor-
adjustment process is far wealthier and far less in need of government
assistance than the deeply troubled and disadvantaged sector targeted
by the original AAA. In 1933, the average income of U.S. farmers was
only about one-half the national average. After six decades of adjustment, this income gap has been eliminated, and in many years farmers
earn more, on average, than nonfarmers. Just over 500,000 commercial
farms with annual gross sales of $50,000 or more produced nearly 90
percent of the nation's agricultural output in the mid-1990s, as shown in
table 4. Net cash income from farming averaged $38,000, and net worth
averaged over $500,000 for the commercial operations in this group with
sales of less than $250,000. Net cash income from farming averaged

Table 4.   Modern Farm Sector Economic Characteristics, 1995

	Annual Sales Value		
	Less than $50,000	$50,000 to $249,999	$250,000 or more
Number of farms	1,534,000	414,000	122,000
Farm characteristics (% of total)			
Farms	74.1%	20.0%	5.9%
Total sales	10.5%	31.4%	58.0%
Government-supported crops	11.9%	43.3%	44.9%
Nonsupported crops	6.2%	18.9%	74.8%
Livestock	8.9%	29.0%	62.1%
Direct government payments	27.0%	40.8%	32.2%
Operator characteristics			
Primary occupation farming (percentage)	39.6%	90.9%	96.7%
Net cash income from farming	−$2,900	$38,000	$303,000
Government payments	$1,275	$7,130	$19,033
Off-farm family income	$30,000	$18,000	$21,000
Total income	$27,100	$56,000	$324,000
Net worth	$255,000	$501,000	$1,020,000

Note: Net cash income from farming includes government payments. Net worth refers to 1991.
Source: U.S. Department of Agriculture, Economic Research Service, Farm Business Economics Report (1996) and Farm Cost and Returns Survey (1991).

$252,000, and net worth over $1 million, for the larger-size commercial farm units with sales of $250,000 or more.[22]

Government Programs and Agricultural Modernization

Government programs contributed to agricultural modernization and productivity growth, but the programs that contributed the most were not farm commodity-support programs. Far more important were the public-sector investments in education and technology, the primary sources of productivity growth (as shown in figure 6). The New Deal supply-control and commodity-support programs led to an increase in farm asset values but not to any significant increase in agricultural productivity.

One possible contribution of the commodity programs to agricultural modernization could be reduced market price instability and enhanced investment by risk-averse agricultural producers. Clarke (1994) claims that the price assurances farmers received from New Deal commodity programs, together with government-assisted improved credit terms, stimulated investments in tractors and machinery that raised productivity. Clarke contrasts tractor sales of $465 million during 1925–29 with sales of $818 million during 1935–39 and attributes the increased level of purchases to changes in the investment climate brought about by the farm programs. She then argues that New Deal programs also had much to do with "the pace and shape" of the revolution in farm productivity after 1940 (205).

Arguments that price instability and impediments in rural credit markets dampened agricultural investments in the 1920s and 1930s are widely accepted. Less clear is how much increased investment New Deal farm programs actually induced.[23] Clarke, for example, fails to provide an empirical assessment of the influence on prewar tractor sales of the farm programs versus other factors, such as lower real interest rates (from over 4 percent to under 2 percent), time lags inherent in adoption of new technologies as older investments depreciated, and possibly differing *ex ante* price expectations in the late 1920s and 1930s.[24]

22. There are also over 1.5 million farms with annual sales of less than $50,000, but these farms produced only 10.5 percent of the total output in 1995. Most are not commercial operations, as indicated by negative average net cash income from farming shown in table 4.

23. See Shultz (1945) and D. Gale Johnson (1947) for classic analyses of the effects of price instability in the 1920s and 1930s. They argued for price stabilization policies that maintained, rather than elevated, market-based price levels.

24. The late 1930s proved *ex post* to be a much better time for farmers to have made in-

Moreover, capital investments that might be stimulated by price stability have not been the principal determinant of farm output and incomes. Use of intermediate inputs and improved multifactor productivity have been more important sources of growth, as shown in table 3. Gopinath and Roe (1997) further disentangle the sources of growth in agricultural output for the 1949–1991 period. They show that investments in land and capital contributed only 0.03 percent per annum to the increase of agricultural gross domestic product (GDP), holding constant other factors. Use of new intermediate inputs contributed 0.64 percent per annum to such growth, while multifactor productivity improvements are estimated to generate growth of nearly 2.30 percent per annum, all else constant. Thus, investments, which Clarke argues were enhanced by the farm programs in the period following the Second World War, were not the primary source of agricultural growth in that period.[25]

Nor have the farm commodity-support programs had much long-term effect whatsoever on farm wage rates or the rates of return on investments in agriculture.[26] An attempt to increase farm wage rates or ease labor-adjustment pressures by raising farm commodity-support prices shifts the VMP_A or VMP_A' curve upward in figure 7.[27] In the short run, a one-time increase in output prices might hold more labor in agriculture for a few years or might raise lagging farm wages slightly for an equivalent length of time. But to raise labor income on farms in the long run, the shift upward due to higher output price supports would have to raise the wage rate for the entire economy, an unlikely effect in an industrial country where only a fraction of the workforce is in agriculture.[28] As D. Gale Johnson (1973, 1991) argues in perhaps the

---

vestments, especially with short-term credit. Clarke rests her argument about the importance of New Deal programs partly on an assessment that a higher percentage of farms large enough to benefit from having purchased a tractor had actually done so by 1939 compared to 1929. This part of her argument is again flawed by the many circumstances that raise the likelihood of an increase in this percentage over time.

25. Clarke finds similarly that adoption by farmers of hybrid corn in the 1930s, which raised land productivity, cannot be attributed to the AAA farm support or credit programs.

26. As Bruce Gardner (1991) notes, hired labor wages in agriculture have followed the national trend over time but have remained below nonfarm wages. See Gardner 1991 and Melichar 1984 for analyses of farm investment rates of return.

27. For simplicity, the shifts due to the farm output price-support programs are not shown in figure 7 but can be visualized as upward movements of the curves.

28. Figure 7 is drawn out of scale to illustrate this point: it shows agriculture as still employing about one-fifth of the national labor force even in the final equilibrium, but actual farm labor constitutes a much smaller percentage.

best-known critique of American farm policy, the commodity programs would have had to provide more than a one-time increase in price level to permanently expand labor use on farms. The programs would have had to provide continuous increases in real farm output price levels—a policy strategy too expensive to have been seriously considered.[29]

Not that the programs actually enacted were inexpensive. For the forty-year period from 1955 through 1995, inflation-adjusted expenditures on these programs totaled over $450 billion (in 1992 dollars), with direct transfers to farmers of nearly $340 billion. Direct program payments have accounted for nearly 20 percent of total net farm income over these years, and thus a much higher percentage of income derived from the supported crops.[30] A portion of the spending that did not go directly to farmers was largely lost to the economy, holding surplus crops in storage or subsidizing sales of government stocks to foreigners. Farm support programs also generated "deadweight losses" for the U.S. economy by stimulating excessive levels of input use and output supplies, by shifting production incentives among commodities, by shifting resource use within the sector away from idled land, and by exacerbating both on-farm and off-farm environmental externalities associated with production. In the mid-1980s, when farm policy costs were measured in conjunction with international negotiations aimed at disciplining farm subsidies, U.S. farm programs transferred an annual income benefit to producers estimated to be $10 billion less than the costs of the programs to consumers and taxpayers.[31]

If the commodity programs have not raised farm labor returns nor had much effect on the number of farmers in the United States over time, where have the benefits of these programs been concentrated? Instead of affecting returns to mobile factors, such as labor, the billions of dollars spent on farm support programs since the 1950s have mostly

29. Johnson's 1973 monograph, *World Agriculture in Disarray,* describes the distorting effects policy interventions have induced worldwide. Published at the outset of a four-year inflationary spiral and international commodity price boom, it seemed at the time to have misread economic events but has since become widely appreciated for its steadfast interpretation of the fundamental structural changes in agriculture. A second edition was published in 1991.

30. See table 9 in the chapter that follows. Disentangling net farm income among commodities is complicated by the difficulty in assigning the use of many inputs to specific outputs, and by the use of some farm outputs as inputs into other farm production.

31. The welfare costs and benefits of the farm programs in the mid-1980s are presented in table 10. These calculations are based on commodity market price distortions and direct taxpayer costs. They do not include costs associated with environmental externalities.

been captured by owners of the fixed resources in agriculture. Owners of land, farm buildings, and production allotments and quotas have seen the value of their property increased because of government programs. The economic logic is simple. If output prices are pushed upward, while returns to mobile factors of production such as labor are set in national markets and remain relatively unchanged, then the additional revenue that farm output earns becomes a rent—an income gain—attained by owners of the specific factors used in production.[32] These rents are dissipated by rising values of the assets on which they are earned.

A large body of evidence supports the conclusion that the benefits from the farm commodity-support programs have been captured primarily by owners of sector-specific assets in agriculture. D. Gale Johnson (1991) cites conclusions drawn to this effect by prominent agricultural economists Willard Cochrane, Luther Tweeten, and Earl Heady and Leo Mayer. He reports that their assessments are supported by studies of the capitalization of tobacco allotments in land values by J. L. Hedrick and James Seagraves; of the capitalization of the value of restricted production rights for milk and poultry into the price of transferable quotas in Canada by Richard Barichello, Peter Arcus, and T. K. Warley; and of the effects of U.S. farm programs on returns to farm resources by Andrew Barkley and John Rosine and Peter Helmberger. In testimony before the Senate Committee on Agriculture, Forestry and Nutrition in 1995, Tweeten concluded that if market prices followed past trends, land values would decline between 10 and 20 percent were support programs then in effect eliminated, an estimate consistent with the evidence presented in other analytic studies.[33] The large net worth of the operators of commercial farms, shown in table 4, to some extent reflects the higher asset values that farm commodity programs have created.

---

32. Schematically, the total value of agricultural output is given in figure 7 by the area under the VMP_A curve, while the farm wage bill is the rectangle of agricultural wages times the quantity of labor use. The difference is returns to the sector-specific factor.

33. Beech (1996) summarizes other studies confirming the effects of farm support programs on returns to fixed resources in agriculture. These include analysis of the effects of tobacco allotments in Kentucky by Vantreese, Reed, and Skees; of the implicit price of corn base acreage by Herriges, Barickman, and Shogren; of the capitalization of wheat subsidies into land values in Canada by Goodwin and Ortalo-Mange; and of U.S. support programs on land values by Featherstone and Baker; Hoffman, Offutt and Shoemaker; Runge and Halbach; and Shoemaker, Anderson, and Hrubovak. See also Barnard, Whittaker, Westenbarger, and Ahearn 1997.

Reasons to Change the Traditional Programs

The remarkable technological modernization and labor-adjustment process that has transformed agriculture since the Second World War has diminished the rationale for the New Deal–era farm supply-control and price-support programs. By raising the earnings of farm operators, modernization of agriculture has negated the argument that commodity programs help a disadvantaged class of Americans. The benefits from these programs go mostly to owners of agricultural land and other assets. Not all farm operators are owners of land, and owners of land are not necessarily farm operators, but because of the valuable assets they own, the *average* net worth of farm families in the 1990s was roughly four times as great as the average net worth of nonfarm families.

Structural changes in U.S. farming have also nullified several other original depression-era justifications for the commodity price-support programs. In the 1930s, the share of total production on large farms versus small farms was less disproportionate than it has become in the years since then. In 1939, the largest 5 percent of farms were the source of 38.3 percent of total farm sales. By 1995, the largest 5.9 percent of farms were the source of 58 percent of total sales (see table 4). This increased concentration of production capacity has reduced the justifiability of providing subsidies to farmers on a "per bushel of production" or a "per acre" basis. This approach was of dubious equity in the 1930s and has since become even more conspicuously inequitable.

The greater specialization of individual farm units is another change that has rendered traditional commodity programs increasingly inequitable over time. In the 1930s, a significant share of all U.S. farmers could be helped by offering farm support programs for just a few basic crops. In more specialized modern agriculture, many farmers—including those involved in livestock, fruits and vegetables, specialty crops, and other products that account for nearly 60 percent of total farm sales receipts (see table 5)—are not producing the commodities for which price supports or government cash payments are available, so they do not benefit directly from these commodity programs. In 1986, the entire farm sector was suffering through a painful financial crisis, and support program spending increased dramatically. Even so, nearly one-half of all financially stressed farmers received no program payments at all (USDA 1987). As figure 8 demonstrates, since 1986 the levels of assistance have continued to vary widely across diverse agricultural com-

Table 5.   Agricultural Output Values (in Billions of Dollars), 1995

Commodity	Output Value
Crops	105.6
Food grains	11.2
Wheat	9.8
Rice	1.6
Feed grains	26.8
Corn for grain	24.1
Oil-bearing	14.8
Soybeans	14.6
Hay	11.0
Cotton	7.3
Tobacco	2.3
Sugar	1.9
Peanut	1.0
Fruit and tree nuts	10.8
Vegetables	14.7
Other	3.8
Livestock	73.8
Cattle and calves	24.8
Hogs	9.7
Dairy products	20.1
Poultry	14.5
Eggs	4.0
Sheep and lambs	0.4
Other	0.3

Source: U.S. Department of Agriculture, *Agricultural Statistics* (Washington, D.C.: U.S. Government Printing Office, 1997).

modities, resulting in an uneven distribution of program benefits among specialized producers.

Farm programs have also lost their original justification of being essential to the economic health of rural America. The U.S. economy has diversified so much that few rural areas depend heavily on farming. Only about 10 percent of all rural (nonmetro) counties in the United States have been classified as "farm dependent" (deriving at least 20 percent of income from farming) since the 1970s, and no single state has been classified as farm dependent overall. Moreover, in those few counties that are farm dependent, average levels of income and wealth per capita are higher than nonfarm counties. Only a tiny fraction, about 1 percent, of all nonmetro counties are both poor and farm dependent (CNP 1991).

Although one-quarter of all nonmetro counties are classified as poor, farm programs have always been an ineffective weapon against rural poverty. Poor southern black farmers (an exception to the relative ho-

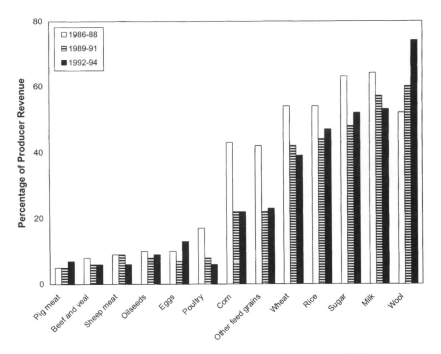

Figure 8.   Levels of Support for Agricultural Commodities, 1986–1994
Source: Organization for Economic Cooperation and Development (OECD), *Agricultural Policies, Markets and Trade: Monitoring and Outlook* (Paris: OECD, various years).

mogeneity within agriculture even in the 1930s) accounted for one-tenth of the total number of farmers in the 1950s. The average farm output levels and incomes of these minority farmers were low, and they owned a relatively small fraction of farmland, so they benefited little from the farm commodity price-support programs. Commodity price supports have played almost no role in reducing this farm poverty, or in preventing the migration of low-income minority farmers from rural to urban areas. By the 1990s, the number of minority farmers in the United States had fallen to under 20,000.[34]

A more important factor in reducing both farm and nonfarm rural poverty rates has been the growth in nonfarm rural employment opportunities. Less than 10 percent of the rural labor force work in farming; the other 90 percent work in such areas as manufacturing, services, or

34. The migration of southern minority farmers to nonfarm residences helps explain the reduced differential of farm versus nonfarm family incomes.

the public sector. Even most rural farm families now derive the larger share of their income from nonfarm activities. Of the average farm household income in 1995 of $44,392, less than $5,000 came from farming. For operators of the 1.5 million places still counted as farms but which have gross farm sales of less than $50,000, income from farming averaged net *losses* of $2,900 in 1995, while nonfarm incomes averaged $30,000 (see table 4). Even on midsized commercial farms, nearly one-third of household income derives from nonfarm sources. Only 15 percent of all U.S. farm households, about 300,000 households in all, derived more income from the farm than from off-farm sources in the 1990s (see Bruce Gardner 1991). Improved educational and skill levels have enabled many who live on farms to earn more of their income from nonfarm employment. This healthy trend has also rendered obsolete the presumption that subsidies to farming are the best way to help rural Americans.

When the rural economy overall is considered, the recent operation of U.S. farm programs may actually have hindered income growth. Land-idling "set aside" and conservation programs—the programmatic descendants of the original AAA supply-control efforts of the 1930s—have taken out of production an average of nearly 20 percent of cropland over the fifty years since the Second World War, which has significantly reduced the tonnage of crops grown in some years. This has exacerbated, not relieved, the labor-adjustment problem in agriculture, and has contributed further to the concentration of farm program benefits in the value of land (Shoemaker, Anderson, and Hrubovak 1989). Acreage controls have also reduced the dollar value of machinery and chemical or seed inputs sold to farmers and the tonnage of crops transported and processed. For every worker still employed on American farms, approximately one upstream agricultural worker off the farm supplies inputs such as fertilizer or farm machinery, and as many as six downstream workers are engaged in agricultural storage, transport, processing, and marketing.[35] Depression-era production control programs hurt rather than help these far more numerous off-farm agricultural workers. By one calculation, land-idling programs have reduced income prospects in rural areas so sharply as to cut the nonfarm population of some counties by 30 percent (Van der Sluis and Peterson 1994; see also Goetz and Debertin 1996).

35. These estimates are derived from intersectoral economic models such as Harrington, Schluter, and O'Brien 1986.

With the passage of time, the production control feature of farm programs became obsolete in an important additional sense. Farmers in the United States are again more dependent on trade than they were in the 1930s. At the time of the Great Depression, U.S. farm exports had been curtailed by trade barriers and diminished foreign demand for more than a decade, so fear of losing foreign markets was not a constraint on implementation of supply-control programs. In 1934–36, the United States was actually a substantial net *importer* of wheat because of drought and poor harvests. Even in the 1950s, when the use of supply controls was expanded substantially for some crops, there still seemed little reason to fear loss of global market shares, because commercial export volumes were still small and because farming in Europe had not yet been modernized and was still recovering from damage done during the Second World War. Commercial export markets were not seen as a sustainable source of demand so much as a potential source of temporary market disruptions (Hathaway 1963).

These circumstances were beginning to change in the 1950s, but the policy error of indifference to foreign competition persisted. Severe damage was felt by U.S. producers when the cotton program controlled production to boost prices, only to see the high prices stimulate more foreign production. From 1949 to 1958, cotton production in the United States fell from 16.1 million to 11.5 million bales, while production overseas increased from 15.2 million to 32.9 million bales. Finally, by the late 1960s and early 1970s, world market constraints on U.S. farm policy became impossible to ignore. Heavily subsidized competitors began challenging U.S. farmers in some export markets, as the European Economic Community (EEC) went from being a net grain importer in the mid-1960s to a net exporter two decades later. At the same time, lucrative new export opportunities emerged in the industrializing nations of Asia, the Middle East, and the Soviet Union, and commercial agricultural exports became, for the first time since the First World War, a significant share of total U.S. farm sales.[36] As table 6 demonstrates, the nominal U.S. agricultural trade balance in-

36. The reemergence of world agricultural markets is consistent with a larger reopening of the international economy. Sachs and Warner (1995) find two major periods of growing global economic integration. The first occurred at the end of the nineteenth century, peaking around 1910. Subsequently, integration regressed to a point where, in 1950, only five countries had fully convertible currencies. Integration resumed in the 1960s and has strengthened particularly since about 1980.

Table 6.   Balance of U.S. Agricultural and Merchandise Trade
(in Billions of Dollars), 1950–1995

	Agriculture	Merchandise		Agriculture	Merchandise
1950	−.19	1.42	1973	5.58	.91
1951	−1.74	4.07	1974	11.74	−5.51
1952	−.65	4.48	1975	12.00	8.90
1953	−1.48	4.90	1976	12.04	−9.48
1954	−1.24	4.89	1977	10.62	−31.09
1955	−.64	4.16	1978	13.41	−33.97
1956	−.59	6.48	1979	15.79	−27.56
1957	.93	7.87	1980	23.21	−25.54
1958	.07	5.12	1981	26.56	−28.07
1959	−.29	2.43	1982	23.61	−36.39
1960	.51	5.92	1983	18.40	−67.10
1961	1.30	6.29	1984	19.11	−112.49
1962	1.38	5.32	1985	11.45	−122.17
1963	1.17	6.21	1986	5.43	−145.08
1964	1.97	7.82	1987	7.23	−159.56
1965	2.11	6.11	1988	14.30	−126.96
1966	2.22	4.78	1989	18.11	−115.25
1967	2.32	4.71	1990	17.66	−109.03
1968	1.66	1.41	1991	15.02	−74.07
1969	.81	1.96	1992	18.11	−96.11
1970	1.13	3.27	1993	18.14	−132.62
1971	1.93	−1.43	1994	17.15	−166.10
1972	2.00	−6.42	1995	24.72	−174.47

Note: Positive balance indicates a trade surplus, negative balance indicates a trade deficit.
Source: U.S. Department of Agriculture, Agricultural Statistics (Washington, D.C.: U.S. Government Printing Office, various years); and U.S. Department of Commerce, Statistical Abstract of the United States (Washington, D.C.: U.S. Government Printing Office, various years).

creased from a $1.93 billion surplus in 1971 to a $26.56 billion surplus a decade later—a remarkable 500 percent increase, even after adjustment for inflation.

The dependence of U.S. agriculture on trade by the mid-1990s is shown for key commodities in table 7. When producing for integrated and competitive world markets, the use of unilateral production controls to try to boost prices to U.S. farmers for export crops becomes self-defeating. Trade policies that limit U.S. imports of agricultural commodities in order to sustain high prices for domestic producers are also harder to justify. Not only do these policies impose substantial costs on consumers, but they close off export and income growth opportunities to some developing countries that are potential markets for other U.S. farm products.

Table 7.   Trade Dependence among Agricultural Commodities, 1995
(Value of Imports and Exports as a Percentage of Domestic Production)

Imports			Exports			
10–25%	5–10%	0–5%	0–10%	10–25%	25–50%	50% or More
Oilseeds	Beef and veal	Wheat	Dairy	Beef and veal	Corn	Wheat
Sugar	Dairy	Cotton	Pork	Poultry	Soybeans	Rice
Tobacco		Fruit and		Vegetables	Cotton	Tobacco
Vegetables		tree nuts			Fruit and	
		Pork			tree nuts	
		Poultry				

Source: Derived from USDA, Agricultural Statistics (Washington, D.C.: U.S. Government Printing Office, 1997).

The Farm Policy Reform Problem

Economic developments and technological change have transformed U.S. agriculture since colonial times. The nineteenth-century export-oriented agricultural expansion collapsed in the early 1920s, but farm support programs were not initiated for more than another decade. Supply-control and crop price-support programs were only enacted in the 1930s after a larger general macroeconomic collapse persuaded voters to elect a Democratic president and Congress promising widespread economic relief. These commodity programs were not the ideal response to the crisis, because farmers were suffering more from a worldwide monetary contraction and collapse of demand than from too much production. The new farm programs were nonetheless an understandable part of the radical shift in policy views—toward an increased role for government in the economy—that emerged from the global crisis. The New Deal–era farm programs were thus somewhat justified, in the context of the times, as a policy response to the agricultural collapse.

The circumstances of agriculture have since changed again, and today bear no resemblance to the era of the Great Depression. The farm sector has experienced such rapid productivity growth since the Second World War that it has prospered even while real farm prices have been driven downward. The number of farms has declined, but earnings of those who remained in agriculture have risen to match nonfarm levels. The supply-control and price-boosting features of the depression-era farm commodity programs had minimal long-term effect on the modernization process and did little to ease the adjustment pains felt by farmers leaving agriculture. These programs became increasingly dysfunctional as they imposed rising costs on consumers and tax-payers, and as they reduced U.S. competitiveness in reemerging world markets. Benefits from the commodity programs were captured largely by the owners of farm assets, especially the owners of high quality farm-land, and farmers eventually became wealthier on average than the consumers and taxpayers paying the costs of farm supports. For these reasons, the New Deal–era programs lost their original rationale, and became unsuited to the needs of the modern farm sector.

Chapter Two

Unilateral Postwar Reforms

IN THIS CHAPTER we turn from the economic history of American agriculture to the politics of farm policy reform. We seek to explain why the attempts made through Congress to reform policy unilaterally between 1948 and 1985 had only limited success, even though the original justifications for the New Deal–era farm support programs were disappearing.

The theories from economics and political science that offer the most insights about the durability of farm programs are those that emphasize the role of organized self-serving political interest groups. The concentration of program benefits into values of land and other agricultural assets provided incentives for farm owners to lobby for continued support. Shrinking farm population size need not weaken such narrow lobby group efforts; shrinking numbers may even (to a point) help solve the problem of taking collective action, thus increasing the political strength of these groups. The political resources needed to perpetuate existing programs are in any case less than the resources needed to create new ones. Once the political influence of farmers was reinforced through the formation of elaborate government institutions to control and manage the farm programs, terminating those programs and withdrawal of program benefits became that much more difficult.

The farm price-support programs did not remain in place for lack of efforts at reform. The four approaches to reform we identified in the introduction—cash outs, buyouts, squeeze outs, and cutouts—have all been attempted at various times. The most radical cutout and buyout efforts were never endorsed by any farm-sector political leaders, and none succeeded. Limited efforts to achieve a squeeze out to more slowly reduce costs and distortions were frustrated in the 1950s, when the high productivity growth in agriculture kept reduced price-support levels above the still lower prices that would have prevailed under free market conditions. The squeeze-out approach was frustrated again in the 1970s, when farm lobbies succeeded in ratcheting up nominal price-support levels to prevent the erosion of their real value by inflation.

The only kind of unilateral reform progress that emerged as politically feasible in the domestic arena after the Second World War was a gradual movement to a cash out that began belatedly in the mid-1960s. For the producers of the major export crops, farm income came to be supported in this period less by rigid high price guarantees and government purchases of commodities, and more by direct cash payments. This was a change in policy instruments that facilitated export competitiveness, but it was not a withdrawal of farm income support. Supply controls and some price supports continued to be used both for exported and particularly for import-competing commodities. When appreciation of the U.S. dollar and high interest rates caused a sharp farm-economy downturn in the 1980s, participation in the farm programs increased, loan rates again became intrusive, more land was idled, and federal spending on cash payments to farmers reached unprecedented levels. Despite this crisis, policy continued moving along an expensive, incomplete cash-out path. To some extent, this partial reform helped the New Deal–era farm programs to survive, even though they were less and less needed on economic, social, or equity grounds, and even though they implied continuing market distortions and large taxpayer costs.

Explaining the Difficulty of Reforming Farm Policy

The life span of a government program, in agriculture or in any other sector, will usually depend upon an evolving balance of political power between those that support the program (typically, those who benefit from it most directly) and those that oppose the program (typically, those who must pay for it or who would like public resources to be used in some other way). Arguments made by economists about efficient resource use or social costs and benefits can often be marshaled by one side or the other to try to tip the balance in this power struggle. Arguments based on history, beliefs, values, or even nostalgic perceptions may be used as well. But the power struggle is better understood as one between interests and organizations, not arguments or ideas.

The importance of organized interest groups is highlighted in one formal model of government price interventions by Grossman and Helpman (1994). Their model assumes that the owners of the sector-specific fixed factors in some industries are organized to capture the benefits of government support by making monetary contributions to government officials, while others are not. The equilibrium policies illustrate the influence of the organized political lobbies. For a small country facing fixed world prices, the policy outcome that maximizes national welfare is free trade, yet a political equilibrium emerges in which the government favors organized industries with import tariffs and export subsidies, while unorganized industries are penalized.[1] The equilibrium policies are chosen because of the government's desire to raise contributions from the organized industries, which it weighs against the negative effects of its interventions on average welfare.[2]

The Grossman-Helpman model assumes that organized industries influence the government only through the monetary contributions they make. In practice, political organizations advance their interests in other ways as well. They provide policy makers with arguments and information favorable to their interests, or are able to instruct and mobilize voters to reward or punish specific legislators on election day. The farm commodity programs that were first initiated in the United States during the 1930s have proved difficult to reform primarily because the defenders of these programs have remained better organized and more effective than the critics over the ensuing years. Numbers of voters matter, but organization (as emphasized by Grossman and Helpman) matters more. If it were only numbers that mattered, farmers would have lost their political power long ago.

The structural transformation that occurs as agriculture modernizes in the context of a growing economy tends to increase the incentive for farmers to organize for political action. As industrial productivity increases and incomes rise, those farmers who fail to make adjustments

1. The Grossman-Helpman model is solved for endogenous policy outcomes in two stages. In the first stage, the organized lobbies simultaneously set schedules of the contributions they will make as a function of the full set of price interventions chosen by the government. In the second stage, the government acts on the contribution schedules offered by the various lobbies and chooses an equilibrium set of intervention policies.

2. Government interventions only take the form of trade policies in the Grossman-Helpman model. The level of protection received by the organized industries (and likewise the degree of disprotection suffered by the unorganized industries) is determined by several structural characteristics of the economy. Obviously, no intervention occurs if there are no organized industries or, less obviously, if every industry is organized—in which case their lobbying efforts perfectly counteract one another. When only a fraction of industries are organized, protection rates are inversely related to the relative importance the government attaches to average welfare versus contributions, and to the proportion of industries that are assumed to lobby. The protection level received by an organized industry rises when supply or demand are relatively unresponsive to changes in prices. The Grossman-Helpman framework has been extended by Dixit (1996) to include domestic policies and by Schleich (1999) to allow choice among domestic and trade policies. Extensions of the small-country model with fixed world prices apply to policies of large countries that affect world price levels and whose governments may or may not cooperate on their policy decisions.

(by postponing adoption of new technologies or movement of their labor out of farming) tend to experience slower income growth than the rest of the economy. These slow-adjusting farmers (feeling themselves caught on Cochrane's treadmill) will have a heightened motive to organize for political action. They will seek policy protection as an escape from the adjustment imperative. This will ally them with the larger low-cost farmers who are not hurt by adjustments, but whose asset values rise if protection is enacted.[3] Farmers will also have increased capabilities to organize for political action as industrialization occurs, because they will become better educated and more wealthy, and paradoxically, because they will be fewer in number.

The reason smaller numbers do not have to be a disadvantage in the struggle to form effective political organizations, and may even be an advantage, is that narrow-based coalitions tend to face lower organization costs to obtain member support.[4] The organizational costs among U.S. farmers have fallen because of information transmittal technology and because increased specialization enables farmers to more easily identify like-minded individual producers, to induce them to accept membership in commodity associations, and to organize them to behave collectively. Moreover, with fewer farms and greater specialization, returns from a particular commodity program tend be concentrated on a smaller number of producers—thus raising program benefits per producer and further increasing individual incentives to participate in lobbying activities. At the same time, as the nonfarm economy has grown in relative size and absolute wealth, farm program budget costs have become dispersed among an increased number of taxpayers, and the effects of these programs on food prices are scarcely noticed. Thus, with industrial development, organized pressures to direct program benefits to farm producers tend to increase, while organized resistance tends to decline.

---

3. Some scholars have seen this political alliance as facilitating modernization indirectly as well as resulting in program budget costs and market distortions. Cochrane and Ryan draw this conclusion when they argue that "the real costs of the programs to society may properly be viewed as the costs of achieving a rapid rate of technological advance in American agriculture"(1976, 391). Rausser (1982, 1992) and de Gorter, Nielson, and Rausser (1992) develop this reasoning into a positive political theory in which levels of output-enhancing public investments (with broad social benefits) are determined in simultaneous equilibrium with income-redistributive policies that benefit only sectoral interest groups.

4. See Olson 1965 for the seminal reference about group size and collective action; and Olson 1985 for its application to agricultural policy.

Quantitative studies confirm the link between industrial development and agricultural protection. Agricultural economists Anderson and Hayami (1986) have measured the extent to which farmers in industrial or rapidly industrializing countries gain protection from governments, relative to nonfarmers. Honma and Hayami (1986) show that variations in indicators of industrial transformation are sufficient to explain 60 to 70 percent of all variations in nominal rates of protection for agriculture across fifteen countries over the 1955–80 period.[5] Their results demonstrate that where the industrial sector has become highly advantaged relative to farming, as in Japan, protection levels for farming are highest; where the industrial sector is less highly advantaged, as in Australia or New Zealand (or to some extent Canada and the United States), rates of farm protection are still positive, but may be relatively low.

The Honma and Hayami comparative study also indicates that as industrialization matures, there may be some limits to growth in levels of farm sector protection. In their analysis, peak protection levels are estimated to be reached when the farm population is below 10 percent and falling toward 5 percent of the total population. The political process will continue to supply increasing levels of protection so long as the farm population remains greater than 5 percent of the total. Once the farm population falls below 5 percent, however, the political system is more likely to offer decreasing levels of protection.

A detailed empirical study for the United States by Bruce Gardner (1987) amplifies the relationship between levels of industrialization and levels of protection for agriculture.[6] Gardner evaluates differences in levels of support among seventeen commodities (measured by the producer price gains resulting from farm programs) in a long-term (1912–80) analysis. He finds that relative support increases systematically

5. The nominal rate of protection measure used by Honma and Hayami (1986) to quantify the level of support provided to agriculture is given by the internal-to-border price ratio (ratios greater than one indicate domestic support for agriculture, while ratios less than one indicate that agriculture is being taxed).

6. Ruttan, for example, had called for such amplification in order to better "understand the rate and direction of the broader historical forces that influence the demand for institutional change" in farm policy (1984, 558). More qualitative assessments of the causes for protection in U.S. farm policy are provided by, among others, Rapp (1988), Tweeten (1989), Moyer and Josling (1990), Hansen (1991), Rausser (1992), Browne et al. (1992), Cochrane and Runge (1992), Swinnen and van der Zee (1993), Brooks and Carter (1994), Browne (1995), B. Delworth Gardner (1995), and Sumner (1995). Batie and Marshall (1989) offer assessments of proposals for several departures from existing policies. Bullock (1992) and Swinnen (1994) provide theoretical and quantitative models.

when supply and demand for a commodity are less responsive to an increase in price, which increases the effectiveness of supply controls and lessens the deadweight losses caused by the market interventions. Protection rises among commodities with increased exposure to international trade (when a larger share of output is either imported or exported), and the overall level of support for agriculture rises when farm income declines relative to nonfarm income in preceding years. Factors that facilitate political organization by commodity interests also are significant. Support levels increase with the size of the average farm unit, with the geographic concentration of production, and with stability of its location over time. Gardner also finds an inverted U-shaped nonlinear relationship between the number of producers of a commodity and the level of support obtained, with less support for commodities with either relatively few or relatively numerous producers.

Economists who study commercial markets are comfortable viewing farm policy outcomes as equilibria determined by interest group competition in an analogous political marketplace.[7] The marketplace metaphor is useful, but it overlooks the importance of specific historic macroeconomic and macropolitical events—such as the Great Depression or the Second World War—that can induce large, discontinuous changes in policy regimes. In their efforts to understand the difficulty of policy reform, political scientists point also to the role of ideas and institutions. Hall (1993) argues that low-order policy reforms can be relatively easy to achieve, but that higher-order reforms are difficult, because existing institutions and long-held ideas must be challenged. Hall's analytic framework emerges from a review of monetary policy change in Great Britain, but it can also help explain a relative absence of farm policy change in the United States. He describes "first order"

7. Some economists are as uncritical of the political marketplace as they are of economic markets. Government policy interventions can be argued to be efficient in a limited sense if they minimize the deadweight losses of income transfers, once redistributive objectives are determined by interest group politics (see Bruce Gardner 1983; Stigler 1988). Wittman (1995) goes further, concluding that nearly all of the arguments claiming that economic markets are efficient apply equally well to democratic political markets. Cochrane and Ryan implicitly had adopted reasoning similar to Wittman, arguing earlier that the extension of farm programs year after year by Congress was "evidence that the people of the United States speaking through their elected representatives were of the collective judgement that farm price and income programs were, on balance, in the public interest, were good for the country, and should be continued" (1976, 392). Taken to their extreme, arguments along the lines of Wittman or Cochrane and Ryan risk becoming absurd: if a government policy exists (in a democratic society) it must be appropriate.

reforms as those in which only the settings of policy instruments change (e.g., farm commodity loan rates go down, perhaps as part of a squeeze-out reform strategy), while the instruments themselves remain in place. A slightly more ambitious "second order" reform takes place when policy instruments are modified (e.g., market-intrusive loan rates are replaced by direct government payments to farmers—a cash-out reform). The only way to get a powerful "third order" reform (e.g., an end to the farm support programs through a buyout or a cutout) is to adopt an entirely new theoretical or ideological vantage point. In Hall's view, movement toward this third order of change will have to come from more than just a routine political contest between organized lobby interests. It will require some form of society-wide contestation over ideas, and that in turn may not happen until existing policies have failed so completely and so conspicuously as to render the existing policy regime untenable.

Goldstein and Keohane (1993) argue that even rational actors maximizing a utility function rooted in material interests will be independently influenced by ideas. Applying this ideas-based approach to the problem of policy durability, some political scientists have hypothesized that ideas will retain power over time partly because they tend to become embedded in political institutions. Goldstein (1993), in a discussion of the durability of U.S. trade policies, argues that ideas, once embedded in institutions, can influence policy even after the interests of their creators have changed. Some analysts of farm policy, such as Bonnen and Browne (1989), have agreed that ideas can be influential long beyond their original moment of formation. They claim that farm groups remain politically powerful in the United States in part because of their ability to mobilize a badly outdated but still potent "mythology" of agrarian values.

Because institutions and ideas both matter, and because both tend to resist change, it is that much easier to understand why farm policies already in place are difficult to reform. Pierson (1994) goes further, arguing that welfare state programs will tend to endure in part because the interest groups that want those programs will actually be strengthened by their operation. Politics can create new programs, but the prior existence of programs also alters politics, through what Pierson calls "feedback" effects. It is easier for organizations to defend programs in existence than to create new ones, because it is easier to motivate political action to preserve tangible benefits that are already being received, and because programs tend to grant financial resources precisely to the groups most likely to lobby for the preservation of those benefits. Pierson's analysis concentrates on pension policy, housing policy, and income support policy, but his concept is also useful for understanding farm program durability. In just this way, the farm benefits received under the original AAA, and the county-level institutions required to implement its supply-control features, gave new organizational opportunities, incentives, and financial resources to the Farm Bureau, and thus helped strengthen the lobby that subsequently worked hardest to keep the programs in place.

A second type of feedback effect needs to be stressed as well. Existing benefit programs can be easier for lobby groups to defend because the governmental apparatus that grows up around them will come to share the lobby groups' interests in program perpetuation. Without farm support programs there would be less reason to have fully staffed Agriculture Committees in Congress, and less reason to maintain a large Department of Agriculture. The programs generate benefits for farmers, but they also generate budgets for government bureaucracies, and they create for congressional committees prized jurisdictions over those budgets—committees that in turn reward the institutions under their jurisdiction for political support. It is thus not surprising to find the Agriculture Committees of Congress and the USDA often working in conjunction with the leaders of farm organizations to keep the government programs in place. The three-sided nexus (farm lobbyists, congressional Agriculture Committees, and the USDA) that so often works to perpetuate existing farm programs has traditionally been described as an "iron triangle." We prefer to call this nexus of program preserving institutions an agricultural "policy establishment." The keen interest of this establishment in preserving its role becomes another factor ensuring the durability of farm policy.

What role do political parties play in the complex process of entrenchment of established entitlement programs? Political parties are organizations that seek to promote the material interests of their most active members and leaders by nominating and supporting winning candidates in competitive elections. To thrive, these parties must find candidates capable, through personal or programmatic appeal, of securing the financial resources and votes needed to win. The United States has a two-party system in part because Congress is composed of representatives of single member districts where election requires only a simple plurality of votes, even if less than a majority. In this system, where runoff elections do not take place, smaller third parties that stand no chance of coming in first (such as a party appealing only to farmers) have no reason to form. In the U.S. system, with farm numbers quite low, the policy positions taken on agriculture by the two parties will therefore more likely be a reflection of larger political principles or responsive to the financial contributions or organizational support of their respective farm constituents, rather than to numerical clout in the voting booth. The interests of these farm constituents can change over time (for example, as the structure of agriculture changes). Farm constituent links to parties can sometimes be reversed even when interests do not change: for example, as the Republican Party—mostly for unrelated reasons linked to race policy issues—makes gains in the once "solid" Democratic South. And because parties with different farm group constituencies can suddenly replace each other in their control of government, they become in our analysis important sources of agricultural policy change, perhaps not of the third-order magnitude (in Hall's terms), but at times of the first order or second order.

The theoretical frameworks of Grossman and Helpman; Olson; Anderson and Hayami; Hall; Goldstein and Keohane; and Pierson help to explain how farm support programs have been able to endure. Since the New Deal, farm sector interests have had ample reasons and plenty of opportunity to lobby for program continuation, and organizing for program protection is easier than organizing for program creation. To succeed in program protection, farmers have only had to be more motivated and organized than the interests within other sectors that might oppose them or lobby for competing programs of their own.

Unilateral Partial Reforms, 1948–1985

Forty years of effort to reform farm policies unilaterally in the United States confirms the difficulty of changing established entitlement programs. Under conditions of the Second World War, farm lobby groups had attained price-support programs for 166 commodities and had been guaranteed that CCC loan rates for 20 commodities would be maintained at 90 percent of parity for at least two more years. The 20 commodities for which continued support was ensured included the 6 basic crops (wheat, corn, cotton, rice, tobacco, and peanuts) plus 14 additional commodities (manufacturing milk, butterfat, chickens, eggs, turkeys, hogs, dry peas, soybeans, flaxseed oil, peanuts for oil, American Egyp-tian cotton, Irish potatoes, and sweet potatoes) for which expansion of production had been solicited during the war. By precedent, the prices of a number of other crops (including barley, oats, and rye) also were expected to be supported at or near 90 percent of parity.

Lost Postwar Reform Opportunity

Agriculture was on the eve of a remarkable transformation at the end of the Second World War. Rural communities had been disrupted by war-induced labor movements, Americans feared a commodity depression, and, as described in chapter 1, the technological transformation brought on by new machinery, hybrid seeds, inorganic fertilizers, and modern farming practices was underway. In this economic and social setting, instead of adopting either a squeeze-out strategy of lower support prices or some variant of a cash-out plan, Congress for a time legislated continuations of high fixed wartime price supports. Farm organizations during this period had a strong motive to keep these high supports in place and were politically better organized than any rivals representing the interests of nonfarm consumers or taxpayers.

The wartime farm price-support legislation first came under significant congressional scrutiny in 1948, after the Republican Party had recaptured control of Congress in the 1946 midterm elections (ending sixteen years of continuous Democratic rule). The Farm Bureau and midwestern Republicans from the nation's most productive farming areas had always been less enamored with supply controls and high price supports than Democrats representing the producers of wheat, tobacco, and cotton. In 1948, a farm bill midwesterners touted as a strategy for long-term adjustment in agriculture was adopted by the Senate. Named for Republican Senator George Aiken (Vermont), this Senate bill provided price-support levels that were flexible between 60 and 90 percent of parity. It revised the parity formula to effectively lower support price levels and included a rule for setting loan rates designed to restore supply and demand equilibrium whenever excess supplies were projected from carryover stocks of the previous year (plus expected new production).

The Aiken proposal to lower price support from a fixed 90 percent of parity was an early attempt to achieve a slow farm program squeeze out. Though it passed the Senate, it was attacked by opponents as an attempt at supply control "through bankruptcy." In reaction, the House of Representatives adopted a bill from its Agriculture Committee chairman, Republican Clifford Hope (Kansas), that continued high fixed loan rates. The Hope bill was favored by southern Democrats and by representatives of both parties from the relatively marginal farming areas in the northern plains states. The Agriculture Act that eventually passed Congress was brokered as a compromise. Its Title I kept loan rates fixed at 90 percent of parity through June 1950. Thereafter, under

Title II , a "long-term" program of Aiken's more flexible levels was to take effect.[8]

The 1948 act was short-lived. The reelection of Harry Truman as president and the return of Congress to Democratic control later that year shifted farm policy momentum back toward the proponents of supply controls and high support prices. The long-term provisions of the 1948 act were superceded by the Agricultural Act of 1949, which contains a major part of the "permanent legislation" for farm policy that remains law a half-century later.[9] The 1949 act extended price supports for the six basic crops at 90 percent of parity through the fall harvest of 1950, effectively nullified the revisions to the parity formula, increased the loan rates corresponding to different levels of estimated supplies, and established mandatory support prices (at various parity levels) for dairy products, tung nuts, potatoes, and wool. Thus, the squeeze-out proposal from the 1948 act was repudiated before it took effect.

The first serious proposal for a partial cash out of price supports was made in 1949 by Democratic Secretary of Agriculture Charles F. Brannan. He recommended continued support for farm income at a high level—but through supply-control measures used in conjunction with direct payments to farmers rather than through price-support guarantees and government takeovers of surplus stocks. The direct payments in the Brannan plan were a cash-out reform, but his plan otherwise implied an enlargement of the government's role in agriculture. Brannan's cash payments were designated not only for producers of traditional supported commodities, but also for producers of livestock and livestock products (see Benedict 1953).[10] This made the Brannan

---

8. See Benedict 1953 for a more detailed account of the crucial 1948 and 1949 farm policy debates. The long-term Aiken program drew on earlier recommendations by the Committee on Postwar Agricultural Policy of the Association of Land-Grant Colleges and Universities, and by the House Special Committee on Postwar Economic Policy and Planning (known as the Colmer Committee).

9. The other cornerstones of permanent legislation are the Agricultural Adjustment Act of 1938 and the Commodity Credit Corporation Charter Act of 1948. These acts are permanent because they contain no termination date, thus they remain in effect unless repealed or suspended by specific subsequent laws.

10. Specifically, Brannan proposed supporting the incomes of producers of eggs, chickens, milk, hogs, lamb, and beef cattle, as well as basic crops. As noted earlier, programs to limit supplies of hogs and beef cattle had been implemented in the early 1930s but livestock products (except dairy) subsequently had been subject to less supply controls and price supports. In part, this reflected the view that livestock was "a processing operation converting feed into secondary products," and was not as vulnerable as crop production (Brandow 1977, 223). Livestock products have been subject to some import controls.

plan for cash payments not only intrusive, but potentially quite expensive compared to existing price-support programs. It also spread support interventions beyond those farm producers already organized to lobby for benefits.

The Brannan plan for cash payments won the endorsement of the National Farmers Union, but it antagonized the Farm Bureau and congressional Republicans who still favored the simple squeeze-out option of lowering price-support levels. Brannan's plan antagonized some Democrats as well, and was summarily rejected by Congress. The idea of moving toward cash payments was thereafter suppressed for a time, and did not reemerge until more than a decade later. Meanwhile, there would be more attempts to seek reform through a squeeze out.

Thwarted Squeeze Out in the 1950s

It took the election of Dwight D. Eisenhower and a Republican Congress in 1952, followed in 1953 by the end of the commodity boom associated with the Korean War, to turn the tide against continued high fixed price supports. Eisenhower entrusted his farm policy to Ezra Taft Benson, an outspoken opponent of regulation and champion of a market-oriented approach.[11] Benson won support from the Farm Bureau, which was increasingly dominated by competitive midwestern producers of corn and other feed grains who were least dependent on the government programs. He echoed the arguments for flexible support prices that mainstream Republicans had been making, without success, since 1948. Benson again urged lower price-support levels, and a more flexible relationship between levels of expected supplies and the percentage of parity that the support programs guaranteed. As market prices were falling after 1953, Benson and the Republicans seemed to prevail. In the Agricultural Act of 1954, Congress replaced support rates fixed at 90 percent of parity with varying rates and a minimum parity level of 82.5 percent. Benson then used his discretion as secretary of agriculture to implement the authorized lower support levels.

The drive for lower support prices in the 1950s can be understood as a concerted effort to control CCC stock holdings and farm program costs, and it again had the features of a squeeze-out reform strategy. Benson and other reform advocates reasoned that if the generosity of farm programs could be reduced even marginally, supply-control intrusions could be avoided and budget costs contained. The number of

---

11. Benson titled his 1960 policy book *Freedom to Farm*.

farmers might fall faster than if higher levels of price interventions were retained, but with employment opportunities expanding rapidly off the farm, moving marginal farmers out of government support programs and out of agriculture would not impose too much of a hardship. Significant numbers of marginal farmers, who knew they were the ones being squeezed out, resisted this logic. These farmers, mostly in the prairie states and in the south, backed by their allies in Congress (including some Republicans as well Democrats), objected strongly to an approach that seemed geared primarily to the interests of large-scale commercial farmers in the midwestern corn belt.[12]

When Congress came back under Democratic control after 1954, flexible price supports went out of favor, and farm program legislation reverted to heavier reliance on supply controls.[13] The most widely used supply-control measure was again acreage idling. While this measure distorted resource use, it was a more fortunate policy choice, and more agreeable to most farmers, than the imposition of direct production or marketing quotas. Farmers typically idled their least productive land and were free to adopt production enhancing technologies on the rest. Thus, land idling only partially restricted supplies while enabling the modernization of the farm sector to continue. The new supply-control initiative was given a conservation-based justification, borrowing from the arguments offered in the 1930s. Under the "Soil Bank," farmers were paid to take crop land out of production on an annual basis (this provision operated during 1956–58) or to idle it under a long-term Conservation Reserve Program. The Conservation Reserve Program of 1956 accepted enrollments of land through 1959 and idled some acreage as late as 1972. At their peak, the short-term and long-term supply-control measures adopted in the 1950s took 27.8 million acres out of production, about 10 percent of national planted acreage (see table 8).

12. Even in parts of the corn belt, the Benson policies were unpopular. In the 1954 midterm elections, and, especially, the 1956 elections, the squeeze-out approach to farm policy cost the Republicans political support from farm districts throughout the Midwest and prairie states (see Hansen 1991).

13. The Agricultural Act of 1956 continued price supports for the basic crops in the 1949 act and raised support levels for four other feed grains: oats, rye, barley, and sorghum. Henceforth, the commodity-support programs would focus on these crops plus sugar, dairy, honey, and wool and mohair. Soybeans, which eventually emerged as a major export crop, also continued to be eligible for price-support loans, but were not subject to acreage supply controls or, later, to receive direct payments. Soybeans accumulated in government stocks in 1957, 1958, 1961, 1967, and 1968, but in all other years market prices remained above the legislated support levels (Cochrane and Ryan 1976, 250).

Table 8.   Crop Acreage (in Millions) Planted and Idled, 1954–1995

	Total Cropland	Planted Acreage	Hay, Other, and Fallow	Acreage Idled under Farm Programs			
				Total	Set Aside	Additional	Long-term
1954	465.0	284.3	180.7	0.0	0.0	0.0	0.0
1955	463.0	282.6	180.4	0.0	0.0	0.0	0.0
1956	461.0	275.4	172.0	13.6	0.0	0.0	13.6
1957	459.0	261.2	170.0	27.8	0.0	0.0	27.8
1958	458.0	256.9	174.0	27.1	0.0	0.0	27.1
1959	458.0	264.4	171.1	22.5	0.0	0.0	22.5
1960	456.0	257.7	169.6	28.7	0.0	0.0	28.7
1961	453.0	242.6	156.7	53.7	25.2	0.0	28.5
1962	459.7	233.3	151.7	64.7	38.9	0.0	25.8
1963	447.0	240.9	150.0	56.1	31.7	0.0	24.4
1964	444.0	237.5	151.4	55.1	37.5	0.0	17.6
1965	442.0	238.0	147.7	56.3	41.9	0.0	14.4
1966	439.1	233.4	142.4	63.3	47.6	0.0	15.7
1967	435.9	251.6	143.6	40.7	25.1	0.0	15.6
1968	439.0	236.6	153.0	49.4	35.7	0.0	13.7
1969	438.0	229.4	150.6	58.0	50.2	0.0	7.8
1970	437.0	229.8	150.2	57.0	53.1	0.0	3.9
1971	435.0	242.8	154.6	37.6	33.8	0.0	3.8
1972	434.0	233.6	138.4	62.0	58.7	0.0	3.3
1973	433.0	255.6	157.8	19.6	15.8	0.0	2.8
1974	432.0	267.0	162.3	2.7	0.0	0.0	2.7
1975	431.0	269.4	159.2	2.4	0.0	0.0	2.4
1976	467.6	274.2	191.3	2.1	0.0	0.0	2.1
1977	469.0	282.4	185.6	1.0	0.0	0.0	1.0
1978	470.5	272.9	179.3	18.3	18.3	0.0	0.0
1979	464.1	283.0	168.1	13.0	13.0	0.0	0.0
1980	457.7	295.2	162.5	0.0	0.0	0.0	0.0
1981	451.3	302.0	149.3	0.0	0.0	0.0	0.0
1982	445.0	297.3	136.6	11.1	11.1	0.0	0.0
1983	444.6	239.8	126.9	77.9	77.9	0.0	0.0
1984	444.1	282.1	135.0	27.0	27.0	0.0	0.0
1985	443.7	280.2	133.0	30.7	30.7	0.0	0.0
1986	443.3	262.8	132.4	48.1	42.6	3.5	2.0
1987	442.9	243.0	123.7	76.2	53.5	7.0	15.7
1988	441.4	241.0	122.7	77.7	44.5	8.8	24.4
1989	439.8	252.1	126.9	60.8	18.4	12.6	29.8
1990	438.3	255.7	121.1	61.5	12.3	15.3	33.9
1991	436.7	249.5	122.2	65.0	17.0	13.6	34.4
1992	435.2	256.2	123.8	55.2	8.6	11.2	35.4
1993	434.1	250.1	124.5	60.6	8.3	15.9	36.4
1994	433.3	254.7	129.7	50.8	1.5	12.9	36.4
1995	432.5	248.9	130.0	56.3	4.9	15.0	36.4

Note: Planted Acreage refers to the fifteen major crops. *Hay, Other, and Fallow* includes "Minor Crops, Etc." and land idling unrelated to farm programs. *Set Aside* refers to acreage of corn, grain sorghum, barley, oats, wheat, cotton, and rice required to be idled annually by voluntary participants for eligibility in price and income support programs. *Additional* refers to land idled annually beyond minimum eligibility requirements under 0, 50 / 85–92 programs initiated in 1985. *Source:* U.S. Department of Agriculture, Farm Service Agency, Economic and Policy Analysis staff, *Land Use Summary* (January 1997).

When land-idling supply-control programs were reintroduced in the 1950s, commercial export sales had not yet reemerged as a large contributor to U.S. farm income, so the danger that other exporters might expand production capacity to offset the U.S. cutback, and then take away U.S. market shares, seemed minimal. The volume of U.S. grain exports was increasing at the time, but in large part only through the use of export subsidies. A new "food aid" program, Public Law 480, was legislated in 1954 as part of farm support policy. The PL 480 program authorized sales of government-owned U.S. farm products to poor countries not for hard foreign exchange, but for the inconvertible currencies of those countries, on concessional credit terms. By 1960, fully 70 percent of U.S. wheat exports were moving on such a nondollar basis. Less than half of all U.S. agricultural export sales went through unsubsidized commercial channels.

The heavy use by the United States of direct export subsidies and the PL 480 export program, thinly disguised as food assistance to the poor, was hardly in the spirit of international free trade. The United States was, by the mid-1950s, a strong proponent of reduced protection for manufacturing, and was in the process of using a new international organization—the General Agreement on Tariffs and Trade (GATT)—to smooth the transition to a peacetime global economy by negotiating the lowering of tariffs on a broad array of manufactured goods. In agriculture, however, the United States initially resisted market-oriented reforms within the GATT, where it insisted that quantitative import restrictions tied to domestic production controls and direct export subsidies be explicitly allowed for agricultural products. In addition, a permanent "waiver" from the GATT rules was given unilaterally to the United States in 1955 so that it could continue to operate its dairy, beef, sugar, and other import-control programs for supported commodities even when there were no domestic production restraints.[14] A pattern of excusing agriculture from market disciplines—the pattern that emerged in the 1930s when the AAA survived while the NIRA did not—was thus still reflected in U.S. trade policy two decades later.

In the end, the attempted squeeze out of New Deal farm programs during the 1950s produced results that were meager and in some ways counterproductive. Although reform advocates succeeded in reducing price-support levels in real terms, technological and managerial im-

14. We discuss the GATT in greater detail in the next chapter; for early developments see Josling, Tangermann, and Warley 1996; and Swinbank and Tanner 1996.

provements cut farm production costs at least as fast, especially for larger commercial farm operations, so the attraction of these reduced price supports remained strong to most farmers.[15] Program participation rates remained high, and the tendency of commodity programs to distort production patterns through supply controls actually increased. Federal price guarantees for wheat in 1961, the year that Eisenhower left office, remained as much as 50 percent above the free market price that would have prevailed in the absence of government commodity loan rates, and for feed grains such as corn, support prices remained 20 to 30 percent above free market levels (Cochrane and Ryan 1976). As a consequence, farmers continued to forfeit their crops to the CCC, and the burden of government-owned stocks continued to rise, as shown in table 9. By 1961, government-owned stocks of corn were more than twice the level of 1953, and total carryover stocks of wheat were equal to more than an entire year's worth of utilization.

Partial Cash Out in the 1960s

Congressional agricultural policies in the Eisenhower era had proven expensive as well as intrusive. Net government expenditures exceeded $3 billion in fiscal year 1955 and were nearly as high in 1956 (see table 9). Continued high program costs through 1960, plus a partisan urge to reverse course, prompted the new Kennedy administration to abandon the faltering squeeze-out strategy. What followed was an important interlude of policy dispute and improvisation, which eventually moved Congress toward a new experiment with cash-out policy reform options—at least for export crops.[16] Henceforth, intru-

---

15. See D. Gale Johnson 1987 for a discussion of the failure of policy to adjust sufficiently to avoid interfering in farm commodity markets in the 1950s.

16. Among the supported commodities, *export crop* refers to the feed grains (primarily corn), wheat, cotton, and rice; and *import competing* refers to sugar, dairy, peanuts, and tobacco. This categorization is a somewhat simplistic expositional device. Corn, wheat, rice, sugar, and dairy products fit relatively neatly into their respective categories; starting in the 1960s, the cash out made the U.S. export crops competitive in world markets, while the import-competing commodities remained protected from international competition, with domestic prices exceeding world market levels. Dairy products (fluid milk, cheese, and other manufactured products) are subject also to complex pricing arrangements under a system of domestic regional marketing orders. Other commodities present complications as well. Exports account for a large proportion of wheat utilization, but a small amount is also imported (primarily from Canada), and domestic producers sometimes seek protection from the import competition. Cotton and tobacco are exported and imported (see table 7) under intricate domestic-production and trade rules. Peanuts have been produced under a two-price system since the 1977 farm bill. A limited quantity (used

Table 9.   Farm Program Expenditures and Net Income (in Billions of Dollars), 1948–1995

	CCC Expenditures	CCC Stocks Held	Direct Payments to Farmers	Net Farm Income	Direct Payments (% Net Farm Income)
1948	−0.20	0.1	0.26	17.7	1.5
1949	0.06	1.1	0.19	12.8	1.5
1950	1.61	2.6	0.28	13.6	2.1
1951	−0.78	1.4	0.29	15.9	1.8
1952	−0.24	1.1	0.28	15.0	1.8
1953	1.83	2.2	0.21	13.0	1.6
1954	1.33	3.4	0.26	12.4	2.1
1955	3.10	4.6	0.23	11.3	2.0
1956	2.94	5.4	0.56	11.3	4.9
1957	1.14	4.7	1.02	11.1	9.2
1958	1.05	4.7	1.09	13.2	8.3
1959	2.85	5.3	0.68	10.7	6.4
1960	1.56	6.0	0.70	11.2	6.3
1961	1.33	5.6	1.49	12.0	12.4
1962	2.05	4.5	1.75	12.1	14.4
1963	3.12	4.7	2.70	11.8	22.9
1964	3.17	4.3	2.18	10.5	20.8
1965	2.65	4.0	2.46	12.9	19.1
1966	1.54	3.1	3.28	14.0	23.4
1967	1.69	1.8	3.08	12.3	25.0
1968	3.20	0.9	3.46	12.3	28.2
1969	4.12	1.2	3.79	14.3	26.5
1970	3.78	1.8	3.72	14.4	25.8
1971	2.82	1.1	3.15	15.0	21.0
1972	3.98	0.8	3.96	19.5	20.3
1973	3.55	0.4	2.61	34.4	7.6
1974	1.00	0.2	0.53	27.3	2.0
1975	0.57	0.4	0.81	25.5	3.2
1976	1.46	0.6	0.73	20.2	3.6
1977	3.81	1.1	1.82	19.9	9.1
1978	5.66	1.2	3.03	25.2	12.0
1979	3.61	1.2	1.38	27.4	5.0
1980	2.75	2.8	1.29	16.1	8.0
1981	4.04	3.8	1.93	26.9	7.2
1982	11.65	5.5	3.49	23.8	14.7
1983	18.85	10.7	9.30	14.2	65.5
1984	7.32	6.6	8.43	26.1	32.3
1985	17.68	8.3	7.70	28.8	26.7
1986	25.81	13.9	11.81	31.0	38.1
1987	22.40	12.3	16.75	37.4	44.8
1988	12.50	4.9	14.48	38.0	38.1
1989	10.50	4.0	10.89	45.3	24.0
1990	6.50	2.1	9.30	44.8	20.8
1991	10.10	2.4	8.21	38.5	21.3
1992	9.74	1.7	9.17	48.0	19.1
1993	16.05	0.8	13.40	43.5	30.8
1994	10.34	0.7	7.88	48.4	16.3
1995	6.03	0.6	7.25	34.8	20.8

Note: Commodity Credit Corporation (CCC) columns refer to fiscal years, whereas other columns represent calendar years.
Source: U.S. Department of Agriculture, *Agricultural Statistics* (Washington, D.C.: U.S. Government Printing Office, various years).

sive market-distorting price supports for these crops would gradually be replaced with income support to farmers in the form of direct cash payments.

The political road toward this cash out was a bumpy one. With excess supplies of grains piling up on the streets of midwestern towns, the Kennedy administration's first move was toward more—rather than less—market intrusion. An "emergency" paid land diversion program was enacted, pushing idled acres to 64.7 million (an astonishing 27 percent of the 233.3 million planted acres) in 1962. Then, in May 1963, the option of less costly but even more intrusive *mandatory* supply controls was put to a vote among wheat farmers. Under the Kennedy administration's mandatory program, marketing certificates would be issued for wheat used for domestic consumption and exports. These certificates would keep the wheat price around $2.00 per bushel, well above the expected equilibrium market price without supply controls. In exchange for the certificate subsidies, wheat acreage would be cut and penalties would be imposed on farmers who overplanted. This mandatory program, if approved by a two-thirds referendum majority, would have reintroduced the most draconian supply-control features of the New Deal–era policies.

The alternative to the administration's mandatory wheat supply-control program that was offered to farmers by the 1963 referendum was a sharp cut in price-support intervention. The price-support level would be only 50 percent of parity, about $1.25 per bushel, under the referendum alternative. Participation in the program would be voluntary, with no penalties for overplanting (except loss of eligibility for the very low loan rate provided). In essence, the referendum alternative to mandatory supply controls was a cutout—an abrupt end of the existing wheat program without any payment of compensation.

More than one million farmers participated in the wheat referendum in 1963, and a 52 percent majority rejected the administration's proposal (see Cochrane and Ryan 1976). This defeat of the proposed wheat program was orchestrated by the Farm Bureau, which attacked mandatory supply controls as a loss of "freedom to farm" (see Hansen 1991). The Farm Bureau argued that Congress would provide a policy more generous than the cutout referendum alternative if the mandatory controls

---

for domestic consumption) receives a support price well above the world market level (hence, our classification of peanuts as import competing), while other peanuts (known as "additionals" and receiving a much lower support level) are exported at world prices.

were rejected. This judgment proved correct when a record-breaking wheat crop in 1963 added to already record levels of carryover stocks. Less than a month after the referendum failed, Democratic Senator George McGovern (South Dakota) proposed a continuation of *paid* land diversions, together with a wheat certificate program based on *voluntary* instead of mandatory participation. Under the McGovern proposals, wheat farmers who observed their acreage allotments would receive certificates redeemable by the CCC for seventy cents per bushel, enough to ensure revenues of two dollars per bushel on the 40 percent of production used for domestic consumption (see *Congressional Quarterly Almanac* 1965; Hansen 1991).

McGovern's proposal for a voluntary program based on redeemable wheat certificates reflected a shift in political sentiment away from reliance on intrusive CCC loan rates to raise market price levels, and toward direct cash payments to farmers that caused less market disruption. This shift in policy had been gaining strength for some time. The largest U.S. grain export companies and lowest-cost farm producers had begun to see damage to commercial sales abroad from high domestic support prices by the early 1960s. These interests were instrumental as early as 1962 in prompting Congress to authorize the secretary of agriculture to reduce loan rates (initially for corn) and to compensate farmers instead with direct payments. Cash payments were also given a larger role in the cotton program, under a plan to bring domestic cotton prices down to world price levels through subsidies to domestic handlers and millers. The legislation authorizing the new wheat and cotton programs was signed into law in April 1964, just in time to apply the redeemable certificates to the spring wheat harvest. The political shift toward a cash out was then reinforced in the 1965 farm bill, which set loan rates near world price levels and continued direct cash payments tied to production quantities for wheat and cotton. The 1965 farm bill also reauthorized payments for voluntary land idling.

This move toward direct payments—a partial cash out—in the mid-1960s spelled the end of the parity concept for setting price-support levels. It allowed domestic consumption to expand (aiding producers of livestock as well as food processors and consumers) and was less damaging to export sales, but it was not a move away from income support for farmers and came to enjoy considerable bipartisan support. Republican agriculturalists in the congressional minority applauded this shift in policy because it provided income to some of their constituents and avoided the most egregious applications of supply controls. Democratic and Republican legislators representing different geographic regions and commodities continued to spar over loan rates, levels of land idling, uses of paid versus unpaid land diversions, and the size of cash payments. But differences arising from these interparty, interregional, and intercommodity disputes were confined to the details of farm policy, and solutions were worked out internally within the agricultural policy establishment. The agriculturalists then presented a unified position to the Democrat majority that was in control of Congress and was willing to bear the incremental costs of the new support programs.

Direct cash payments had never before played so large a role in farm policy as they did following the mid-1960s. When the New Deal price-support programs began to operate in the 1930s, direct government payments to farmers constituted approximately 10 percent of net farm income. The level of payments then declined to less than 3 percent of net income when market prices rose during the Second World War and the Korean War, and remained under 10 percent of net farm income through the late 1950s (as shown in table 9). With the cashing out of farm programs, the share of net farm income derived from government payments rose to more than 25 percent in the second half of the 1960s. Even with these larger direct payments, the shift toward a cash out was incomplete. Market-intrusive policy instruments—particularly supply-control acreage-idling policies—remained in use. An average of nearly fifty-four million acres of crop land were idled annually under supply-control programs during 1965–69.

The move to provide expensive new cash payments to farmers proceeded in the 1960s despite significant slippage in numerical clout of the farm lobby in Congress. The landmark *Baker v. Carr* Supreme Court ruling of 1962—the "one man, one vote" decision—curtailed the overrepresentation of rural districts in state legislatures across the country, and eventually reduced the overrepresentation of rural districts in the U.S. House of Representatives as well. As late as 1966, rural districts still constituted 83 percent of an absolute House majority, but by 1973 they would make up only 60 percent of a majority (see Destler 1980). Despite this shrinking political base, and also despite growing federal budget deficits and concerns about inflation by the late 1960s, farm organizations retained the power to preserve commodity-support programs that—under the cash-out approach to policy—became increasingly expensive to taxpayers. These programs survived in part because farm program spending, although increasing in absolute terms and growing steadily larger in *per farm* terms (even within payment limitations), was not growing as fast as federal spending in other areas. Increased spending on health, education, and housing under President Lyndon Johnson's Great Society initiatives, and on defense during the mid-1960s escalation of the Vietnam War, gave proponents of farm spending plenty of room to hide their own modest budget increases. Even though nominal outlays increased, the share of the total federal expenditures going to farm programs actually fell, from about 3.5 percent during the decade of the 1950s to only 2.0 percent by the late 1960s.

Rather than this gradual cash-out approach to reform, could the failed squeeze-out strategy of the 1950s have yielded by the mid-1960s to a more decisive buyout or cutout of the traditional farm support programs? A buyout, with its larger up-front payments to farmers, was never seriously attempted during the 1950s or 1960s, although it was on several occasions discussed and even advocated as an attractive option. Postwar agricultural economists offered various proposals for the government to buy or cut its way out of farm price-support guarantees. One such proposal, in 1954, recommended that the government issue price-support quotas to farmers, then repurchase the quotas, devaluing them each time by the buyback price (Brinegar and Johnson 1954). A more serious buyout strategy was endorsed eight years later, in 1962, by the Committee on Economic Development. It proposed an "adaptive program for agriculture" that would have dropped support prices immediately. Farmers were to be compensated over a period of five years through a "temporary income protection program," and a costly retraining and adjustment assistance program was designed to ease the burden of the expected one-third reduction in the total farm labor force. Farm groups found the proposal repugnant, press comment was adverse, and the idea died (see D. Paarlberg 1964).

Thus, farm policy practitioners focused by the end of the 1960s on a gradual and partial cash out of the New Deal–era price-support programs for export crops, backed by a still-heavy reliance on supply-control acreage reductions. Reform advocates who promoted more extensive changes encountered resistance. The Republican administration of Richard Nixon pushed for more ambitious reform when farm legislation came up for renewal in 1970, but this was blocked by the Democratic Congress. The Nixon administration sought authority to set support prices anywhere from zero to 90 percent of parity, while still endorsing, according to Secretary of Agriculture Clifford Hardin, "long-range resource adjustment involving voluntary land retirement"

(*Congressional Quarterly Almanac* 1970, 635). Congress insisted on retaining a stronger price-support floor than the administration proposed. In the 1970 farm bill, direct cash payments were continued to producers of wheat, feed grains, and cotton who voluntarily set aside some of their acreage, and farmers who met overall acreage reduction requirements were given flexibility to plant whatever crops they chose on land they retained in production. Direct payments remained above 20 percent of total net farm income in the early 1970s, and sixty-two million acres were idled in 1972.

An Illusory Squeeze Out in the 1970s

When a remarkable international commodity price boom in the early 1970s suddenly made planting for the world market more lucrative than participation in the government support programs, it momentarily appeared that something of a farm program squeeze out was going to be achieved. This proved to be only an illusion: the commodity price boom was temporary, and advocates of more generous farm support programs were able to use the temporary boom as an opportunity to boost the levels of guaranteed price supports.

Farm commodity prices began to rise sharply in late 1972 and peaked in mid-1974. Crop prices nearly doubled during this short period. The 1970s farm price boom was part of an overall macroeconomic shock, generated in part by the Nixon administration's 1971 decision to abandon the gold standard and devalue the U.S. dollar, which led to the collapse of the Bretton-Woods regime of fixed exchange rates. Mismanaged election-year wage and price controls and lax Federal Reserve policy, together with simultaneous peaking of business cycles around the world, drove up the prices of many primary commodities, including gold, copper, petroleum, bauxite, and tin. In agriculture, grain markets were also pinched in 1972 following a series of secretive purchases of U.S. wheat by the Soviet Union. These export sales were subsidized unnecessarily by the Department of Agriculture and political repercussions swirled around what came to be called "the great grain robbery" (see R. Paarlberg 1985; Hansen 1991). Still, the global farm price boom mostly grew out of the larger macroeconomic phenomena that affected all commodity markets (Schuh 1976).

The commodity price boom quickly pushed market prices above the nominal support levels provided by the 1970 farm bill. As a result, cash payments to farmers declined, surplus government stocks were sold, and export subsidies were (belatedly) terminated. It seemed at the time that the government was being extricated from its involvement in agriculture by the new market conditions. Democratic Senator Herman E. Talmadge (Georgia), chair of the Senate Agriculture Committee, warned farm program lobbies in February 1973 that "the pressures on us to do nothing—to let existing legislation expire and eliminate permanent legislation on the books—is extremely great"(*Congressional Quarterly Almanac* 1973, 290). But the proponents of farm policy reform failed to take the necessary steps in the early 1970s to extend this temporary market eclipse of farm programs into a more lasting squeeze out. False anxieties about future world food supplies contributed to this failure. The price inflation and temporary tightening of markets were misread as a "world food crisis," and the 1973 farm bill was written, for the first time in thirty years, with the objective of *stimulating* agricultural production.

Farm policy reformers inside the Nixon administration at one point proposed to use the opportunity presented by high market prices to eliminate direct cash payments to farmers. Under their proposal for the 1973 farm bill, cash support payments would be phased out over three years, while price-support loan rates would be retained at modest levels, along with the authority for direct payments for land idling if commodity stocks again began to accumulate. In effect, the Nixon administration tried to use high market prices to achieve a cutout. The Democratic Congress, seeing this proposal for what it was, instead reaffirmed the cash payments approach by adopting the concept of "deficiency payments" to export crop producers, calculated as the difference between market prices for a crop and a legislated "target price."

Once target prices were embraced, debate centered on the levels at which they would be established. The original levels were well below the high market prices prevailing in 1974 (see figure 9). This seemed to be a victory for a passive squeeze-out reform strategy, and total farm program expenditures fell to less than $1 billion as market prices peaked. Reform advocates hailed this temporary suspension of program activity as the dawn of a new era of market-oriented agriculture. But the reformers' hopes were disappointed. Farm support program beneficiaries anticipated continued inflation and succeeded in obtaining an escalator for nominal target prices in the 1973 law.[17] This pro-

---

17. The inflation escalator included a downward technical adjustment to offset measured increases in farm productivity, something of a concession to reform-oriented squeeze-out proponents.

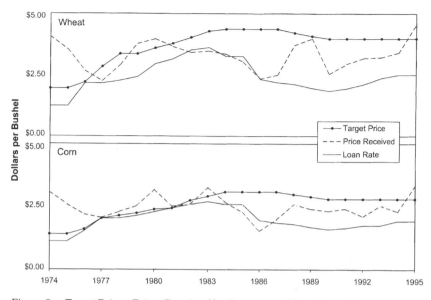

Figure 9.   Target Prices, Prices Received by Farmers, and Loan Rates for Wheat and Corn, 1974–1995
Source: U.S. Department of Agriculture, *Agricultural Statistics* (Washington, D.C.: U.S. Government Printing Office, various years).

tected them from a squeeze out of their income support through an inflationary erosion of an entitlement guarantee made only in nominal terms.[18]

With both a quick legislated cutout option rejected and the likelihood of a slow inflation-driven squeeze out diminished, the 1973 Agriculture and Consumer Protection Act was for most crops just a continuation of the earlier partial cash-out approach to farm policy. Support mechanisms remained tied to market prices, to farmers' planting decisions, and to possible requirements for participation in annual supply-control acreage idling. For one import-competing crop, however, a cutout reform was seemingly achieved. With world sugar prices above domestic support levels, the House of Representatives failed (in June 1974) to extend the U.S. sugar price-support program scheduled to expire at the end of the year. Yet even this apparent cutout of one commodity program would be rescinded a few years later.

18. Pierson labels this kind of inflation-driven entitlement loss "decrementalism" (1994, 20).

Any illusion of a squeeze out ended when market prices collapsed in 1975. Because the instruments of farm support were still in place, commodity programs became burdensome again. Lobby pressures for a further strengthening of farm support began to mount with nonfarm price inflation unabated and farmers caught in a "cost-price" squeeze. As agricultural prices were falling, Republican President Gerald Ford vetoed another measure that would have raised nominal target prices and loan rates.

When the 1973 farm bill came up for renewal in 1977, sharply increased target prices and loan rates were still being proposed by the agricultural lobby in Congress. The administration of Democratic President Jimmy Carter (elected in 1976) unsuccessfully resisted these proposals on budget grounds. The 1977 farm bill not only raised nominal target prices and loan rates, it also tied future rates to increases in farm production costs. The apparent cutout of the sugar program was reversed when Congress reinstituted sugar support at a level above world prices.[19] This was followed by yet another "emergency" act in 1978, which raised the wheat target price by sixty cents per bushel and increased the loan rate for cotton.[20] Together the adjustments made in 1977 and 1978 undercut any remaining hope that farm program benefits could be squeezed away through inflation. Federal government CCC farm program outlays jumped back to nearly $4 billion, demonstrating that a lasting squeeze out had not been achieved from the opportunity created by the 1970s commodity price boom.

How did farm interests manage so readily to block any diminution of the partially cashed-out commodity-support programs during and after the price boom in the early 1970s? For one thing, farm organizations aware of their diminished independent voting power in Congress were clever enough to forge links with other interest groups that were then getting stronger. Urban constituencies that might otherwise oppose farm support expenditures were transformed from adversaries into allies: in a classic legislative "logroll" they agreed to a mutually beneficial package in which farm supports and spending on food stamps and other nutrition programs would be voted forward together (Ferejohn 1986; Browne 1988). Several reform-minded secretaries of agriculture

19. The new sugar support program guaranteed producers a minimum of 13.5 cents per pound at a time when the world market price had fallen to 10 cents.

20. More drastic intervention was considered (but eventually rejected) by Congress. A radical new farm organization, the American Agriculture Movement, made its presence known by camping out in Washington to demand strengthening of the farm programs.

fought against this convergence of lobbying interests in the 1970s by offering to give the rapidly expanding food stamp budget to the Department of Health, Education and Welfare, but the Agriculture Committees of Congress would have none of it. USDA spending on domestic food programs quickly exceeded total spending on farm programs, but farm organizations, which valued the urban district support that was bought in this fashion, did not complain too much.

In addition to such logrolling tactics, farm interests managed to protect their programs by taking maximum advantage of the period of macroeconomic instability. When inflationary monetary growth and strong international markets drove up prices, the farm organizations responded by demanding higher levels of underlying guarantees for loan rates and cash payments. This demand was easy for Congress to satisfy at the time (as during the Second World War) because the higher support levels at first implied no actual increase in short-term spending outlays. The larger farm spending outlays would only come later when the boom finally ended.

The growth of farm subsidies in foreign countries—especially in Western Europe—was also used by U.S. farm groups as a new device for maintaining their own high support levels. When, in the 1970s, the EEC transformed from a net importer to a net exporter of sugar, and began using export subsidies to dump its excesses onto the world market, sugar producers in the United States were given an excuse for demanding the restoration of their own protectionist program. Taking up a line they would also use effectively during the 1986–93 GATT negotiations, U.S. farmers argued they should not be asked to accept *unilateral* market-oriented reforms without guarantees of comparable reforms in competitor countries.

In retrospect, why didn't reform proponents attempt to use the opportunity presented by high market prices in 1973 to offer a buyout to farmers? The commodity price boom generated unexpected farm budget savings, and reform advocates might have tried to capture unspent farm subsidy dollars to offer to farmers as an up-front inducement to abandon permanently the partially cashed-out support policies of the 1960s. This sort of thinking later emerged when prices were unexpectedly high during the 1995–96 farm bill debate, but not during the 1970s commodity boom. The erroneous world food crisis mentality temporarily undercut the drive to end farm subsidy policies. A common view was that the era of low food prices had come to an end—along with the era of low energy prices. Moreover, Congress had not yet organized its budget procedures around projections of future spending, or around future spending caps. The Congressional Budget Office (CBO), which eventually would be charged with providing budget expenditure forecasts, was not created until 1974. CBO forecasts would be used by agriculturalists in 1995–96 to capture projected expenditures otherwise lost under circumstances of a sharp rise in market prices. But in 1973, no one was yet thinking that the farm sector might have a claim on what would otherwise be *unspent* support payments.

Costly Cash Out in the 1980s

The 1977 and 1978 farm bills pushed up nominal target prices and loan rates, but with inflation still running at high levels the increased costs of the farm programs were moderate. Less land was being idled than previously (just under twenty million acres in 1978 and 1979) to control commodity supplies and, not incidentally, the budget costs of deficiency payments. The White House shifted back into Republican hands after 1980, and market conditions strengthened and acreage idling was suspended in 1980 and 1981. David Stockman, the budget director for the new Reagan administration, signaled an intent to mark farm program spending for sharp reductions, as one part of the administration's attempt to reduce government spending as a share of national income.

To cut the level of projected farm program spending, an "omnibus" farm bill that included essentially all commodities (tobacco remained the exception) would be subject to explicit expenditure limitations set by a congressional budget resolution. The Reagan administration proposed an outright elimination of income support through target prices and deficiency payments, and it sought discretionary authority to lower, not raise, price-support loan rates. This was a stark cutout proposal, one that Republican as well as Democratic agriculturalists in Congress refused to accept. Even so, when the new four-year Agriculture and Food Act of 1981 was passed it seemed fiscally disciplined at the time. Budget hawks in the administration and Congress had whittled down the estimated cost of the bill from $16.6 billion in one early House version to just $11 billion. The new farm bill provided *nominal* increases in target price levels of 6 percent annually, but these increases seemed austere to most observers given the U.S. economy's 13.5 percent inflation rate the previous year.

What the authors of the 1981 farm bill failed to anticipate was the looming end to high inflation, already being effected through a tightening of monetary policy at the Federal Reserve Board. By 1982, tight monetary policies had driven up real interest rates and thrown the U.S. economy into a recession. The high real rates of interest also pushed up the foreign exchange value of the dollar (by roughly 70 percent in nominal terms, and 40 percent in real terms, between 1980 and 1985) making U.S. farm products less competitive in world markets. For U.S. farmers, this was a painful blow. Anticipating that the export boom of the 1970s would continue, many farmers had borrowed heavily to expand production. But when agricultural exports, which had peaked at over $43 billion in 1981, fell to just $26 billion by 1986, commodity prices and land values collapsed. Farmers who had earlier borrowed against inflated land assessments suddenly found their debts unserviceable and their livelihoods threatened by foreclosure. With tight monetary policy in the 1980s, the U.S. farm sector slumped into its worst financial crisis since the Great Depression.

The unanticipated collapse of exports and the farm financial crisis in the mid-1980s put enormous stress on the farm support programs. As the U.S. dollar appreciated and exports dropped, U.S. farm commodity prices fell to the level of the newly raised loan rates set in place by the 1981 farm bill, and would have fallen further without these price guarantees (see figure 9). This caused a substantial buildup of government-held commodity stocks, as well as massive government cash outlays, when farm output was diverted from commercial markets into storage under CCC loans. Annual expenditures increased to $11.6 billion in fiscal 1982 alone.

To constrain the rapidly rising costs of the farm support programs, and to rein in the accumulation of CCC commodity stocks, the Reagan administration first fell back on the traditional strategy of imposing more supply controls. The secretary of agriculture used discretionary authority to divert 77.9 million acres from production in 1983 (see table 8). This repeated the earlier boom-collapse policy pattern of the 1950s, when failure to lower high wartime support prices resulted in renewed reliance on acreage idling to control supply. But with increased dependence on international markets for farm products in the 1980s, the supply-control strategy proved even less successful than before. Foreign producers responded to the world price floor set by U.S. loan rates by increasing their own planted area, and the U.S. share of world grain trade fell from 54 to 36 percent.

The Reagan administration also made use of an expensive new payment-in-kind (PIK) mechanism in which government-owned stocks were given to farmers (in effect, given *back* to farmers) in lieu of cash payments. The distributed PIK commodities, treated as "off budget" for accounting purposes, were valued at more than $10 billion in 1983. During fiscal years 1982–84, budgeted farm program expenditures amounted to nearly another $38 billion.

Faced with these more intrusive supply-control programs and higher off-budget and budgeted outlays, the Reagan administration tried again to cut farm subsidies sharply in its submission to Congress for the 1985 farm bill. It proposed a repeal of the permanent 1949 farm program legislation, a lowering of loan rates, and a phasing down of direct payments to achieve a reduction in spending from $60–85 billion projected under existing programs to just $20–35 billion. This proposal, amounting to a severe four-year squeeze out (perhaps a prelude to a cutout) failed quickly—it was labeled "dead on arrival" by Republican as well as Democratic members of Congress—and was ignored.[21] Instead, with political sympathy for financially stressed farmers running high in 1985, agriculturalists in both parties competed to offer more aid—despite the already record levels of farm program costs. The higher underlying support levels that the farm lobby had been able to engineer during the earlier boom thus proved relatively easy for them to defend during the bust.

The 1985 farm bill debate in Congress nevertheless became an important one. With the Reagan administration's cutout approach rejected, a struggle emerged between those who wanted to aid farmers by restoring U.S. competitiveness with lower loan rates versus those who preferred a more determined use of supply controls. The first approach followed the partial cash-out strategy, while the second would have revived the interventionist programs of the New Deal era. Pursuit of the partial cash-out strategy prevailed in the end. Lower loan rates meant fewer market distortions, and on this account the 1985 farm bill was a victory for policy reform. But this cash-out reform move did not come cheaply. Farm groups were politically powerful enough to insist that target prices remain as high as ever, even though loan rates were lowered. This implied even larger cash deficiency payments to farmers, which diminished the magnitude of the reform victory in 1985. Con-

21. Although the Senate was under Republican majority control in 1985, both the Republican chair of the Senate Agriculture Committee, Jesse Helms (North Carolina) and the ranking member of the House Agriculture Committee, Republican Edward Madigan (Illinois), introduced the administration's bill "by request," indicating they did not support the proposals.

taining the rise of these payments eventually required new supply-control market intrusions as well.

The 1985 farm bill fixed nominal target prices for two years, then permitted only modest (2 to 5 percent) yearly declines in the last three years of its five-year duration. Meanwhile, under the so-called Findley Amendment, the secretary of agriculture was authorized to lower loan rates immediately by up to 25 percent, and then to keep them in the range of 75 to 85 percent of an "Olympic" moving average of past market price levels, in order to make U.S. farm exports more competitive in world markets.[22] With the gap widened between loan rates and target prices, the five-year cost of the new farm bill was estimated at $52 billion at the time, and extension of the PIK program would eventually add another $17.5 billion to total costs during 1987–89. To keep these costs from escalating even higher, requirements were established for an *unpaid* Acreage Reduction Program (ARP) of land set asides as an eligibility criterion for receiving price-support loans or deficiency payments. Acreage bases and set-aside requirements were specified on a crop-specific basis, so the planting flexibility that had temporarily been provided by earlier farm bills was lost. Over forty million acres were idled under these crop-specific acreage set-aside requirements in 1986, 1987, and 1988.

Another costly cash-out dimension of the 1985 farm bill was the introduction of a generous new "marketing loan" program for cotton and rice. These price-support loans could be paid back at world market prices instead of CCC loan rates, meaning they would carry higher budget costs if the world price fell below the loan rate. The introduction of marketing loans (mandatory for cotton and rice but at the discretion of the secretary of agriculture for feed grains and wheat) again increased U.S. competitiveness in international markets, since farmers could now sell their products abroad instead of forfeiting them to the government. Yet it also provided wealthy producers with a convenient loophole to avoid per-farm payment limitations and was too expensive and inequitable to be easily classified as a step in the direction toward farm policy reform.

A new export subsidy scheme, the Export Enhancement Program (EEP), was also institutionalized by the 1985 farm bill, requiring the sec-

22. For example, 1985 target prices for wheat and corn were lowered slightly over four years, from $4.38 and $3.03, respectively, to $4.10 and $2.84 by 1989. Loan rates dropped immediately from $3.30 and $2.55 in 1985 to $2.40 and $1.92 in 1986. The Olympic moving average, which was adopted for setting future loan rates, drops the lowest and highest of the past five years and takes the average of the remaining three.

retary of agriculture to use $2 billion worth of CCC stocks as export bonuses over three years. Farm-sector proponents of the EEP claimed it would have dual effects: it would reduce grain stockpiles, and it would give the United States a weapon against specific subsidized export sales from Europe with the stated intent of raising the cost of European farm policies and bringing this troublesome competitor to the bargaining table for agricultural trade negotiations. The Reagan administration initially opposed the EEP, but dropped its opposition in exchange for crucial votes in Congress for omnibus budget legislation. In this farm lobby victory, the administration's Office of Management and Budget (OMB) classified the EEP (like the PIK) as off budget. This politically convenient decision was based on the argument that the government already owned the CCC stocks being given away, and that the export subsidy outlays would be offset by direct savings on storage expenses, and by indirect savings on future deficiency payments, as domestic prices were pushed up by the subsidization of exports.[23]

Thus, in the context of a continuing macroeconomic crisis, the relatively generous terms of the 1985 farm bill led to a sharp increase in farmer dependence on government program participation, more cash payments, more acreage set asides, and more trade distortions. Just as the inflation of the 1970s had created the momentary illusion that the government was finally getting out of agriculture, its abatement in the early 1980s and the expensive and intrusive interventions that followed the 1985 farm bill created something of the opposite illusion: that reform progress had been reversed and the government was moving back into a much more costly and market-distorting role again. Temporarily, the government's involvement in agriculture did increase. The annual wheat acreage base eligible for program payments rose from an average of sixty-three million acres under the 1970 and 1973 farm bills to nearly seventy-eight million acres by the mid-1980s, which meant that during the most costly farm program years the national wheat acreage base actually exceeded the largest acreage ever planted (see Thompson 1990). Farm program participation expanded further under the exceptionally generous provisions of the 1985 farm bill, despite gradual ero-

23. Bruce Gardner (1996) provides a comprehensive evaluation of the political origins, operation, and economic effects of the EEP. An ad hoc targeted export subsidy program using CCC wheat stocks to augment commercial sales had been created earlier (in 1983) as an off-budget program under discretionary authority of the secretary of agriculture. In chapter 3, we discuss the failure of international negotiations under GATT to discipline export subsidies of the Europeans as one cause of these U.S. export subsidy policies.

sion in the real dollar value of per-bushel deficiency payments. For corn, the principal feed grain produced in the United States, the percentage of production acres enrolled in federal farm programs more than doubled from around 40 percent in the late 1970s to nearly 90 percent by 1987. Direct subsidies to corn farmers during this same period jumped from 4 percent to nearly 70 percent of the total market value of U.S. corn production.

How did farm groups succeed yet again, in 1985, in extracting such generous benefits from the political system? The farm financial crisis of the 1980s generated broadly based public support for farmers, which eased the political problem considerably. Additional support for farmers had been generated by a 1980 partial embargo on U.S. grain sales to the Soviet Union following the Afghanistan invasion. And in Congress, although members from farm districts were fewer in number than ever before, they found a new logrolling partner to help defend the farm programs: the environmental lobby, which had emerged from the 1970s with considerable political clout.

It was something of a challenge for the farm lobby to overcome the mistrust between farmers (protective of their private property rights) and environmental activists (ready to impose sharp government regulations). Yet, the advantages seen by some farm groups from idling land to boost prices dovetailed neatly with the interests of environmentalists in idling land to reduce soil erosion, groundwater contamination, and loss of wildlife habitats. The legislative coalition that was forged between farm and environmental groups in the 1980s renewed an old partnership that was effective in the 1930s and again in the 1950s. Farm groups helped revive this alliance in the 1980s by welcoming inclusion in the 1985 farm bill, with only token protestations, of language for several environmentally "green" measures. These measures included so-called sod buster and swamp buster provisions that could hypothetically withdraw benefits from farmers who plowed fragile lands or filled in wetlands, as well as various other "conservation compliance" requirements. In return, the farm lobby won environmentalist support for a new Conservation Reserve Program (CRP). The 1985 CRP authorized cash rental payments to farmers to idle forty-five million acres of erodible cropland for a ten-year period. Environmentalists applauded the benefits that long-term land idling would provide, while farmers and their lobbying organizations understood that a large long-term *paid* land retirement would lessen the need for unpaid annual ARP set-aside requirements. The 1985 farm bill was followed by a torrent of activity to attract voluntary land enrollments in the new CRP, with high rental rates as the main inducement.

The conservation compliance measures and CRP of 1985 helped transform many of the environmental interest groups from potential enemies of farm programs into helpful allies, and in this new relationship farmers lost very little. The conservation compliance provisions, though potentially onerous, were lightly enforced by state Soil Conservation Service offices staffed with sympathetic agriculturalists from the USDA, rather than by regulators from the Environmental Protection Agency. Participation in the CRP was voluntary and, since the rental rates per acre offered by the government for CRP land were typically higher than the prevailing market rental rates, participation could be lucrative.[24]

Considered with the increased shares of total national production that were enrolled in the farm commodity-support programs during the 1980s, initiation of the new CRP reflected a desire by the Agricultural Committees in Congress that farmers *not* be squeezed out of programs: without broad participation, the ARP requirements and long-term land idling would not have the intended supply-restraining and price-boosting effects. In this regard, a certain amount of strategic gamesmanship transpired between Congress, the USDA bureaucracy, and the farmer participants as program benefits mushroomed. The motives of Congress and the USDA are mixed—one goal is to support farm income while another is to control budget costs. Farmers have a simpler strategic problem of choosing from a menu of voluntary programs to maximize their present and future gains. Protecting future gains naturally required maintaining future program eligibility, which sometimes induced farmers to plant certain crops even when short-term market conditions should have discouraged doing so. The voluntary nature of the farm programs, in combination with their heavy reliance on acreage reductions, produced needless costs and distortions. In order to lure farmers into voluntary participation in the unpaid annual ARPs, the government had to raise program benefits for crops on permitted acres to high levels. This encouraged farmers to apply excessive chemical inputs on permitted acres, which in turn led to calls from environmentalists for a paid conservation reserve. But the CRP was also made

24. See Thurman 1995 for a cogent argument against policies that couple policies designed to achieve environmental objectives to programs designed to provide income support to farmers or to restrict supplies.

voluntary, so its rental payments per acre had to be made even higher than other land rental rates to induce farmers' participation. Since these other rental rates embodied program payments, the government was constantly bidding against itself to secure voluntary farmer participation in various acreage reduction schemes. The cost to taxpayers of farm programs and market intrusiveness rose at the same time.

Amid these costly policy malfunctions, it was easy to overlook the important gains that were made under the 1985 farm bill, including the crucial lowering of loan rates for export crops. The 1985 farm bill also took several important first steps toward "decoupling" cash payments to farmers from planting decisions. The program acreage bases and the yields per acre that would be eligible for deficiency payments were effectively frozen, denying farmers the old option of increasing production levels in the short term to boost their eligibility for government support in the longer term. Further decoupling was made possible by a little noticed "zero certification" provision that allowed farmers to plant any nonprogram crop other than fruits or vegetables on their base acreage while maintaining that base in the commodity programs (see Cochrane and Runge 1992). Yet another new provision in farm program law, known as "50-92" (later "0-85"), entitled wheat and feed grain producers to collect 92 (later 85) percent of the deficiency payments on their permitted acreage even if they used half (later all) of those acres for conservation purposes rather than planting crops.[25] This allowed yet more decoupling of program payments from cropping decisions. Thus, the steps taken in 1985 to lower loan rates and to begin to decouple deficiency payment eligibility from production decisions ensured that the earlier progress toward a cashing out of farm program benefits for export crops—and hence toward a less market-intrusive future for U.S. farm programs—was continued under the 1985 farm bill rather than reversed, even if at a very high short-run cost.

1985 Buyout Proposals

The large cash outlays for farm programs in the 1980s again raise the question of why reform advocates did not attempt a buyout. Did reformers miss a chance to use these large expenditures to secure more

---

25. Rice and cotton farmers, however, were still required to keep at least 50 percent of their base acreage in production in order to collect deficiency payments. The 50 percent minimum was extended to ensure adequate domestic input supplies for rice and cotton processors.

far-reaching restrictions on future programs? Several buyout initiatives were proposed in the course of the 1985 farm bill debate, but the only one that survived—a federal buyout of dairy cows—was a buyout in name only.

Dairy producers had been as successful as any of the farm lobby groups in ratcheting support levels upward during the commodity price boom of the 1970s. They gave the name "buyout" to one of their 1985 proposals for perpetuating the dairy programs. Congress approved their "whole herd buyout" scheme, a program that required the government to buy (and then slaughter or sell for export) entire herds of dairy cows, in return for promises from individual farmers that they would stay out of the dairy business—but only *for five years*. This program operated for 18 months and ultimately removed 1.3 million of the nation's 11 million dairy cows from milk production, allowing the government to reduce its purchases of surplus milk by roughly one-half. Dairy organizations supported this program as a supply-control measure—it was by no means a buyout that ended a farm sector intervention program. It was expensive in the short term, although a part of the cost was offset by assessments on producers. It was also widely criticized for the unnecessary subsidies it gave to older dairy farmers who were planning to retire soon anyway, it was poorly targeted (more than one hundred individual dairy farmers received government payments greater than $1 million through the program), and it angered livestock producers who feared a depressive effect on meat prices (and who were as a consequence promised $250 million worth of government red meat purchases).

Something closer to a real buyout scheme was briefly debated but ultimately rejected by Congress in 1985. This bill, introduced by Republican Senator Rudy Boschwitz (Minnesota) and Democratic Senator David Boren (Oklahoma), replaced all conventional commodity program support expenditures with fixed payments to farmers. The "transition payments" under the Boschwitz-Boren proposal would be fully decoupled from both market prices and planting decisions. The distribution of these payments would be based solely on the past acreage and yield histories of individual farmers. The Boschwitz-Boren decoupled transition payments were offered as a de facto buyout; they were calculated to be generous at the outset (large enough to prevent any first-year loss of farm income above a farmer's variable costs), but then they would be cut sharply, to only one-half of their original level within five years, at which time the farm sector would be expected to survive essentially on its own.[26]

The Boschwitz-Boren transition payment buyout scheme was killed in the Senate Agriculture Committee, having been broadly rejected by all farm groups, including the Republican-leaning Farm Bureau that eleven years later would endorse a remarkably similar decoupled payment scheme in the 1996 FAIR Act. The reasons for rejection of this Boschwitz-Boren buyout in 1985 were straightforward. With the farm sector in the depths of a severe financial crisis, most farm program beneficiaries were in no mood to experiment with a such a radical plan. Opposition to the Boschwitz-Boren buyout approach also developed around its projected short-term cost to taxpayers. The CBO estimated that the buyout would cost an unprecedented $51 billion over its first three years, higher budget costs than anticipated at the time under continuation of existing deficiency payment programs.[27]

As the farm bill debate progressed through 1985, falling market prices eventually led the projected costs of other farm bill proposals to reach similar levels to the decoupled Boschwitz-Boren payments, and the farm bill actually passed by Congress in the end was even more expensive—it cost taxpayers $25.8 billion in its first year alone. But at the time the Boschwitz-Boren buyout was first being presented, these huge costs had not yet been incurred, so it was the decoupled transition payments approach that looked too expensive. From a political perspective the Boschwitz-Boren bill actually lost both ways: in the eyes of budget officials it was initially too generous, yet in the eyes of farmers it was not generous enough compared to the available alternative of continuing the existing support programs.[28]

---

26. Boschwitz and Boren proposed loan rates of $2.20 and $1.90 per bushel for wheat and corn, respectively, $0.50 per pound for cotton, and $5.50 per hundredweight for rice. Decoupled payments were to start at $1.42 and $0.94 per bushel for wheat and corn, $0.18 per pound for cotton, and $4.26 per hundredweight for rice, then fall 10 percent per year from 1987 through 1991.

27. Some critics also rejected the Boren-Boschwitz plan because they doubted that the promised reduction in transition payments would ever take place. As originally introduced, the bill contained a loophole that allowed the secretary of agriculture to continue the initial payment levels if poor market circumstances precluded the reductions.

28. After the bill was defeated in the Agriculture Committee, Boschwitz brought it to the Senate floor as an amendment to the farm bill then working its way through Congress. It was defeated 42 to 48 on November 22, 1985. Democrats voted against the amendment 3 to 39, while Republicans gave Boschwitz a sympathy vote of 39 to 9.

The strongest opposition to the Boschwitz-Boren buyout proposal came from Democratic populist farm groups (especially northern plains wheat producers) whose membership lived in communities so heavily dependent upon farm support programs that a full transition to the market—even if generously supported through cash payments in the short term—simply held no appeal. These groups championed the 1985 Harkin-Gephardt Bill, a scheme for mandatory supply controls, and rejected Boschwitz-Boren because they said it would cost the taxpayer too much money, produce windfall gains for big agribusiness companies (who would get access to low-priced commodities), and reduce farmers to the status of welfare recipients. The Farm Bureau joined in condemning the welfarelike aspect of the decoupled transition payments, and in the years that followed it became anathema in many farm circles even to mention the concept of decoupling.

The Reform Problem after the 1985 Farm Bill

Established entitlement programs that have lost their original rationale but are defended by well-organized beneficiaries are always difficult to reform. In the case of farm commodity-support programs, the concentration of benefits in agricultural asset values has provided strong incentives for owners of those assets to seek to perpetuate the original interventions. The labor adjustments brought about by agricultural modernization, and farm incomes that lagged behind nonfarm incomes into the 1960s, gave farm interests a political motivation to support the commodity programs, even though these programs were not effective in addressing the long-term adjustment problems the farm sector faced. Reforms in farm policy since the Second World War have been incremental, incomplete, and often costly. Through 1985, the principal reform was a partial cash out that allowed intrusive loan rate price guarantees to fall for export crops.

When reformers made more direct efforts to cut farm programs sharply (as in 1970, 1981, and again in 1985), well-organized farm lobbies said no. Proposals were occasionally made to buy out the farm support programs instead, but these either failed to gain serious political attention (in the 1950s and 1960s), were not really a permanent buyout at all (the 1985 whole herd dairy buyout), or were rejected by budget officials as too generous and by farmers as not generous enough (the 1985 Boschwitz-Boren decoupled payments proposal).

A substantial effort to achieve a squeeze out was made by a Republican Congress in 1948, and again in the early 1950s by a Republican pres-

ident and Congress. This squeeze out would have lowered farm program costs and distortions by moving to lower and more flexible price-
support levels, without any cash compensation to the farmers for
whom price supports were being reduced. Yet the rapid productivity
growth occurring in agriculture meant production costs were falling
even faster, so even at lower real price-support levels, rates of participation in the farm programs continued to increase, surplus stocks continued to accumulate, and the squeeze-out strategy proved inadequate to
achieve less intervention. Higher market prices during the worldwide
inflationary boom in the early 1970s did prompt many farmers to stop
using the government programs temporarily. It briefly appeared that a
more passive squeeze out was underway, but the impression was illusory. Farm organizations used this interlude of higher prices to ratchet
up underlying levels of promised government support, as they had
during the Second World War.

The illusory squeeze out of the 1970s was followed in the 1980s by a
seemingly massive setback for reform. Under the intrusive 1985 farm
bill, program participation increased and budget costs hit record highs,
even while markets sustained damaging distortions as a result of new
acreage restrictions and renewed export subsidies. But, in retrospect,
the 1985 farm bill outcome was not a step backward for reform. While
costly in the adverse macroeconomic context in which it operated, the
principal thrust of the 1985 farm bill was to continue moving down the
reform path of a partial cash out. Rather than seek to protect farm income with mandatory supply controls or high loan rates that would
have reduced U.S. competitiveness in world markets, the 1985 farm bill
dropped loan rates sharply for export crops and supported farm income with more cash payments. By reducing the market intrusiveness
of price-support levels, the shift to more reliance on cash payments under the terms of the 1985 farm bill allowed exports to grow, and was
therefore reform progress of a certain kind.

The reform limitations of this partial cash out of farm policy are evident in at least three dimensions. First, the cash out was extended only to
one category of commodity programs: those supporting export crops—
primarily wheat, corn, cotton, and rice. For dairy and highly protected
import-competing crops, including most conspicuously sugar and
peanuts, no cash out was yet underway. Farmers continued to receive
protection for these crops through market-intrusive import restriction
policies and domestic production quotas that functioned in the traditional way—by burdening consumers rather than taxpayers.

Second, the cash out was incomplete, even for export crops. The payments to farmers were not fully decoupled either from market prices or planting decisions, so they continued to distort market outcomes. In order to contain the budget cost of the cash support payments, the government too often found itself relying even more heavily on supply controls.

Third, the cash payments made under the commodity programs were poorly disciplined and poorly targeted. Government payments on supported commodities accounted for more than 20 percent of *total* net farm income in the late 1960s, and for an even higher percentage throughout most of the 1980s. Under the 1985 farm bill, 15 percent of all these payments were received by less than 2 percent of U.S. farms with annual gross sales of more than $500,000. At the other extreme, nearly one-half of all U.S. farms under financial stress during this period received no direct payments at all. Cash payments were poorly disciplined because participation in farm programs was voluntary, which meant the government had to offer deficiency payments high enough to ensure participation when it sought to reduce crop acreage with unpaid land set asides, and to bid against the deficiency payment benefits when it sought to enroll farmers in long-term paid land retirements.

Thus, the farm policy reform problem was anything but resolved after the 1985 farm bill. The disappointment surrounding unilateral efforts prompted reform advocates to seek an important change in venue. For most of the decade that followed, farm policy reform was pursued most conspicuously through an international negotiation in GATT, rather than through unilateral domestic measures in Congress. Yet, it would be the limited unilateral partial cash-out progress at home that would, in the end, define what the GATT negotiations could produce to advance the reform agenda.

Chapter Three

Seeking Reform by International Negotiations

By 1986, REFORM ADVOCATES had grown weary of seeking policy change unilaterally through congressional channels dominated by the farm lobby. The cash-out approach embraced in the 1985 farm bill had reduced market-distorting loan rates, yet at an intolerable cost to taxpayers. For some, this proved that U.S. farm support entitlements were impervious to significant reform. For a cohort of more visionary (or perhaps simply more dogged) reformers, a different conclusion was drawn: perhaps farm policy reform could never advance at home without the prior negotiation of an international agreement imposing parallel reforms on competitors and trade partners abroad. A round of GATT multilateral trade negotiations was scheduled in 1986, so these undaunted reform advocates decided to take the problem of farm policy liberalization into the international arena. One of the original architects of this internationalization strategy, Daniel G. Amstutz, the undersecretary of agriculture for international affairs and commodity programs and later a top U.S. agricultural negotiator, argued: "[W]e must reject the 'go it alone' approach, and move toward a global solution. The new round of trade negotiations is a major opportunity for making that move. . . . [T]he international bargaining table is where the solution lies" (1986).

In this chapter, we discuss the farm policy reform gains that resulted from the 1986–93 round of GATT negotiations (called the Uruguay Round, because it was launched by a ministerial meeting in Punta del Este) and from the domestic U.S. implementation legislation that followed in 1994. We first examine the earlier history of agricultural trade negotiations in the GATT, noting the minimal impact such negotiations usually have had on farm policy. We explore the reasons that convinced reform advocates in 1986 that the next round of negotiations would be different, and point to some distinctive circumstances in agriculture in the late 1980s—in the United States and elsewhere—that seemed to promise a greater chance for success through the internationalization approach. We then summarize the conduct of the negotiations, and analyze the content of the Agreement on Agriculture that finally emerged.

Once they were underway, the international negotiations in the GATT did not speed reform in the United States, but did to some extent in Europe. In part because policies there were even more distorting than U.S. policies at the time the negotiation began, the larger burden of making concessions during the negotiation fell on the Europeans. Farm lobbies in the United States actually found a powerful new excuse for resisting unilateral reforms as the negotiations proceeded: they argued that such reforms would be a unilateral giveaway of bargaining leverage. They even asked for more subsidies and supports from Congress, as "bargaining chips" to win a better international deal.

The modest new disciplines of the Uruguay Round Agreement on Agriculture that finally emerged from the lengthy GATT negotiations in 1993 also underscore the difficulty of using international negotiations as an indirect means to speed domestic policy change in the United States. Compared to the reforms introduced unilaterally under the 1985 and 1990 farm bills, few, if any, constraints on U.S. policy were imposed by the final multilateral Agreement on Agriculture, or by the trilateral North American Free Trade Agreement (NAFTA) completed in 1993 while the Uruguay Round negotiations were still underway. To secure congressional approval for the full set of GATT agreements in 1994, including U.S. participation in the newly formed World Trade Organization (WTO), President Clinton then had to make written promises that no significant new policy reforms would be sought by his administration in the upcoming 1995 farm bill debate. In this sense, the Uruguay Round exercise did more to constrain policy to the status quo in United States than to speed the process of reform.

Early GATT Exemptions and Limited Agricultural Reforms

The original GATT, founded in 1947, gave nations seeking nondiscriminatory and liberalized trade policies a set of common standards to follow and also a venue in which to negotiate steadily more ambitious standards. In the area of manufacturing trade, the GATT worked well. Seven successive negotiating rounds over four decades reduced average U.S. tariffs on manufactured trade from their original postwar level above 40 percent down to an average level of less than 5 percent by 1985. In the area of agriculture, however, the GATT had never been able to serve as a comparably effective instrument of reform. One reason had been the original U.S. preference in the 1950s for explicitly *illiberal* farm trade rules and practices in the GATT (see Josling, Tangermann, and Warley 1996; Swinbank and Tanner 1996). When the EEC then formed its Common Agricultural Policy (CAP) in 1962, these illiberal rules provided no disciplines. Europe's more highly protected and subsidized farmers started taking market shares away from U.S. agriculture later in the 1960s, and at this point a new U.S. interest in tightening the GATT's farm trade rules belatedly emerged. By then, however, highly protected European farmers had joined the most highly protected U.S. farmers in demanding a continuation of lax GATT disciplines on agriculture.

In repeated rounds of multilateral negotiations in the 1960s and 1970s (the Dillon Round, the Kennedy Round, and the Tokyo Round), U.S. reform advocates were able to gain little in the way of new disciplines on policy through the GATT. One initially obscure exception was an agreement made in the 1961–62 Dillon Round of negotiations, when the EEC pledged not to impose import duties on soybeans (a high protein oilseed), manioc, and other nongrain feed ingredients that were minor components of livestock feeds at the time. This concession, which eventually became consequential, was only made by the EEC because the CAP had not yet been fully formed, and Europe was still a net grain importer, so protection against alternative feed sources was not yet needed by European grain producers. When the steep common wall of CAP protection later formed, EEC negotiators began guarding against leaks in that wall with greater determination.

The 1963–67 Kennedy Round of multilateral trade negotiations was the first in which U.S. reformers pushed hard through the GATT for significant agricultural trade liberalization—but only so hard as they could within the limits set by what was then a Cold War imperative to maintain cooperative relations within the NATO alliance. These reform efforts accordingly met little success. For the first several years of the Kennedy Round, EEC negotiators in Geneva lacked the authority even to discuss agricultural trade concessions, because internal policy decision making in Brussels was paralyzed by a dispute over voting procedures in the Community's Council of Ministers. This dispute was eventually resolved when the EEC agreed that a "unanimity rule" would be applied to major policy decisions. This gave France, with its large number of farmers, an effective veto over significant reforms in agriculture.

The EEC also found it hard to negotiate seriously on agriculture during the Kennedy Round because it was at that moment moving toward much higher common internal farm price levels. Between 1959 and 1968, as the farm-pricing system was gradually effected, cereal protection levels within the EEC increased from 14 to 72 percent (Malmgren 1972). In these circumstances, all the Europeans could propose in the

Kennedy Round of agricultural negotiations was a freeze on margin of support (*montant de soutien*). This idea was rejected because it would have placed the EEC, with common producer prices at roughly twice the world level, legally on a par in the GATT with less protected markets such as Australia, where producer prices for exported farm products were essentially at the world level. The EEC proposal also would have legitimized its uniquely disruptive use of *variable* import levies, which were recalculated daily to stabilize internal prices —at a cost of more instability in the world market.

The United States had little to offer of its own in the way of concessions on agriculture in the Kennedy Round. Congress had willingly delegated unprecedented tariff-cutting authority for the upcoming negotiations in the Trade Expansion Act of 1962, but most farm trade barriers were *nontariff* measures, such as import quotas or export credits and subsidies. It was only in the limited area of tariff reductions that the Kennedy Round made some modest progress concerning agricultural reform. The United States made tariff concessions covering $610 million of agricultural imports, in return for concessions from others covering $870 million of its exports. Negotiations on EEC variable levies and on other nontariff farm trade barriers proved fruitless.

U.S. reform advocates again encountered difficulties in the 1973–78 Tokyo Round GATT negotiations. This round of negotiations began during an inflationary interlude and commodity price boom. Budget pressures to reduce farm support levels were temporarily eclipsed during this period, both in the United States and in Europe. When U.S. negotiators tried to prepare an offer of reform (in U.S. dairy and livestock programs, in return for EEC concessions on grains) that they hoped would interest their EEC counterparts, the plan leaked out, and angry objections from dairy and livestock producers led Congress to place tighter restrictions on executive branch authority in the negotiation of nontariff agreements (see Destler 1980).

In the end, the Tokyo Round produced only two significant achievements for U.S. agriculture. Japan agreed to tariff concessions on $1.2 billion in U.S. agricultural exports, and to relax some of its quota restrictions on imported farm products, particularly beef and citrus. The new Code on Subsidies and Countervailing Duties—intended to tighten the GATT's permissive rules—was also adopted by GATT countries in the Tokyo Round. This new code clarified the GATT definition of what would count as a "more than equitable" share of the world market for a country subsidizing its agricultural exports, and did a better job of defining the previous representative period for determining such shares. The new code also created an elaborate multilateral mechanism for settlement of disputes over subsidy policies, but this mechanism failed its first test when the United States subsequently tried to use it to impose effective disciplines on EEC wheat flour export subsidies. When the United States brought its complaints to the GATT, it took nearly six years for the newly created dispute settlement mechanism to produce, in 1983, what proved to be an empty and ambiguous nonverdict. It was at this point, with international commodity prices sharply falling, that the United States initiated direct retaliation against the EEC with a disruptive wheat flour export subsidy program of its own. Thus, through the mid-1980s at least, GATT agreements had done little to discipline interventionist agricultural policies in the United States or elsewhere.

Hope for Progress in the Uruguay Round

At about the time of the wheat flour decision, the GATT Committee on Trade in Agriculture began to prepare for the handling of farm policy issues in the event of a new round of negotiations. The export subsidy dispute motivated the United States to press for disciplines through this committee, and after suffering farm district losses in the 1982 midterm election, interest in a GATT deal intensified in the Reagan administration. Soon after its bold 1985 farm program cutout proposal was rejected by Congress and transformed into yet another expensive (yet only partial) cash out, preparations began within the GATT for the launching of the new round of multilateral trade negotiations. U.S. officials preparing for this new round in 1985 and 1986 came to believe that significant progress on agriculture might be negotiated, despite the history of past GATT failure to secure reform agreements. Their belief rested largely on the worldwide collapse of commodity prices following the end of the Tokyo Round in 1979. It was presumed, because of this collapse, that the EEC (which was evolving in membership and was coming to be known simply as the EC and then, after 1992, as the European Union or EU) might now be almost as ready for farm policy reform as the United States.[1] The Reagan administration's unilateral reform effort

1. The original EEC was one of three European Communities, but "Economic Community" and "EC" were often applied to it alone by the end of the late 1960s. The EEC formally adopted the name European Community when the Treaty on European Union was signed in Maastricht in February 1992. Original member countries in 1957 were Belgium, France, Germany, Italy, Luxembourg, and the Netherlands. Denmark, Ireland, and the United Kingdom became members in 1973; Greece in 1981; Portugal and Spain in 1986; and Austria, Finland, and Sweden in 1994.

had fallen short in Congress in 1985, but perhaps a multilateral reform agreement could at last be negotiated through the GATT.[2] At a meeting of the contracting parties in Geneva in November 1985, a preparatory committee was established to determine the objectives, subject matter, and modalities of this new round; with enthusiastic U.S. support, the new round was scheduled to begin in September 1986.

Compared to U.S. farm programs in the mid-1980s, supports for farmers in Europe under the CAP were far less cashed out. European consumers, as opposed to taxpayers, still carried most of the burden of EC policy, as shown in table 10. Still, by the time the Uruguay Round began in 1986, the CAP had become a sufficient burden to European taxpayers as well as consumers to generate substantial internal pressure for reform. As the European Community became a net exporter in one farm product market after another under the production stimulus of its high internal prices, so-called export restitutions (which became more expensive after the 1980s fall in world prices) had to supplement import levies as a CAP protection device. Real annual farm program budget outlays in the European Community doubled between 1975 and 1986, and consequently it was forced in 1986 to increase the value-added tax revenue base from 1.0 to 1.4 percent of national income. In 1987, still more revenues were needed to cover rapidly growing farm spending obligations, yet—despite high spending on export subsidies—stocks of agricultural commodities continued to accumulate (see Blandford 1990; Koester and Tangermann 1990).[3]

Shared U.S.-EC interests in farm policy reform were most obvious in the area of export subsidies. The 1983 retaliation in kind against EC wheat flour export subsidies had been followed in 1985 by U.S. initiation of the new multibillion-dollar Export Enhancement Program (EEP), signaling the onset of a mutually destructive export subsidy competition in world wheat markets. Neither the United States nor the European Community profited from this competition, because the subsidies offered to gain a relative export advantage mostly just offset one

2. Some analysts have implied that U.S. reformers sought to internationalize the process in 1986 not because they had given up on unilateral reform, but because they wanted to generalize what they believed to be inevitable U.S. reforms (due to budget pressures) to Europe through an international agreement (see IATRC 1994). Our assessment is that the Reagan administration was genuinely pessimistic about further opportunities for unilateral reform progress after the 1985 farm bill experience and saw the international negotiation strategy as an alternative, rather than a supplement.

3. Cereal stocks in the European Community doubled between 1980–81 and 1986–87 (Swinbank and Tanner 1996).

Table 10.   Annual Farm Program Benefits and Costs (in Billions of Dollars), 1986–1987

	Producer Benefits	Consumer Costs	Taxpayer Costs
United States	26.3	6.0	30.3
European Community	33.3	32.6	15.6
Japan	22.6	27.7	5.7

Source: U.S. Department of Agriculture, Economic Research Service, *Economic Implications of Agricultural Policy Reforms in Industrial Market Economies* (August 1989), table 8.

another, or displaced competitor exports into markets where subsidies were not being offered.[4] The big winners from this competition were wheat-importing countries—such as Egypt, Russia, and China—who made purchases at artificially cheap prices. The big losers were a number of smaller wheat-exporting nations, especially those that did not offer their own direct export subsidies. Australia was a leader among these nations, and in 1986 took steps to form a new group of fourteen "nonsubsidizing" countries. The Cairns Group (named for the Australian city where they first met) proceeded to push the GATT for sharp reductions in export subsidy use.

Arguments that the upcoming Uruguay Round of GATT negotiations might provide the best possible venue for seeking farm policy reforms were also given a boost in 1985 by the publication of a new study from the influential private Trilateral Commission. Coauthored by reform-minded scholars from the United States, Europe, and Japan, this study emphasized the importance of simultaneous farm policy reform actions by all industrial nations (Johnson, Hemmi, and Lardinois 1985). A similar emphasis on coordinated multilateral action was at the same time emerging from within the developed-country Organization for Economic Cooperation and Development (OECD). The OECD had undertaken a new Ministerial Mandate on Agricultural Trade in the mid-1980s, an initiative that helped put multilateral farm policy reform onto the Group of Seven (G-7) agenda. At the May 1986 Tokyo Economic

4. Neither the EC export restitutions nor the U.S. export subsidies were very efficient methods to help domestic farmers. For the United States, much of the subsidy value of EEP—about 40 percent—went directly to foreign customers. An estimated 70 to 90 percent of the exported bushels would have been sold anyway, even without a subsidy attached, and the EEP was never a cost-effective tool of leverage against the European Community. For every added dollar the United States spent on EEP trying to take wheat markets away from the European Community, Brussels could fully offset the EEP by spending only 23 cents (see Koester and Nuppenau 1987; Epstein and Carr 1991; Haley 1991; Bruce Gardner 1996).

Summit of the G-7, agriculture actually received more discussion time than any other single issue. President Reagan was persuaded, following this summit, to endorse international negotiations as the most promising path toward farm policy reform. "No nation can unilaterally abandon current policies without being devastated by the policies of other countries," Reagan stated. "The only hope is for a major international agreement that commits everyone to the same actions and timetable" (Rapp 1988, 50).

The new enthusiasm for internationally coordinated farm policy reform was based in part upon scholarly study and modeling exercise research results, which showed that multilateral reforms would be less painful to farmers than unilateral reforms undertaken without international cooperation. Although most farm sector protection came at the expense of domestic consumers and taxpayers, as indicated in table 10, a substantial portion functioned simply to offset the illiberal policies of other nations. When the Uruguay Round began in 1986–87, it was estimated that over 40 percent of U.S. gross subsidy benefits given to producers merely offset the depressive effects on world prices of subsidy policies in other countries, particularly the European Community. Roughly one-third of the European Community's gross support of farmers was performing a similar policy offset function. If the United States and the European Community agreed to cut subsidies at the same time, the burden on their own farmers of ending subsidies could thus be reduced. Economic simulation models indicated that a unilateral agricultural policy liberalization would have withdrawn an estimated $26.3 billion from the U.S. farm sector in 1986–87, while a complete multilateral liberalization (eliminating all support and trade interventions among all industrial countries) would have deducted only $16.2 billion—implying a 38 percent reduction in lost benefits from international cooperation. Likewise, a unilateral liberalization would have taken away $33.3 billion from the EC farm sector, while a multilateral liberalization would have withdrawn only $22.7 billion (Blandford 1990, table 9-3).[5]

An international sharing of the policy reform burden among farm producers in all countries would thus reduce the actual burden producers in any one country would have to bear, and it was hoped that this would reduce farm sector resistance to reform. Yet reduced pain is still pain,

5. Johnson, Mahe, and Roe (1993) derive status quo policies as the expected outcomes when U.S. and EC decisions are modeled in a noncooperative game theoretic framework, and provide similar estimates of the net costs. See also Tyers and Anderson 1992.

and the diminished burdens implied by cooperative as opposed to unilateral liberalization still made the option of reform unattractive to most
farm groups. Farm policy liberalization, even if multilateral, would
take some income away from most industrial country farm sectors in
the short run, and reduce farm asset values in the long run. Estimates of
the anticipated price and production effects for the U.S. and EC farm
sectors following a simultaneous farm policy liberalization in all industrial countries from a 1980–82 base period are shown in table 11. These
figures indicate that except for U.S. feed grain farmers, the combined
price and production consequences of even a multilateral liberalization
on agriculture would still have been adverse. Farm asset owners in developed countries thus lacked a collective self-interest in liberal reform,
even from a fully cooperative multilateral reform. They did not have the
mutual interest in reducing protection that had long facilitated trade
liberalization in the manufacturing and service sectors, where production and exports tended to expand rather than contract in the aftermath
of a mutual liberalization.

While farm sector resistance to even multilateral reform would be expected, enthusiasm among reform advocates for the international negotiations was sustained by an implicit assumption about the policy
process: farmers would find it more difficult to block reforms if those actions were taken through an international negotiation and embedded
in a binding multilateral trade agreement in the GATT. Presumably,
grounding farm policy reform in a multisector international negotiation would take the policy initiative away from illiberal domestic agricultural sector political coalitions and dilute the veto power they might
seek to exercise over the final outcome. By internationalizing the farm
policy reform problem into the GATT, the day-to-day policy initiative

Table 11.   Estimated Trade Liberalization Effects (% Change from 1980–82 Base)

	Wheat	Feed Grains	Dairy	Sugar
Prices				
United States	−11	−1	−36	−25
European Community	−15	−22	−27	−30
Production				
United States	−3	+6	−22	−7
European Community	+3	−20	−10	−17

Note: This table presumes full liberalization. The actual Uruguay Round result fell far short of this objective.
Source: Rod Tyers and Kim Anderson, *Distortions in World Food Markets: A Quantitative Assessment* (Canberra: National Center for Development Studies, ANU, 1986).

might be transferred from rent-seeking domestic farm lobbies—both in Washington, D.C., and in Brussels—to reform-minded trade officials negotiating in search of mutual advantage in Geneva. Farm lobby strength would then be diluted further, thanks to the multisector content of the Uruguay Round. Agriculture would be just one of fifteen separate groups in the larger international negotiations, so the other sectors (such as manufacturing, services, and intellectual property) with strong interests in a liberalizing outcome overall would pressure agriculture to cooperate. Particularly during the final negotiation and ratification stage, agriculturalists who tried to block reforms in their sector would presumably be isolated and weakened, because their intransigence would begin to threaten the gains made in all the other components of the tightly packaged final agreement. In the United States, congressional "fast-track" approval procedures would further neutralize farm lobby objections by allowing the president to seek GATT-agreement implementing legislation on the basis of a deadline-driven, no-amendment, limited debate, up-or-down vote.

In more abstract language, advocates of U.S. farm policy reform were hoping to use an international negotiation to transform their domestic challenge into a "two-level game." Negotiations initiated at the international level in Geneva would open up new space for achieving reform outcomes at the domestic level. Political scientist Robert Putnam (1988) has pioneered the study of this kind of "synergistic linkage." His favorite example is the 1978 G-7 Economic Summit in Bonn, where an international exchange of pledges on energy policy change and macroeconomic stimulation facilitated the subsequent task of implementing such policy changes at home.[6] Putnam makes no formal claim as to when or how often the international game board can be used by national leaders to weaken domestic opposition in this fashion, but U.S. policy reformers who sought to internationalize the agricultural policy process in 1986 were clearly hoping to create another successful synergistic linkage.[7]

6. For a largely supportive view of Putnam's interpretation of the Bonn summit pledges see Ikenberry 1988. The nonenergy part of the Bonn deal was later challenged on substantive grounds, because inflation followed in 1980–81 (see Dobson 1991). Still, from a procedural perspective, the example of the 1978 summit shows how prior agreements abroad can at times weaken political opponents of change at home. Synergistic linkage has also been asserted in the case of the U.S. Structural Impediments Initiative (SII) with Japan (see Schoppa 1993).

7. The Grossman-Helpman (1994) model of trade policy formulation by governments under the influence of contributions from organized interest groups (described in the pre-

Balanced against the hope that international negotiations would provide a forum in which to achieve reform of agricultural policies in 1985 were several practical problems with the internationalization approach. One problem was that agriculturalists might never quite lose control of the policy process, even though trade officials in the Office of the U.S. Trade Representative (USTR) were nominally in charge. Partly to appease farm lobbies in Congress and partly for lack of its own in-house expertise on agriculture, USTR routinely subcontracted the day-to-day handling of farm negotiation issues to officials in the USDA Foreign Agricultural Service. This outcome diminished the extent to which negotiators were insulated from domestic farm group pressures.

A second danger was that an international negotiation would give domestic farm lobbies a new argument for resisting liberal reforms at home—claiming a need to halt any unilateral reform that might hurt the "bargaining power" of U.S. negotiators in the GATT. Third, international agriculture bargaining could prove contentious enough to block or slow down agreement on the larger and more important manufacturing and service sector issues at stake in the Uruguay Round—perhaps enough to offset any reform gains that might eventually be made in the farm sector. Only the conduct and outcome of the negotiation itself would reveal whether the final payoff from an internationalized reform strategy would prove positive or negative.[8]

Uruguay Round Negotiations, 1986–1993

The Uruguay Round negotiations were launched formally at Punta del Este in September 1986. The major participants in the agricultural

---

vious chapter) can also be extended to cooperative behavior among the governments. The noncooperative political equilibrium policies chosen by governments will impose excess costs on one another as each government tries to exploit opportunities to exercise monopoly power over the international terms of trade. Cooperation between governments eliminates these costly elements from their equilibrium policies, which improves their ability both to satisfy organized lobbies and to provide increased average welfare. This cooperation is another way of explaining what Putnam calls positive synergistic linkage.

8. Even on theoretical grounds there was room for ambiguity about the outcome to be negotiated. In the Grossman-Helpman model, for example, some organized industries (which condition their political contributions on the policies in both countries) may end up with higher levels of protection when there is cooperation between the governments (Grossman and Helpman 1995; Schleich 1997). Increased protection is particularly likely in the formal model when the industry is relatively powerful in both countries and domestic subsidies as well as trade interventions are used by governments. These stylized conditions are characteristic of U.S. and EC agricultural policies.

negotiations, including the United States, the European Community, Japan, and the Cairns Group, stated their opening positions in 1987. A midterm review conference in Montreal in December 1988 deadlocked in large part because of disagreements over agriculture. Negotiating progress in other areas (including trade in services and intellectual property) proved difficult so long as prospects for a U.S.–EC agreement on agriculture seemed uncertain. Two more years passed, and a ministerial conference in Brussels, in December 1990—originally scheduled to bring the round to an end—was adjourned without result due to a continued deadlock concerning agriculture. Not until the United States and the European Union finally came to terms on agricultural issues at a series of bilateral meetings in Washington, D.C., late in 1992 and 1993 (known as the Blair House I and II meetings) was the way clear for the Uruguay Round Agreement on Agriculture to be completed. Only then, in December 1993, could the rest of the round be completed as well.

The opening phase of the Uruguay Round negotiations on agriculture, which lasted from the summer of 1987 to the December 1988 midterm review deadlock, was dominated by discussion of a surprisingly extreme position taken at the outset by U.S. negotiators—the so-called zero option to eliminate over ten years all domestic and border measures that distorted world agricultural trade. A second phase, which began early in 1989 and lasted through the failed 1990 Brussels ministerial, was marked by a softening of this extreme U.S. position, but not enough to satisfy the Europeans. A third phase began early in 1991 and eventually culminated in the Blair House meetings. During this phase, the European negotiating position on agriculture in the GATT shifted dramatically following unilateral internal farm policy changes. The U.S. position also softened further, enough to produce an agreement the European Union was willing to accept in December 1993.

Negotiating the Uruguay Round Agreement on Agriculture sped the pace of liberal reform somewhat in Europe, but it had little or no short-run reform impact on U.S. farm policy. In some instances, in fact, the international negotiation may have even slowed the pace of U.S. farm policy reform. In the long run, the Uruguay Round will aid U.S. agriculture by stimulating world income growth and hence farm product demand, and it may also provide some modest constraints on future U.S. intervention policies. This would be reform through a two-stage process over time, rather than through the two-level process identified by Putnam (1988).

Zero Option and Arming to Disarm

Little or no progress was made in the 1987–88 phase of the Uruguay Round, mostly because of the extreme nature of the U.S. zero option proposal. Formally presented in July 1987, this was a plan to eliminate all production- and trade-distorting farm subsidies over ten years after an agreement was reached. The zero option permitted direct farm income support payments that were completely decoupled from production decisions and market prices, but its most extreme interpretation precluded public support for investments in agricultural research, education, or provision of market information services. The Reagan administration officials who devised this proposal already knew, by the time of its formal presentation, that it would be an unacceptable starting point for the European Community and Japan (both had communicated as much earlier in the year at the G-7 economic summit in Venice), but they went forward with it just the same. The zero option went far beyond the terms of the Punta del Este Declaration under which the negotiations had been launched; it went far beyond any agreement yet considered seriously in the OECD; it went beyond any position yet taken by the Cairns group; and most obviously it went beyond anything remotely acceptable to the Agriculture Committees of Congress.

Why did the Reagan administration make such a radical and untenable farm policy proposal at the start of the GATT Uruguay Round? The zero option did make some political sense for the Reagan administration as a means to jolt GATT negotiators out of the overly cautious, incrementalist style that had failed to produce significant reforms for agriculture in the past. It also made some procedural sense for a second-term, lame-duck Reagan administration to take an extreme position at the start, because it would clear the way for the new president in 1989 to make his own decisions over what concessions to consider more seriously in the GATT.

Paradoxically, the extreme zero option also made short-term political sense for handling those U.S. domestic farm lobbies who were nervous about the GATT process. This proposal reassured these groups in three different ways. First, it was so unlikely to be accepted abroad that it posed no real threat at home. Second, because it prohibited all distorting subsidies, U.S. negotiators could claim they were not making arbitrary decisions about which countries, which regions, or which commodities had to bear the heaviest burdens of reform. Third, it did not rule out the replacement of production and trade-distorting subsidies with fully decoupled cash payments. The zero option could thus be presented to extreme reformers as a cutout proposal, but at the same time it could be presented to farm groups as nothing more than the foundation for a decoupled cash out, leaving U.S. farm income subsidies unharmed.

Whatever the tactical calculations that originally generated the zero option, it was a gambit that deadlocked the agricultural negotiations for eighteen months, through the December 1988 midterm review conference in Montreal. As this phase of the negotiation developed, representatives of some of the most protected U.S. farm producers actually began to endorse the zero option, since they knew it would produce such a deadlock. During the run-up to the GATT midterm review, the U.S. Trade Representative, Clayton Yeutter, signaled his readiness at one point to compromise the zero option and move closer to the more realistic Cairns Group position, which focused on first disciplining export subsidies to secure an "early harvest" of partial reforms in Montreal. Many U.S. farm groups (including heavily protected sugar and dairy producers, with the least interest in liberalization) complained to the secretary of agriculture, arguing that only the zero option could guarantee them a "level playing field" in international trade. Under pressure, Yeutter adhered to the zero option at the midterm review, which prolonged the deadlock. This was a kind of synergistic linkage between international negotiations and domestic farm lobby strength that reform advocates had perhaps not anticipated. The negotiations were being manipulated by—rather than weakening—protectionist U.S. farm lobbies.

It was unfortunate that the Reagan administration's opening proposal came to be known as the zero option, because this was also the name for the administration's position in an arms control negotiation with the Soviet Union concerning the removal of intermediate range nuclear forces (INF) in Europe. Farm lobbies welcomed this chance to equate their subsidies to armaments; it gave them a rare opportunity to depict farm subsidies as instruments vital to some national interest. Unilateral reform could now be likened to the folly of unilateral disarmament, or as an unwise yielding of potential bargaining leverage in the negotiations. Domestic farm subsidies are not at all like nuclear arms—they are deployed primarily against consumers and taxpayers at home rather than against competitors abroad. Yet with the arms control metaphor in play, farm lobbies could even start asking for *additional* subsidies, as bargaining chips to strengthen the hands of U.S. negotiators in Geneva. They likened their "arming to disarm" effort to the Reagan administration's deployment of Pershing II and cruise missiles in Europe to strengthen the hands of U.S. INF negotiators.

The bargaining chips argument was used effectively by U.S. farm lobbies while the GATT negotiations were underway. Trade Representative Yeutter was persuaded by domestic farm lobbies to expand use of the EEP in 1987 as a "tactical tool" to pressure EC negotiators at the GATT bargaining table. In 1989, the Democratic chair of the Senate Agriculture Committee, Senator Patrick Leahy (Vermont), rejected a proposed $2 billion reduction in U.S. domestic farm subsidies by representing it as a giveaway of bargaining leverage. "If that is not telegraphing unilateral disarmament I do not know what is," Leahy said ("Yeutter Vows" 1989, 18). In the EC likewise, powerful farm organizations rejected price cuts (recommended by the European Commission) in 1989–90, by calling first for "reciprocal measures taken by our GATT partners" (USDA 1989, 8). In 1990, Yeutter, then the secretary of agriculture, was pressured into accepting a new marketing loan program for soybeans and other oilseeds. Yeutter was instinctually a strong free trader and had earlier opposed this new domestic price-support program, but he finally yielded to the argument that it would provide more "leverage" for the United States in the GATT negotiations (*Inside U.S. Trade* 1990, 20). Still later in 1990, U.S. farm lobbies attached a "GATT Trigger" provision to that year's new farm bill, which obliged the secretary of agriculture to spend more on export subsidies in the event of a failed Uruguay Round.[9]

The international negotiation was thus producing plenty of synergistic linkage in the United States, but it was mostly negative rather than positive from a farm policy reform viewpoint. Reform advocates had been hoping to use the GATT negotiations abroad as a path toward smaller subsidies at home, but farm lobbies were instead using the negotiations as an added pretext to avoid domestic subsidy cutbacks— and even as a means to seek larger subsidies.

Comprehensive Proposals and Modest Unilateral Reforms

Early in 1989, soon after the Bush administration took charge of U.S. policy in the GATT, the zero option position was abandoned. This move allowed the deadlocked talks to resume, and in the second phase of the negotiations that followed, the United States produced a more realistic comprehensive proposal (in October 1989). But EC negotiators were unable to respond in an adequate and timely fashion, which doomed

---

9. See also R. L. Paarlberg 1995 for an analysis of the ratcheting up of the EEP subsidies during the Uruguay Round.

the December 1990 Brussels ministerial to another disappointing dead-lock.

The lack of progress in this second phase of the GATT negotiations on agriculture was in part a timing problem. The high internal farm budget pressures within both the United States and the European Community during the initial 1987–88 phase, which had sustained a sense of reform urgency, were much reduced by 1989–90. A summer drought in North America in 1988 drove up crop prices and temporarily reduced govern-ment commodity stocks and farm budget outlays. In the European Community, farm budget pressures were also diminished in 1988 by a unilateral reform measure (a so-called stabilizer agreement for cereals) plus a further 25 percent increase in EC revenues (Moyer and Josling 1990). These half measures brought just enough short-term budget re-lief to weaken interest in a GATT agreement both in Washington, D.C., and in Brussels.

Did the ongoing international negotiations prompt the domestic re-form in the European Community in 1988? When evaluating the impact of the GATT negotiations on the internal farm policy reforms, the se-quence of events is instructive. The European Community acted unilat-erally in 1988 to embrace a partial reform of its cereal policies at a time when it did not yet have any guarantee that credit would be given for this reform in any final Uruguay Round agreement. It was not until April 1989 that the United States agreed to recognize unilateral mea-sures (such as the EC stabilizer reform) undertaken since Punta del Este as fulfilling part of the commitments each country would make to re-duce farm supports (Swinbank and Tanner 1996). It is thus difficult to at-tribute the reform step taken unilaterally by the European Community in 1988 to the negotiations in the GATT.

The United States also undertook modest unilateral reforms as the GATT negotiations passed through their second phase, especially when Congress passed a new farm bill (the Food, Agriculture, Consumption and Trade Act) in 1990 to replace the expiring 1985 legislation. Yet the driving force behind this new farm bill was a difficult domestic budget battle, not the Uruguay Round. With an estimated budget deficit of $161 billion, and with a threat looming of automatic across-the-board spend-ing cuts under the terms of the new Gramm-Rudman law, Congress opted in 1990 to consider farm legislation renewal within the frame-work of larger budget reconciliation legislation (see Cochrane and Runge 1992). The budget reconciliation process obliged Congress to cut $13.6 billion from projected farm commodity program spending levels during the next five years. Congress responded with a 15 percent reduction in the number of acres on which deficiency payments for program crops would be made (payment acres). In partial compensation for this scheduled reduction in payments, farmers were given greater flexibility in what they were allowed to plant on the acres that were no longer eligible for payments (called flexibility or flex acres).

Actual budget savings proved elusive, however, when the new 1990 farm bill provisions were implemented. Rather than cutting $13.6 billion from the projected spending baseline, CCC spending under the 1990 farm bill eventually exceeded that baseline—in large measure because of deficiency payments that exceeded expectations but also partly due to unanticipated crop disaster assistance payments (see Bruce Gardner 1995). The unexpected disaster relief expenditures during 1990–94 led to new crop insurance legislation in 1994 and increased pressure for budget discipline in the 1995 farm bill debate. At the time, however, the 1990 farm bill was enacted for budget reasons, and largely outside the dynamic of the ongoing GATT negotiations. Yeutter and other policy makers had always promised the farm lobby that U.S. policy would be made in Washington, not in Geneva. An account prepared by the International Agricultural Trade Research Consortium (IATRC) concluded that the 1990 farm bill was enacted "for purely internal reasons in response to domestic political and budget pressures" (1994, 32).

As modest unilateral reforms moved forward seemingly independent of the GATT (or in some cases were slowed down by the GATT), it was the failure of the European Community to present a timely and credible counteroffer to the U.S. comprehensive proposal in phase two of the negotiations that most disappointed advocates of a faster reform pace and more substantive change. At this late stage in the negotiation, with the planned final 1990 Brussels ministerial conference only months away, and with the interests of other sectors increasingly at risk due to the agricultural deadlock, protectionist farm lobbies on both sides of the Atlantic (and elsewhere) should have seen their positions weakened. Yet farm lobbies remained in firm control, most conspicuously in Europe. During the months just prior to the Brussels ministerial, the Council of Agricultural Ministers met seven different times to consider the issue, but still granted only minimal new negotiating authority to the European Commission. As a consequence, the commission's final offer was submitted late, and it fell far short of the reform demands then coming both from the Cairns Group and from the United States.

The United States was calling, in October 1990, for a 75 percent reduction in internal support levels and for a 90 percent reduction in export subsidies. The European Community offered only a 30 percent reduction in internal support and no explicit assurances at all concerning export subsidy restraint. The European Community also included an objectionable "rebalancing" demand opposed by the United States, which would have reduced market access for the nongrain feed ingredients (such as oilseeds and corn gluten) that were being sold into the European Community duty-free under the much earlier Dillon Round agreement.

Why didn't industrial interests inside the European Community, especially the German industrial interests that sought a successful liberalizing Uruguay Round outcome overall, mobilize enough influence at this point to override the Council of Agricultural Ministers? German Chancellor Kohl did involve himself in the struggle between the commission and the farm ministers, but tellingly he did so on behalf of German farmers, not GATT progress. Kohl sought concrete guarantees from the commission president that any losses in farmers' incomes from a GATT agreement would be compensated. A German national election was scheduled in six weeks' time, and Kohl's traditional base of support included numerous farm constituents. The German Farmers Union traditionally delivered 80 percent of its vote to the parties (the CDU and the CSU) that made up Kohl's governing coalition (Patterson 1997).

European Cash Out Breaks the International Deadlock

The failure of the 1990 Brussels Ministerial ushered in the third and final phase of the Uruguay Round. During this phase, the European Community embraced more sweeping unilateral internal CAP reforms (the 1991 MacSharry reforms, named for their author, Ray MacSharry, the EC agriculture commissioner), which lowered internal cereal support prices and imposed annual acreage controls, while compensating farmers with direct cash payments. These important MacSharry reforms, in effect an EC movement toward a cash out, became the foundation for the final GATT agreement. When the United States, at Blair House in 1992, subsequently agreed to consider the new European cash "compensation payments" effectively exempt from any Uruguay Round constraints on farm supports (along with U.S. deficiency payments), the path was cleared at last for an international agreement.

The MacSharry reforms were a relatively clean cash out of the CAP's high internal cereal price guarantees. Internal support prices were to be lowered by 29 percent, and farmers were promised cash payments as compensation against losses in income. To qualify for these compensation payments, farmers were required to set aside a portion of their land (originally 15 percent) as a supply-control measure.

The extent to which the Uruguay Round may have triggered the MacSharry reforms remains uncertain and controversial. As argued by Coleman and Tangermann (1997), the European Commission was in part trying to lay the foundation for a GATT agreement when it settled on its decision to lower intervention prices. However, a plan for a cash out of EC cereal policy had been brewing inside the commission for many years and might eventually have been implemented even without an Uruguay Round negotiation. A shift toward supporting farmers with cash compensation payments rather than price guarantees had been strongly promoted by the commission in a paper published in 1985, the year before the Uruguay Round began (Koester and Tangermann 1990). The deadlock between the commission and the council over Uruguay Round negotiating options late in 1990 may have helped the commission revive this option, but the decision to exempt compensation payments from Uruguay Round disciplines would not be made until the first Blair House meeting in November 1992. Thus, the cash out was not a certain path toward a GATT agreement at the time the commission began promoting the idea.

The official—but not credible—explanation given by the European Commission for proposing the MacSharry reforms was a need to reduce CAP expenditures. Although budget pressures on the CAP were intensifying in 1990–91 when the reform was being prepared, the short-term consequence of any cash-out reform would of course be more rather than less budget exposure.[10] A more likely explanation for the timing of the MacSharry reforms is international pressure, but not exactly through the Uruguay Round. As an alternative to lowering intervention prices for cereals, the commission had for years been looking for ways to shut off the duty-free entry of nongrain feed ingredients (including U.S. oilseeds) into the EC market under the concession the Europeans had carelessly given away in the 1961–62 Dillon Round. In the 1980s, the European Community began offering heavy subsidies to its own domestic oilseed producers in hopes of displacing imports, but the U.S. oilseed

10. One alternative explanation accepts the fact of budget pressures on the CAP, but then presents the MacSharry reforms as an effort by pro-French forces inside the commission to preempt what might otherwise have been a pro-German method of dealing with those pressures. French advocates inside the commission, fearing the CAP budget crisis was going to trigger harsh production controls, advocated the MacSharry cash-out approach instead (see Patterson 1997).

industry claimed this was an impairment of the zero-duty binding, and appealed to U.S. trade law in order to force a confrontation. In December 1987, the American Soybean Association filed a petition against EC oilseed policy under Section 301 of U.S. trade law, an action that eventually obliged the U.S. government, in January 1988, to bring the dispute to the GATT. The U.S. case was strong. Oilseed production had more than quadrupled in the EC under the lavish 1980s subsidies, and U.S. exports of soybeans and soybean meal to the European Community had simultaneously gone into decline (USDA 1992).

In January 1990, the GATT, in a decision made entirely outside the Uruguay Round process, adopted a panel ruling that EC oilseed price supports had indeed nullified the Dillon Round zero-duty binding, and the European Community had to modify its domestic oilseed support policies. At the December 1990 Brussels ministerial, the United States then in effect reaffirmed this outcome by again rejecting the EC proposal for rebalancing as part of an Uruguay Round agreement. This forced the European Community to look for new ways to contain its internal cereal surplus.

The first EC attempt at oilseed reform, initiated in December 1991, was a cash out that lowered internal oilseed prices (closer to world market prices) and offered compensatory direct payments to farmers engaged in oilseed production. The United States requested that a GATT panel be reconvened to evaluate whether these direct payments were still a production inducement. In March 1992, this second panel confirmed that European (now EU) policy continued to deprive U.S. growers of the earlier Dillon Round concession, and when the European Union tried to reject this second ruling, the United States threatened retaliation with sanctions in the amount of the estimated trade damages incurred by U.S. soybean producers—$1 billion (USDA 1992). What followed was a dramatic bilateral trade conflict, an important transatlantic test of political will that would have been played out even without an Uruguay Round. Facing a credible threat of U.S. sanctions, the European Union had to abandon the idea of sustaining high internal grain prices by blocking imports of nongrain feeds. Reducing internal grain prices then became the only available option. The European Union resigned itself to this course of action in May 1992, when it at last embraced the proposed MacSharry reforms for grains. A small GATT concession carelessly made by the Europeans in 1962 thus gave the U.S. government, under totally different circumstances thirty years later, the foundation that it needed to threaten bilateral trade retaliation to preserve the original concession. It was this credible threat of U.S. retaliation in a highly charged trade dispute, more than any linkage to the Uruguay Round negotiations, that generated external pressures in 1991–92 for CAP reform.

The embrace of the MacSharry reforms did not bring all EU foot-dragging in the Uruguay Round to an end. The "Draft Final Act," submitted by the GATT Director General Arthur Dunkel, had become the basic negotiating text for the agricultural discussions after December 1991. It took a subsequent weakening of anticipated GATT disciplines at the Blair House I meeting in November 1992 to bring European consent, and even then French objections to this first Blair House agreement (a charge that the commission had exceeded its negotiating authority), backed by vocal rural interest groups and parliamentary pressures, led to yet another full year of delay. Not until the already weak conditions contained in the original Blair House agreement were weakened even further, in December 1993 (the Blair House II agreement), was a final Uruguay Round Agreement on Agriculture completed, and with that the rest of the Uruguay Round negotiations were concluded as well (see Josling, Tangermann, and Warley 1996).[11]

Ironically, this final weakening of the original Blair House agreement in 1993 was in part an artifact of the U.S. fast-track procedure that reformers had been counting on to produce a strong GATT outcome. The new Democratic Clinton administration had inherited the Uruguay Round negotiations after the 1992 elections and was under pressure to secure a final agreement before December 15, 1993, when the most recent congressional extension of fast-track negotiating authority was scheduled to expire. If no GATT agreement had been concluded by that date, the president would have had to make a new set of potentially wide-ranging promises and concessions to Congress to secure yet another extension of fast-track authority to complete the Uruguay Round. In order to reach an acceptable agreement in Geneva by the fast-track deadline, President Clinton had to allow compromises that weakened the final Agreement on Agriculture.

The agreement that brought this third phase of the negotiations to a close was thus the product of a number of factors other than the positive synergistic linkage anticipated by reformers. Farm lobbies and agricul-

11. The crucial Blair House II concession was to increase the quantities of EU grain that would be eligible for export subsidies each year during implementation of the agreement. At the time these annual limits were agreed to, they were expected to be fully utilized. No rules were written about whether unused subsidies could be "rolled over" for future use, which the EU later would assert was its right.

tural ministries on both sides of the Atlantic had retained control of the negotiating positions of their governments almost from start to end. Perhaps the strongest evidence for this assertion is found in the terms of the final agreement, which implied little in the way of significant policy reform, particularly for the United States.

The Final Uruguay Round Agreement on Agriculture

The final agricultural agreement required varying degrees of farm policy reform within three different areas: levels of internal support, levels and forms of border protection (market access), and levels of export subsidization (see WTO 1994). Reaching an international agreement on reforms in these areas had proven a difficult task that tested the energy and ingenuity of negotiators on all sides. Yet upon examination, the reforms themselves were only modest in substance, and many would likely have been attained through unilateral actions even if there had never been an Uruguay Round.

Levels of Internal Support

The architects of the Uruguay Round intended to discipline behind-the-border as well as at-the-border measures that distorted farm commodity production and trade. This pursuit of internal farm support reductions used up more negotiating time than any other single agricultural issue, and in the end specific limits were established. Parties to the agreement committed to a reduction (using a specially constructed index) of their "trade-distorting" internal farm supports—their Aggregate Measurement of Support (AMS)—by 20 percent from a 1986–88 base over the six-year implementation period of the agreement (1995–2000).[12] As an unprecedented discipline on internal supports, this represented a significant *technical* breakthrough for the GATT.[13]

However, the support-level commitments proved to be less than a substantial reform breakthrough, because they added little or nothing to the pace or content of reforms that would have been undertaken

---

12. This AMS index purportedly represents the total value to farmers (in local currency) of trade-distorting domestic supports, calculated against a fixed external reference price from the base period, and aggregated across all policy instruments and all commodities (see IATRC 1994).

13. According to the IATRC evaluation, "For the first time in any sector, multilateral agreement has been reached to identify the types of domestic programs that are judged to have little or no impact on trade, and to accept commitments to place a ceiling on and to reduce support provided through other more trade-distorting domestic policies" (1994, 87).

without the Uruguay Round. The negotiated outcome was much less than the 100 percent reduction in trade-distorting supports sought under the early U.S. zero option, and also much less than the 75 percent reduction sought by U.S. negotiators at the time of the 1990 Brussels ministerial. It was even substantially less than the 30 percent reduction the Europeans offered at Brussels, which was rejected by the United States as inadequate at the time. The AMS commitments were carefully written to go no further than the modest internal support-level reductions that were being undertaken anyway, for which "credit" was now given in the GATT. The European Union insisted upon using a 1986–88 base period for calculating AMS reductions so that it could count toward its final GATT obligation the modest internal support reductions achieved unilaterally under the 1988 stabilizer reform. Once credit for this earlier reform was given, existing European wheat and feed grain policies would automatically be in compliance with the 20 percent AMS GATT reduction commitment, and would require no additional reform (FAPRI 1992).

The AMS commitment also excluded a wide range of subsidies judged to have no or at most minimal distorting effects on trade or to have a public-good dimension. These subsidies were allowed under a so-called green box of permitted policies.[14] The green box exemptions covered such policies as fully decoupled income payments to farmers; "safety net" crop and income insurance programs; environmental programs (including the CRP); publicly supported research; advisory, inspection, and marketing services; domestic food aid; and support for environmental and regional development.

The AMS index for calculating internal support, which was already weakened by the granting of credit for earlier reforms and by the numerous green box exemptions, was further diluted during the final stages of the Uruguay Round. The 1992 Blair House agreement effectively exempted from AMS calculations a belatedly created "blue box" of permitted policies comprising two large domestic cash subsidy programs—U.S. deficiency payments and EU compensation payments.[15]

14. The green box derived its name from a "traffic light" metaphor the negotiators had adopted, under which "red" policies were prohibited, "amber" policies were limited, and "green" policies were not restricted under the Uruguay Round agreement.

15. This Blair House decision went well beyond the earlier agreement to exempt green box policies from the AMS index, because both U.S. deficiency payments and EU compensation payments created production incentives. They were excused from counting toward the AMS so long as they were made under "production limiting programs," based

Deficiency payments, of course, had been the principal instrument of U.S. domestic farm support since the 1970s, and compensation payments were just then becoming a principal means of domestic farm support in the European Union under the 1992 MacSharry cash-out reform plan.

Thus, the final terms of the Uruguay Round internal support reduction commitment were sufficiently weak to oblige neither the United States nor the European Union to contemplate any additional internal policy liberalizations for the duration of its six-year implementation period.[16] In 1993, even before the MacSharry reforms had been fully implemented, the European Commission estimated that its AMS index was already below its formal commitment level for the year 2000. The United States was in an even safer position, thanks to unilateral reforms it had already undertaken (in the 1985 and 1990 farm bills) before and during the Uruguay Round—changes that grew out of a combination of tightened market conditions plus internal budget pressures. The European Union and the United States were not alone in having already more than satisfied the final Uruguay Round internal support stipulations. Japan, because of its earlier unilateral cuts in rice purchase prices, was also free from any new internal support reduction burden, and Canada had already done twice as much unilaterally as the new GATT agreement required (IATRC 1994). Thus, the OECD in 1995 was forced to conclude that the Uruguay Round agreement might not lead to a further reduction in the level of support to farmers.

Border Protection

One of the most widely noted features of the final Uruguay Round Agreement on Agriculture was a requirement that all border protection measures be converted immediately to bound tariffs (limits that cannot

---

on fixed area and yield, and made on 85 percent or less of base production. These conditions exactly matched the deficiency payment provisions of the 1990 farm bill. For a criticism of this exemption decision, see Sanderson 1994.

16. Still more weaknesses were introduced at the end of the negotiations, when it was decided that AMS commitments would not have to be made for each commodity individually, as called for in the previously authoritative 1991 Dunkel draft version of the negotiating text. Instead, it was determined that a single sectorwide commitment would suffice. Under the umbrella of such a sectorwide aggregate, the negotiating countries would find it easier to continue offering generous support for politically sensitive commodities, while claiming credit for larger reductions in less sensitive commodity areas, thus potentially slowing reform and worsening policy distortions between commodities (see Hathaway 1994).

be increased without negotiation with other countries). In addition, market access opportunities had to be provided through low or minimal duties for imports equal to 3 to 5 percent of domestic consumption. These newly bound and minimal tariffs, as well as those that had been bound earlier, then had to be reduced by 36 percent, on average, over the six-year implementation period.

The conversion of nontariff agricultural border protections to bound tariffs ("tariffication") was again an important technical achievement from the standpoint of consistent GATT rule making across sectors, and one that required significant changes in the instruments of protection for agriculture used by national governments.[17] But from the standpoint of achieving actual reductions in the level or variability of border protections, this move toward bound tariffs was at the outset surprisingly empty. First, some exemptions were made (Japan and South Korea were allowed to avoid any tariffication obligations for rice). Second, when the parties formally presented their planned tariff schedules in 1994, it was clear that "dirty tariffication" was widely underway. By taking advantage of an outdated 1986–88 base period that exaggerated existing levels of protection, and by cleverly selecting data points that pushed effective protection-level calculations even higher, most nations were able to establish bound tariffs so high that they would exceed the recent level of real protection from nontariff instruments even after the 36 percent reduction to which they were committed. For the European Union, for example, the 1986–88 base period generated initial tariffs above 150 percent for wheat and coarse grains; above 200 percent for beef, sugar, and skimmed milk powder; and above 300 percent for butter. Table 12 provides World Bank calculations of the permitted year 2000 protection levels for the European Union, compared both to recent and to historical levels (see also Sanderson 1994).[18] When the Economist Intelligence Unit examined these and other tariff schedules in 1995, it concluded that the impact of the Uruguay Round on world agricultural trade would be much smaller than originally assumed (EIU 1995).

The minimum access provisions of the agreement were similarly weakened. Largely at the insistence of the European Union, countries

17. Prior to the Uruguay Round, bound tariffs had covered only 42 percent of the farm imports of developed countries, and only 27 percent of the imports of developing countries (see Hathaway 1994).

18. Actual tariffs need not be as high as tariff bindings, of course, but for protected commodities the limits are often imposed.

Table 12.   Border Protection of EU Agriculture

	Bound Tariffs after Uruguay Round (%)	Nontariff Protection before Uruguay Round	
		1986–88 Average (%)	1979–93 Average (%)
Wheat	170	106	57
Rice	195	103	82
Feed grains	102	89	74
Sugar	297	234	150
Meat	96	96	93
Dairy	289	177	128

Source: Merlinda D. Ingco, "Tariffication in the Uruguay Round: How Much Agricultural Liberalization Was Achieved?" *World Economy* 19 (1996): 425–46, and background paper presented at the International Agricultural Trade Research Consortium, Washington, D.C., December 1994.

were allowed to avoid additional imports of sensitive products by grouping them with less sensitive items, rather than measuring access by individual tariff lines. Countries were also permitted to count special trading relationships that existed under their old quota systems as meeting their new minimum access commitments. The limited imports allowed under low duties were labeled *tariff rate quotas* (TRQs). To meet the tariffication requirement, the TRQs allowed low tariffs on imports up to the old quota amount, then placed prohibitively higher tariffs on overquota amounts. The U.S. sugar import quota system had been converted, with country-by-country quotas replaced by comparably small country-by-country TRQs, prior to the Uruguay Round agreement. Subsequently, TRQs were used to preserve the essence of the quantitative restrictions under the prior U.S. Meat Import Law, and under import restrictions on dairy products and peanuts (see Hathaway 1994; and Sumner 1995).[19]

The new tariffication rules in the Uruguay Round agreement were also weakened through the Special Safeguard Provision (Article 5 of the Agreement on Agriculture), which protects tariffication markets against import surges or unusually low world prices. Importers can apply additional duties if imports exceed a certain percentage of the preceding three-year average (called the trigger level) or if import prices

19. The U.S. overquota tariff levels on these products were set at high levels (peanuts, 123 percent; sugar, 84 percent; dairy products, 70 to 95 percent).

drop below a trigger value. The European Union has reserved the right to use the Special Safeguard Provision to protect markets where variable levies have been removed, and many of the EU trigger prices are higher than the external prices the European Union used to calculate its tariff equivalents. For such reasons the European Union is able, under the Uruguay Round agreement, to manage a new import regime at the border not much different, either in level or in variability of protection, from the old system of variable levies (IATRC 1994).

Export Subsidies

Except during brief interludes of high world grain prices (such as 1973–74), Europe consistently used direct restitutions (subsidies) to its exporters to bring the price of its surplus commodities down to the (usually much lower) world price level. The United States, with its support programs more cashed out, was less dependent than the Europeans on direct export subsidies after the 1960s; yet at the depths of the world commodity price collapse in 1985, the United States joined in offering such subsidies—especially for wheat and wheat flour—under the Export Enhancement Program. Halting this self-defeating export subsidy competition had been a high priority for reform advocates in the United States, the Cairns Group, and also to some extent within Europe when the Uruguay Round negotiations began in 1986.

Hopes were high initially that the Cairns Group would serve as a useful prod to accelerate export subsidy reform. Such pressures were felt, but the Cairns Group was effectively excluded from the final bilateral Blair House deal, which established only modest export subsidy reduction obligations. The U.S. and EU negotiators agreed at Blair House that the volume and value of directly subsidized farm exports were to be reduced by 21 percent and 36 percent, respectively, over the six-year life of the agreement (from the base levels that had prevailed in 1986–90), and that products not subsidized during the base period would not be subsidized at all. This was much less than the 100 percent reduction sought by the United States in its original zero option proposal, less than the 90 percent reduction the United States had called for in its modified proposal of October 1990, and even less than the modest 24 percent (volume) reduction called for in the December 1991 Draft Final Act.

On the positive side, the agreement provided quantified restrictions that went beyond the existing equitable share rules that GATT panels had previously been unable to effect or enforce.[20] European negotiators had so strongly resisted any limits on volume of subsidized exports during the Uruguay Round that these modest limits, when finally accepted, represented a significant negotiating achievement. As late as the 1990 Brussels ministerial, the Europeans were unwilling to accept any quantified export subsidy disciplines. The European Union changed its position only after it had independently adopted the MacSharry reforms. These reforms diminished EU reliance on export subsidies (especially in value terms) because domestic EU prices were brought more in line with world price levels. But if EU prices exceeded world prices by any amount, the temptation to abuse export subsidies would remain, so a constraint on export subsidy volumes had to be negotiated as well. This volume constraint finally became acceptable to the European Union once the MacSharry reforms had been embraced (promising a smaller EU cereal surplus in future years), and once the terms of the agreed-upon quantity limit had been relaxed at the Blair House meetings. By the time the GATT agreement took effect in mid-1995, the European Union's annual subsidized volume of wheat and feed grain exports was already 11 to 20 percent below what it would have to be in the first year of the agreement.[21]

Several factors in addition to the 1991–92 MacSharry reforms made the export subsidy component of the final Uruguay Round agreement relatively painless for the European Union. One of these—the 1995 entry into the European Union of Austria, Finland, and Sweden—had been counted on by EU negotiators. These countries had historically maintained internal cereal price supports even more lavish than those of the CAP, so they were expected under CAP prices to produce less grain and hence begin absorbing more from other EU countries— grain that otherwise would have been exported with subsidies (Anderson 1993). Also, when the historical grain exports of these new members were cleverly added to the EU's baseline (from which the re-

20. The agreement precisely states what forms of export subsidies are to be disciplined and that member countries are prohibited from circumventing their commitments. However, the agreement does not specifically bind the use of export credit or export credit guarantees—it only commits the countries to "work toward internationally agreed disciplines and to abide by those disciplines once they are established" (WTO 1994). International food aid, when provided in accordance with international guidelines, is not disciplined either.

21. According to an official EU statement in June 1995, "Following the reform of the CAP in 1992, this [new GATT accord] is not expected to have any significant impact on European agriculture" (*Agra Europe*, 30 June 1995, P3).

quired GATT cuts had to be made), the baseline itself was increased by about 7.5 percent.

In the United States as well, the new GATT restrictions on export subsidies were painless to accept in the short run. In fact, they were much less constraining than a number of other factors that were altering U.S. export subsidy policy. In fiscal 1995, the year before the GATT restrictions came into effect, U.S. congressional appropriations for the EEP had been cut to $800 million—an effective 37 percent reduction from the actual outlays of two years earlier, and well below the new ceiling on spending imposed by the Uruguay Round ($959 million in fiscal year 1996, the first year actually disciplined by the new agreement). Internal budget constraints, not the GATT, were thus the driving force behind the reductions that took place in U.S. export subsidy authority.

Setting the Stage for Future Reforms

In sum, the reform requirements written into the final Uruguay Round Agreement on Agriculture were technically innovative (internal support limits) and conceptually ambitious (tariffication), but otherwise they were watered down and riddled with exemptions. The negotiations may have helped move the European Union toward a cash out of some of its farm supports, but in the United States little added reform can be attributed to the Uruguay Round exercise. Because of scrutiny from the U.S. farm lobby, the final terms of the agreement were written to not exceed the domestic reforms that had already been undertaken in the 1985 and 1990 farm bills. In the meantime, the conduct of the negotiation had given U.S. farm lobby groups new arguments to resist some reforms and to expand export subsidies to even higher levels.

Will the Uruguay Round Agreement on Agriculture contribute to accelerated or more meaningful policy reforms in the future? The agreement included a commitment on the part of the signatory parties to continue the process of achieving "substantial progressive reductions in support and protection" in 1999 (WTO 1994). Perhaps these follow-on negotiations will produce a more significant second installment of reduced AMS levels, larger TRQs, lower bound tariffs, and smaller export subsidy allowances.[22]

22. One incentive to conclude another agreement on agriculture will come from expiration in 2003 of a "peace clause" established by the Uruguay Round. For the preceding nine-year period, agricultural policies in conformity with the provisions of the Agreement on Agriculture are protected (by its Article 13) from various challenges under more

Moreover, even without further negotiations the modest terms of the Uruguay Round agreement could eventually become a more significant policy constraint in Europe, which would benefit the U.S. farm sector. Beyond the six-year implementation period of the agreement, if EU membership is enlarged to include some high-potential farm producers such as Poland and Hungary, the export subsidy constraints negotiated in 1993 might eventually become a significant source of policy reform pressure. Bringing in the central European countries will subtract rather than add degrees of freedom to the EU's Uruguay Round obligations. A 1995 European Commission paper forecast the impact of a phased enlargement beginning in 2000 that would extend the CAP in its current form to the ten associated countries of central and eastern Europe. Between 2000 and 2010, under this scenario, the associated countries would roughly double their net surplus of cereals (under the stimulus of CAP policies), and the net surplus for the EU-25 as a whole would reach an untenable sixty-five million tons—compared to just seventeen million tons for the EU-15 in 1994. Because the European Union could not use export subsidies to dispose of this much surplus grain in 2010 under the terms of the Uruguay Round agreement, either the agreement would have to be relaxed or further internal reforms would be required. At this point, internal EU budget constraints alone could be enough to force further CAP reform, but a previously negotiated international commitment might reinforce these reform pressures. As with the Dillon Round zero-duty oilseed binding, an international commitment that is of little significance when originally negotiated can become, in the fullness of time, a serious policy constraint. This is the two-stage game dynamic; it can work to advance reforms in the future even when negotiations fail to trigger the instant domestic reforms of Putnam's (1988) two-level game process.

Even without such follow-on progress, the Uruguay Round agreement by itself can be counted as a success for U.S. agriculture. This success did not come so much from an acceleration of policy reform progress in the farm sector as from the further liberalization of trade overall, accomplished through the *nonagricultural* components of the final agreement. The Council of Economic Advisors (CEA) and USTR

general WTO rules. Once this interim period ends, individual countries will have greater opportunities to remedy agricultural trade grievances unilaterally or under the WTO dispute settlement procedures.

projected in 1994 that the Uruguay Round final agreement would increase world income in real terms over a ten-year period, compared to what otherwise would be achieved. (U.S. GAO 1994).[23] It was precisely this promised increase in world income (which would come mostly from the trade-expanding effects of nonagricultural parts of the final agreement), rather than the weak agricultural reforms imposed on the European Union or elsewhere, that was used by U.S. officials in 1994 to try to persuade farm-state members of Congress to ratify the Uruguay Round commitments. Based primarily on projections of worldwide income gains from the overall agreement, USDA calculated in 1994 that U.S. farm exports would grow substantially due to the Uruguay Round, and that U.S. farm income would increase as well (USDA 1994).[24]

It is consistent with the continued political power of U.S. farm groups to see the Uruguay Round as speeding the pace of farm policy reform in Europe but not in the United States, all the while generating liberal reforms in nonfarm sectors that can provide still more income benefits to U.S. farmers. The original goal of reforming U.S. domestic farm policy tended to get lost in the process. In two related trade policy events—the negotiation and ratification of NAFTA during 1990–93, and the final congressional ratification of the Uruguay Round final agreement in 1994—U.S. domestic farm policy reform goals also met frustration.

NAFTA and Agriculture

During the early phase when the GATT negotiations were bogged down on agriculture and other disputes, trade officials in the Reagan administration devised another international strategy for promoting liberalization. Alongside the pursuit of a multilateral trade agreement in the GATT, free trade agreements would be pursued with selected individual countries, both for the bilateral economic benefits these agreements would provide and as a means to keep pressure on major trade partners (the Europeans and Japan) in the Uruguay Round. A free trade agreement was reached with Israel in 1985 and with Canada in 1988. The reform of U.S. domestic agricultural policy was not an objective in these agreements. Although relatively minor agricultural tariffs were

23. The world economy was estimated to expand because of the Uruguay Round agreements between 2.5 percent (assuming low underlying economic growth) and 5.0 percent (assuming higher growth).

24. Annual farm exports were estimated to be $4.7 billion to $8.7 billion larger by 2005 because of the Uruguay Round, with annual U.S. farm sector income $1.9 billion to $2.5 billion higher by 2005.

scheduled for elimination, the more restrictive nontariff barriers were left in place.

The opportunity for a third free trade agreement arose when Mexico approached the United States in 1990. Mexico had been undertaking a unilateral reform of its own agricultural policies, and levels of Mexican trade protection had been reduced significantly. Other aspects of Mexican economic policy were undergoing liberalization, and a trade agreement with the United States (by far Mexico's dominant trade partner) was sought to help lock in these reforms. The Bush administration seized this opportunity to negotiate a wide-ranging bilateral bargain with Mexico, and Canada subsequently joined the negotiations for a North American Free Trade Agreement.

The NAFTA negotiations offered enticing opportunities to some U.S. agricultural exporters, but at the same time aroused some sensitivities concerning imports. Mexico was potentially a lucrative market for feed grains, wheat, soybeans, and other U.S. farm products against which it had traditionally maintained a protectionist regime of import licenses and quotas. However, Mexico was competitive in the U.S. market for winter vegetables, and might expand its exports of these and other specialty crops if U.S. barriers were reduced. Complementarities outweighed competition between the U.S. and Mexican farm sectors, and so the NAFTA negotiations were launched with the bold objective of eliminating both tariff and nontariff barriers to trade in all agricultural products (see Grennes and Krissoff 1993). Canada resisted such a broad approach because it was not willing to give up its nontariff barriers, particularly on dairy and poultry products. As a result, separate agreements among the three countries were negotiated on agriculture in NAFTA, with the previous limited free trade agreement for agriculture between the United States and Canada left intact.

The NAFTA negotiations concluded in August 1992, while the Uruguay Round remained deadlocked. For Mexico and the United States, the agricultural trade provisions of NAFTA called for conversion of all nontariff barriers to TRQs. In an important difference with the eventual Uruguay Round agreement, all of the overquota tariffs would be phased out completely within adjustment periods of five, ten, or, in some cases, fifteen years. NAFTA, unlike the Uruguay Round, produced a timetable for moving toward genuine (albeit bilateral) agricultural free trade—but domestic income and market support policies were left beyond its reach.

The timetable for trade liberalization itself was to be a gradual one.

For the commodities that had been protected by import quotas or licenses, market access levels under the initial TRQs were based on 1989–91 trade quantities and were scheduled to increase by only 3 percent compounded annually. High overquota tariffs provided protection against additional imports in the short and medium run. Reflecting the influence of various import-competing U.S. and Mexican producer interests, corn, dry edible beans, milk powder, and peanuts were classified as particularly sensitive commodities and received fifteen-year adjustment periods. Intense negotiations also focused on complex protective TRQ transition mechanisms for sugar. Mexico agreed to raise its external sugar tariff to the U.S. overquota level by the seventh year of the agreement and would subsequently gain potentially unlimited access to the U.S. market if it achieved a net production surplus. Special tariff phaseout and TRQ mechanisms were also developed for citrus and other horticultural products.

The continued political power of U.S. farm interests was particularly visible in the debate over NAFTA implementing legislation in Congress. The Clinton administration took control of the NAFTA approval problem in 1993, and to satisfy Congress (particularly House Democrats who expressed the most intense opposition), it went so far as to re-open the bargain. New "side agreements" with Mexico were negotiated on the environment, labor, and import surges, as Clinton had promised during the presidential election campaign a year earlier—and despite fast-track procedures that were supposed to have guaranteed to the Mexicans an up or down congressional vote without any further U.S. demands. Most U.S. agricultural lobby groups supported NAFTA, but opposition remained strong among some import-competing farm groups, including fruit and vegetable producers in Florida, sugar and peanut producers nationwide, and northern plains wheat farmers, who were angry that Canada had escaped renegotiating its free trade agreement on agriculture with the United States. The Clinton administration appeased these groups with a variety of side deals, and by extracting still more concessions from Mexico. These new concessions helped to ensure passage of the implementing legislation, by a safe 234 to 200 majority in the House, but they further weakened the negotiated provisions for opening agricultural markets under NAFTA.[25]

---

25. See Orden 1996 for an analysis of the NAFTA agricultural negotiations, including the late deals made to win support from some of its opponents. At one point, over thirty members of Congress, including almost the entire Florida congressional delegation of ten

Ratifying the Uruguay Round Agreement in Congress

The 1993 ratification struggle in Congress over NAFTA was a prelude to the 1994 struggle to secure final implementing legislation for the larger Uruguay Round agreement. In each case, farm lobby groups used the requirement for a favorable congressional vote to seek policy gains. In NAFTA, they primarily sought a weakening or slowdown in the timetable of bilateral liberalization for some import-competing commodities. In the Uruguay Round, where little or no liberalization was being imposed on U.S. agriculture by the international agreement, farm lobbies played out a more opportunistic strategy: they sought to boost outlays for GATT legal export subsidy programs and to extract from the Clinton administration an advance endorsement of generous domestic farm support programs prior to the 1995 farm bill debate.

Much of the early part of the Uruguay Round implementing legislation debate in 1994 revolved around a "pay-as-you-go" budget rule, designed by Congress in 1990 to prevent new legislation (including trade agreement implementing legislation) from adding to the federal budget deficit. Under this constraint, Congress had to find approximately $11.5 billion in savings or new tax revenues (over a five-year period) to offset the lower tariff revenues implied by the final Uruguay Round agreement. Farm policy reform advocates inside the Clinton administration went into the debate hoping this pay-as-you-go requirement, plus the fast-track procedure, would give them leverage to obtain significant farm subsidy reductions (of the kind the international negotiation itself had failed to deliver). Early in 1994, as a contribution to the pay-as-you-go offset, the administration proposed a reduction from 85 percent to 75 percent in the base acreage eligible for commodity program deficiency payments.

Farm lobby organizations and farm-state members of Congress stopped this effort dead in its tracks. Leaders from twenty-one separate agricultural lobbying groups warned immediately they would with-

---

Democrats and thirteen Republicans, opposed NAFTA primarily because of the agricultural provisions. With their support, U.S. sugar producers won the inclusion of consumption and production of high-fructose corn sweeteners (HFCSs) in the evaluation of Mexico's net surplus status. This technical concession seemed to preclude any likelihood of substantial Mexican sugar exports to the United States throughout the fifteen-year phase-in period, but in 1998 Mexico asserted it had not explicitly accepted domestic HFCS consumption as part of the calculation, and sought increased access to the U.S. sugar market.

draw their support for Uruguay Round implementing legislation if agriculture were asked to pay a "disproportionate share" of the five-year budget cost of the trade agreement.[26] Farm-state members of Congress rallied immediately behind this lobby initiative. Sixty members of the House of Representatives, including the entire Rural Caucus, warned the Clinton administration against its plans to cut agricultural spending. When seventeen of eighteen members of the Senate Agriculture Committee signed a similar letter, the administration was beaten on the issue.[27]

When the administration backed away from its failed effort to use the GATT implementing legislation to impose extra spending cuts on farm programs in June 1994, the farm lobby sensed it had enough of an upper hand to switch from a defensive to an offensive strategy. As the price for their support for the implementing legislation, House and Senate Agriculture Committee members, led by Representatives Jill Long (Democrat; Indiana) and Pat Roberts (Republican; Kansas), began demanding farm program extensions and increases in farm support spending, or at least promises from the president to request such extensions and increases in the future. At a mock markup of implementing legislation in July 1994, the House Agriculture Committee assembled and approved an ambitious wish list of proposed amendments to the final implementing bill, including a shift of funds (about $1 billion) into GATT-legal (green box) export programs, a recommendation to curb imports of peanut butter, and also a commitment to use the EEP (along with a subsidy program called the Dairy Export Initiative Program, or DEIP) to the maximum extent allowable under the new GATT rules.

In the Senate, Democratic Agriculture Committee Chair Patrick Leahy focused narrowly on a plan to secure a producer-financed export

26. The agriculturalists argued that 5 percent was a reasonable share (versus the 25 to 40 percent share some in the administration were seeking), because reduced agricultural tariff revenue contributed only 5 percent of total anticipated revenue losses.

27. The pay-as-you-go rule was partly to blame for the administration's weakness. This rule was more strict in the Senate than in the House, because there it stipulated offsets over ten years (not just five). In order to circumvent this onerous ten-year rule for Uruguay Round implementing legislation, the Clinton administration had to ask for a rules waiver from the Senate, which required more than a simple majority. Sixty senators would have to vote in favor in order to override an objection on the floor. For this reason, the implementing legislation battle was to be fought most keenly in the Senate, and the Clinton administration had to consider seriously the threats of a withdrawal of support from seventeen out of eighteen Agriculture Committee senators.

subsidy for dairy products, while other senators met in small groups and put forward their wish lists separately. Democrat Tom Daschle (South Dakota) soon recruited twenty-six senators to cosponsor a parallel version of the House Agriculture Committee's fund-shifting proposal. Republican Senator Thad Cochran (Mississippi) and four other Agriculture Committee members went further. They proposed that the implementing legislation for the Uruguay Round be amended to include an extension of the existing U.S. farm commodity programs, a proposal promptly supported by the American Farm Bureau Federation. Cochran and the Farm Bureau were attracted to the *nonamendable* nature of the fast-track implementing legislation and were hoping to pass the equivalent of a new farm bill through Congress without having to face any floor challenges. A few reform-minded agriculturalists in Congress were offended by these obviously extortionist farm lobby tactics. Republican Senator Richard Lugar (Indiana) charged his colleagues with "taking advantage of fast-track procedures to achieve an expansive and extraneous legislative agenda" ("Administration Offers" 1994, 3).

The Legislative Submission and Side Promises

The Clinton administration's strategy in the end was to satisfy these farm lobby demands only in part through the formal language of Uruguay Round implementing legislation, and mostly instead through a set of side promises specified in letters from administration officials to key House and Senate members. The formal legislative submission, sent to Congress on September 24 (the last possible moment under fast-track authority) did not include the extension of 1990 farm bill commodity programs (as sought by Senator Cochran), nor did it include most of the wish list of amendments originally adopted in the mock markup by the House Agriculture Committee. It did, however, include an extension of EEP authority through the year 2001, and explicitly widened the circumstances under which the EEP could be used.[28]

A September letter from Agriculture Secretary Mike Espy and Acting Budget Director Alice Rivlin to the chairs and ranking minority members of the House and Senate Agriculture Committees meantime made

28. The implementing bill also extended DEIP export subsidy authority through the year 2001, but did not provide for the producer-financed (and possibly GATT-illegal) Leahy dairy export subsidy plan.

side promises in five different policy areas. Concerning the budget, the letter included a reassurance that the administration planned to maintain spending on USDA programs, taking into consideration "reductions made in agriculture budgets in the past and during the GATT round" (30 September 1994). The Espy-Rivlin letter also announced a one-year voluntary extension of existing CRP contracts due otherwise to expire, and promised that the administration would propose a full reauthorization and extension of the CRP in 1995. Espy and Rivlin reaffirmed the implementing legislation commitments on the EEP and DEIP, reiterating that the administration intended "to request that Congress make available funds for these programs to the fullest extent permissible under GATT." This latter statement indicated once again how the Uruguay Round binding on direct export subsidy spending had unfortunately come to be seen, at the insistence of the U.S. farm lobby, as something of a floor as well as a ceiling. In addition, through the Espy-Rivlin letter, the Clinton administration promised to propose increases of $600 million for green box and other GATT-legal agricultural programs, including a combination of direct spending, direct credits, and credit guarantees.[29] The administration's very modest legislative concessions and stronger but still somewhat vague side promises were sufficient to produce the intended effect. Four days after the Espy-Rivlin letter was sent, a coalition of seventeen agricultural groups, led by the Farm Bureau, urged Congress to implement the Uruguay Round agreement.[30]

Republican Election Victory and Final GATT Approval

The administration's struggle for Uruguay Round implementation was not quite finished in early October 1994. Senate delays on nonagricultural matters put off the vote until after the November midterm election. The election results were a bombshell. For the first time in forty years the Republicans won majority control of both the House of Repre-

29. This pledge was a bit misleading, because on the surface it gave an impression that the farm lobby had secured about 60 percent of the $1 billion worth of fund-shifting earlier demanded by the House Agriculture Committee. In fact, the $600 million figure was total "program activity," including contingent programs such as export credit guarantees—which did not always require actual outlays. The administration promise implied only about $150 to $200 million in actual expenditures.

30. Among the farm commodity groups, support was secured from corn, cotton, and rice producers, but wheat, soybean, and milk producers for the moment held back. Senators Cochran and Daschle were among the members of Congress that joined in the GATT endorsement, along with Representative Long.

sentatives and the Senate. This dramatic change in party control was destined to reshape pending efforts to reauthorize U.S. farm policy when the new 104th Congress convened in 1995–96. For the remainder of the lame duck 1994 congressional session, however, it did little to alter the bargain that had already been struck: a bipartisan acceptance by the Agriculture Committees of the Uruguay Round agreement, sweetened by a long list of administration side promises.

Postponement of the implementing legislation vote into the lame-duck session did reopen the administration's bidding efforts to win the support from a few key Senate Agriculture Committee holdouts who had not yet committed on the issue—including Republican Bob Dole of Kansas, who was scheduled to become, after his party's capture of the Senate, the new majority leader. Immediately after the November election recess, Dole began negotiating the terms of his support for the GATT implementing legislation directly with the White House. Dole received enough from his negotiations to offer an endorsement at a high-profile Rose Garden press conference in late November.[31] With his endorsement the Senate vote on the GATT could go ahead on December 1, with a safe margin for victory. A key preliminary vote to waive Senate budget rules passed by a 68 to 32 margin, in effect with 8 votes to spare. The actual implementing legislation vote passed by an even safer 76 to 24 margin (with 26 votes to spare).[32] This was hardly as decisive as the 90 to 4 endorsement that the earlier Tokyo Round GATT agreement had been given by the Senate in 1979, but it was nonetheless a victory for free trade. The House of Representatives had voted earlier, on November 29, to accept the GATT implementation bill by nearly a two-to-one margin (288 to 146).

The outcome of this Uruguay Round implementing legislation

31. These same assurances, together with the earlier commitments on the EEP, were also enough to secure support for GATT from Pat Roberts, who would soon become the chair of the House Agriculture Committee.

32. The eight-vote margin on the budget waiver raises a possibility that the administration gave away more than it had to in its negotiations with individual senators, perhaps including those with strong farm interests. However, many of the senators that made specific farm-related demands as the price for their vote were not bluffing. When the administration decided not to go along with Leahy's dairy self-help initiative, the support of both Vermont senators was lost. When the administration rejected Senator Cochran's demand that the implementing legislation be used to extend the programs of the 1990 farm bill, two of the senators who had joined in making this demand voted against the budget waiver.

process confirmed that seven years of GATT negotiations abroad had done little to diminish or dilute the power of U.S. farm lobbies at home. The Uruguay Round agreements had taken little or nothing away from the farm groups, and when it came time for Congress to vote to implement these agreements, farm lobbies took advantage of the opportunity to extract significant forward-looking concessions from the administration.

The Reform Problem after the Uruguay Round

The Uruguay Round exercise may have advanced liberal farm policy reform somewhat in the European Union, but it did little to alter the pace or trajectory of reform in the United States. The terms of the final Agreement on Agriculture did not go beyond reforms that had already been undertaken unilaterally before the negotiations began (in the 1985 farm bill) or undertaken for budget reasons (in the 1990 farm bill) while the negotiations were underway. In some cases, the Uruguay Round may have actually slowed the pace of U.S. reform. Had there been no international negotiations, the EEP export subsidy program might well have been terminated when market prices strengthened after 1988; instead, the EEP was kept alive and then even expanded in 1992 for bargaining purposes in the Uruguay Round.

The Uruguay Round negotiations seemed at first to be providing an opportunity to move U.S. and European policy in the direction of a fully decoupled cash out (of the kind envisioned in the 1985 Boschwitz-Boren bill or the U.S. GATT zero option). A formal distinction was drawn in the Uruguay Round between distorting subsidies subject to restraint under the AMS and nondistorting (green box) subsidy policies, including decoupled cash payments. Yet this opportunity to promote a decoupled cash out was substantially compromised at the end of the negotiations. Under pressure created by expiration of fast-track legislation, the United States and the European Union agreed at Blair House on the blue box exemption, under which cash payments not fully decoupled (U.S. deficiency payments as well as EU compensation payments) were allowed to escape discipline. Market-distorting production controls were even set as one condition to be fulfilled before these cash payments gained their blue box status.

The international negotiations also failed to curb U.S. farm lobby power in the implementation phase. Rather than being weakened by two-level-game synergistic linkages, U.S. farm lobbies were able to use the vote on Uruguay Round implementation in Congress as a setting in which to make new demands for strengthened or extended subsidies. Thus, at the end of the Uruguay Round process, little had been gained from the internationalization strategy itself, to speed or extend reform of U.S. agricultural policy.

Chapter Four

The 1996 FAIR Act

THE LONG INTERNATIONAL NEGOTIATIONS of the Uruguay Round produced little U.S. policy change beyond the slow and incomplete cash out for export crops that had been underway since the 1960s. Proponents of reform had many reasons to argue that redesign of farm policies ought to go beyond these limited accomplishments, but few observers in the summer of 1994 expected there would be anything more than modest additional adjustment in the pending 1995 revision of the 1990 farm bill.

Expectations about farm policy were unsettled by the Republican election victory in November 1994, but the implications of the new Republican control of Congress were for a time uncertain. Some forty years earlier, a Republican Congress managed, on several occasions, to lower the high fixed price supports inherited from the Second World War, but the support levels had not been lowered enough to contain budget costs or squeeze farmers out of government programs. Republican administrations had argued in the 1970s and 1980s for cutouts of farm support, but Democratic control of the House of Representatives, and nearly continuous Democratic control of the Senate, had blocked those efforts. Would a Republican Congress now embrace radical reform? This seemed unlikely, since Republican agriculturalists in Congress had consistently joined to support farm bills more generous than those proposed by their own presidents. A Republican-controlled Senate had been unwilling to support President Reagan's farm bill cutout proposal in 1985.

Also, a reversed partisan balance had to be considered in the new di-

Our description of the farm policy debate is based on extensive interviews conducted during 1994–96, on first-hand observations of many of the public events we describe, and on numerous primary source materials. Where not cited specifically, the source materials include the interviews, press reports and briefings, congressional hearings, and draft legislation. Two newsletters published by Sparks Companies, Inc., *SCI Washington Report* and *SCI Policy Report*, were valuable sources of information. See Orden, Paarlberg, and Roe 1996a; 1996b; and Hagstrom 1996 for earlier summary assessments of the farm bill debate. See also Stuart and Runge (1997) and Schertz and Doering (1999).

vided government. Whereas mostly Democratic Congresses had pursued modest cash outs of farm programs in the past, defying Republican administrations professing to favor more reform, the 104th Congress would be controlled by Republicans, but face a stand-pat Democratic administration. If the Republican Congress sought a significant squeeze out, buyout, or perhaps even a cutout blocked earlier by Democratic control, could it overcome the opposition of a president who had committed himself to farm program continuity?

The farm bill that eventually emerged under the altered partisan circumstances of the 104th Congress was the Federal Agriculture Improvement and Reform (FAIR) Act of 1996.[1] This chapter describes the key events of the policy process leading to the 1996 FAIR Act. We save for subsequent chapters a full analysis of alternative explanations for the FAIR Act outcome, and of its implications for future reform.

The Republican Congress

Prospects for agricultural policy reform seemed strengthened by the November 1994 Republican election victory. The unexpected shift to Republican control of Congress suggested that a political consensus in favor of a smaller federal government had gained ground nationally. The Republican leadership, having won majorities in both the House of Representatives and the Senate for the first time in forty years, pressed its election-campaign agenda of fiscal discipline, lower taxes, and devolution of government responsibilities from the federal level back to the states, an agenda that Republican zealots described as "revolutionary." Cuts in federal spending programs were implied by this agenda, and seventy-three freshman legislators converged on Washington to implement the mandates of the "Contract with America," a ten-point program the Republican House candidates had endorsed prior to the elections. The governance philosophy of this new wave of Republicans marked entitlement programs, including those for agriculture, for scrutiny.

When the 104th Congress convened in January 1995, an omnibus bill to constrain government spending and balance the federal budget became the principal vehicle around which the Republicans organized their legislative program. Policy debate took on a sharply partisan tenor in a setting in which the stakes for the new leadership included forging

1. See *U.S. Statutes at Large* 1996. For an excellent summary of the FAIR Act, see Young and Shields 1996; for a brief synopsis, see the appendix to this book.

a lasting governing majority. Within the Agriculture Committees, bipartisan cooperation became more difficult than it had been. The new Republican majorities were not necessarily going to endorse extension of the old farm programs, and Democrats responded by rallying in defense of the past interventions.

Following the 1994 election, the Clinton administration appeared to conclude that taking a leadership position on balancing the budget (as it had when it successfully pushed a budget act through the House with only Democratic votes in 1993) had not been rewarded politically, and should be left to the Republicans. In agriculture, the administration quickly backed away from the proposal floated by its budget director (in October 1994) to reduce farm support payments by as much as $16 billion over five years.

Consistent with commitments made during the negotiations over the implementing legislation for the Uruguay Round, the five-year budget submitted to Congress by the president in February 1995 was supportive of agricultural spending. Projections by the administration's Office of Management and Budget (OMB) showed declining expenditures on farm deficiency payments because of strong market demand and anticipated renewal of the ten-year CRP contracts that were soon to expire. The only additional fiscal discipline imposed by the president's budget was inclusion of unspecified policy changes to reduce CCC outlays by $1.5 billion in 1998–2000, the distant "out years" of the legislation. This was a cut of less than 5 percent of the $37.7 billion of CCC spending on commodity and export programs expected by the OMB over five years.[2] The administration's generous positions were reiterated by a new secretary of agriculture, Dan Glickman, in his March 1995 confirmation hearings. An eighteen-year veteran of Congress from Kansas, Glickman promised to be "an advocate for agriculture."

The administration followed up in May with guidelines for farm pol-

2. The budget and farm bill debates during 1994–96 focused mostly on potential cuts to expenditures on the commodity-support and export programs. As we have described in historical context, farm program spending also includes other components. The bulk of spending comprised three broad categories by the mid-1990s: In addition to the commodity and export programs, the OMB projected that $9.9 billion would be spent for conservation programs and $9.3 billion for crop insurance subsidies. The Congressional Budget Office in February 1995 made somewhat different assumptions about land usage, and the CBO projected more CCC spending on commodity and export programs ($41.1 billion) and less for conservation ($8.5 billion) (see Manfredi 1995).

icy (USDA 1995). The guidelines called for maintaining the traditional program structure of target prices and loan rates, modified by a phased-in flexibility allowing farmers to plant alternative crops on their base acreages without losing program eligibility. In a concession to the prospect of further budget pressure, the administration acknowledged that additional needed reductions in outlays could be achieved by increasing the percentage of nonpayment acres beyond the 15 percent stipulated in the 1990 farm bill. The guidelines also recommended extension of the CRP, with new enrollments through 2000 of the most environmentally sensitive land. Thus, the administration endorsed a range of proposals for modest changes but failed to take a leadership role in seeking either sharp budget cuts or fundamental reform of the farm support programs.

A much more aggressive reform agenda was articulated by Republican Richard Lugar, the new chair of the Senate Committee on Agriculture, Nutrition and Forestry. Soon after the November election, Lugar signaled his intent to thoroughly reevaluate the objectives of farm programs, and the policies used to attain these objectives. In his own reform proposal, Lugar recommended that $15 billion be saved from anticipated expenditures over five years by eliminating the EEP and by lowering target prices by 3 percent each year. This was effectively a squeeze-out approach, if not a full cutout. Lugar held a series of hearings in February and March 1995 to showcase his recommendations, but the hearings also served to demonstrate the limited support for bold reform among both Democrat and Republican members of the Senate Agriculture Committee.

The dispute about agricultural policy spilled over to the Senate Budget Committee, which in May passed a resolution with the broad objective of balancing the budget in seven years, based on February 1995 spending and revenue projections by the CBO. Emphasizing fiscal discipline, the Senate budget resolution called for eliminating the federal deficit without either raising or lowering taxes. For agriculture, Lugar's proposed budget cuts were rejected as too severe. Spending on CCC commodity-support and export programs was initially projected by CBO at $41.1 billion over five years, 1995–2000, and $56.6 billion over seven years, 1996–2002. The Senate budget resolution then required reductions from the CBO projections of only $8.8 billion in five years and $11.8 billion in seven years.

On the House side, the new chair of the Committee on Agriculture,

Pat Roberts, represented a rural wheat-growing district in Kansas and was considered, far more than Lugar, a strong proponent of support programs for agriculture. Roberts indicated in early 1995 that he wanted to "take a look at what works and build from there"(McLeod 1995). At the annual meeting of the American Farm Bureau Federation in January, Roberts outlined his objectives for agricultural policy within the framework of the broader Republican (particularly House) agenda.

Roberts's three main objectives were to ensure that farm commodity programs were not singled out for disproportionate budget cuts, to direct any farm spending cuts toward deficit reduction rather than other spending programs, and to seek relief for farmers from what he called a tidal wave of environmental mandates.[3] Based on discussions with his committee majority and the House Republican leadership, Roberts presented these objectives as part of a new "policy ledger" for agriculture. On the negative side of the ledger, Roberts told farm constituents, would be less direct federal support expenditures and, possibly, elimination of the domestic supply restrictions affecting sugar and peanuts. Offsetting these negatives, on the positive side of the ledger, would be lower taxes and interest rates from an overall package of deficit reduction and tax policy reforms targeted specifically toward farmers—including capital gains tax relief and higher health-care deductions for the self-employed. Farm policy would be redesigned to be less burdensome, particularly by increasing planting flexibility on base acreage and by eliminating requirements for unpaid annual ARP land set asides. Paid land diversion through the CRP would be renewed, and regulatory relief would be provided by revisions to legislation on wetlands, endangered species, coastal management, and private property rights. Roberts never mentioned decoupled support payments among his early proposals.

Despite his vocal endorsement of the full House Republican policy and fiscal agendas, Roberts led efforts in Congress to defend the programs under the jurisdiction of the Agriculture Committee. He could live with further cash outs of farm commodity supports, but had no in-

3. Roberts's constant refrain on the budget was that only farm program spending had declined an average of 10 percent annually since 1985. He and other agriculturalists conveniently ignored the fact that the costly cash-out years of the mid-1980s were an inflated measure from which to assess farm program spending reductions.

terest in a squeeze out, or a cutout, or even a buyout. Nor did he have any interest in the Contract with America commitment to turn welfare programs such as the federal food stamp program over to the states in the form of block grants. In late February, after a contentious fourteen-hour session to mark up legislation, Roberts announced an agreement with the House leadership to retain food stamps as a federal entitlement (Hagstrom 1995).

Roberts also did his homework in political arithmetic. Claiming that thirty-three of the freshman Republican members of the House (including twenty-four who had defeated Democratic incumbents) came from districts with a significant agricultural base, Roberts reminded his colleagues of the election defeats suffered in the 1950s when Republicans had attempted a farm program squeeze out through lower CCC loan rates. He developed a strategy to convince the Republican leadership that holding its majority in the House of Representatives after the 1996 elections might depend on taking a supportive approach to agriculture in the new farm bill.

What Roberts faced, however, was a Republican House majority leadership determined to make good on its campaign pledge to cut spending and taxes. Unlike the Senate, House Republicans sought a balanced budget resolution that included tax cuts of more than $350 billion. Greater reductions in aggregate spending would be required to balance the House budget with such tax cuts, compared to the Senate budget resolution requirements. Attempts by Roberts and other congressional agriculturalists to defend farm programs thus faced potentially strident opposition in House committees and on the House floor. A group of reform-oriented Agriculture Committee members was led by Representative John Boehner (Ohio), who represented the leadership as chair of the Republican Conference. The House Budget Committee initially targeted agricultural spending for cuts as severe as those proposed by Lugar and rejected by the Senate.

Even under pressure from the House leadership's commitment to tax cuts, Roberts and his supporters managed to whittle down the proposed reduction in projected agricultural spending from $16 billion to $12 billion over five years by the time House Budget Committee chair John Kasich (Ohio) called a Republican retreat to review a draft budget resolution in early May. In subsequent negotiations, Roberts and Kasich settled on a modest cut for agriculture of $9 billion over five years, and a much larger cut of $17 billion over seven years (Maraniss and Weisskopf 1995). Their agreement allowed for a reexamination of the agricultural budget if other Republican policy promises were not delivered upon.[4]

When the differing budget resolutions passed by the Senate and House went to a conference committee in early June, the Republican majority reached a compromise on tax cuts, agreeing to lower taxes by $245 billion as part of a legislative package projected to balance the budget by 2002. The exact level of spending cuts for farm programs was not resolved by the budget resolution. The House adopted targets that mandated a reduction of projected expenditures on agriculture of $8.5 billion over five years and $13.4 billion over seven years. In the Senate, only aggregate savings by the Agriculture Committee on farm and nutrition programs were specified: $29.2 billion over five years and $48.4 billion over seven years. Under the Senate instructions, more money could be spent on farm support programs than under the House instructions, if expenditures on programs such as food stamps were reduced severely enough.

Nor did the aggregate caps on anticipated spending in the budget resolution mandate how the proposed spending cuts were to be obtained. Farm lobby groups and their congressional advocates among the Republicans had found it easy to work in unison so long as the issue was preserving aggregate spending for agriculture within the constraint of the new majority party's emerging budget commitments. This unity would splinter among competing regional and commodity interests when specific policy options had to be considered.

"Freedom to Farm" versus Traditional Policy Instruments

Not all legislative proposals on farm policy came from support program advocates. One prominent coalition of farm program critics early in 1995 proposed a virtual elimination of some of the traditional agricultural supports. Republican Dan Miller (Florida) and Democrat

4. Roberts obtained a nonbinding amendment to the budget resolution that linked both sides of his policy ledger. This sweeping escape-clause stated that budget reductions for agricultural programs would be reexamined if land values on January 1, 1998, were less than 95 percent of their values on the date of adoption of the resolution; if regulatory relief sought in the areas of wetlands regulation, the Endangered Species Act, private property rights, and cost-benefit analysis of proposed regulations were not enacted into law; if new legislation had not been enacted providing capital-gains tax reductions, increased estate-tax exemptions, and mechanisms for averaging income for tax purposes; if there had been any U.S. government interference in international markets; or if NAFTA, GATT, and other international trade agreements had failed to lower export subsidies and reduce import barriers of foreign governments.

Charles Schumer (New York) led almost 100 House cosponsors of a bipartisan bill to end the domestic sugar price-support program. They negotiated an early promise from Roberts to allow a vote on their proposal when the farm bill reached the House floor. In June, Republican Representative Dick Zimmer (New Jersey) joined Schumer to introduce broader legislation to end farm subsidies. Their Farm Freedom Act proposed that deficiency payments be phased out by lowering target prices 5 percent per year. In effect, Zimmer and Schumer were seeking a cutout of the farm support programs. Aggregate outlays for deficiency payments were capped during the transition period under this proposal, then eliminated in the sixth year. The sponsors claimed that over five years their proposal would save $29 billion and end income transfers to farmers.

The budget mandates of the Senate and House Agriculture Committees lay between the extremes of the subsidy cutout in the Zimmer-Schumer bill and the generous budget proposal of the Clinton administration. To meet the congressional budget objective, the traditional support policies would require some modification.

One unexpected option that circulated around the House Agriculture Committee in early June was an unsigned three-page outline of a reform proposal. Titled the Freedom to Farm Act, this proposal renewed historic Republican themes such as planting flexibility, but it also revived the controversial full decoupling approach that had been rejected in 1985—and it took a novel approach to the budget issue. Compared to previous calls for scaling back existing programs to achieve some level of anticipated savings, the Freedom to Farm Act turned the budget process upside down. Instead of detailing measures to reduce anticipated program expenditures, the Freedom to Farm Act described a means to capture money for agriculture that might otherwise go unspent. By June 1995 crop prices had begun to rise, meaning that traditional deficiency payments were about to shrink automatically to lower levels than projected by the CBO. The Freedom to Farm Act sought to lock in all the expenditures for farmers that were permitted by the earlier budget resolution—a total of $43.2 billion—before this automatic shrinkage took place.[5]

To lock in the projected expenditures, the Freedom to Farm Act pre-

---

5. The spending that the Freedom to Farm proposal sought to lock in was the full $56.6 billion projected in the CBO budget baseline of February 1995, less the budget resolution mandated cuts of $13.4 billion.

sented a straightforward decoupling alternative to existing deficiency payments for the feed grains, wheat, cotton, and rice. Over a seven-year period, a fixed entitlement would be paid to farmers on an annual basis, with individual payments determined by past support program participation. The Freedom to Farm payments would be made regardless of levels of market prices and independent of production decisions. With the fixed support payments "decoupled" from economic activity, farmers would not have to be concerned about maintaining program base acreage or meeting ARP requirements (although they would have to continue certain conservation practices to remain eli-gible for the payments). The Freedom to Farm payments would last for the seven-year "transition" period, with aggregate annual expenditures falling one-third from $7.6 billion in 1996 to $5.0 billion in 2002. Under the Freedom to Farm Act, the EEP would be reauthorized, and minimal price-floor guarantees would be provided by retaining nonrecourse CCC loans— but at 70 percent of the Olympic five-year moving average of past prices, instead of 85 percent as stipulated by the previous farm bills. The permanent legislation from 1938 and 1949 would be suspended until 2002, and a national commission would be established to make recommendations about the appropriate long-term role of the government in agriculture.

The fixed decoupled payments under the Freedom to Farm Act guaranteed producers a seven-year contractual income stream and, like the Zimmer-Schumer Farm Freedom Act, promised budget discipline through a firm cap on future farm program expenditures. The budget cap of the Freedom to Farm Act was more generous to farmers, and it provided more immediate production flexibility than the Zimmer-Schumer bill. With farm commodity market prices strengthening and end-of-year carryover stocks suddenly projected to be near record low levels, prices were likely to remain strong for at least another year. , This is what made the guaranteed payments under the Freedom to Farm Act more lucrative in the short run than anticipated deficiency payments under continuation of the 1990 law, or under any similar legislation. Prospects for strong farm exports and prices in subsequent years compounded the potential short-term windfall that might be delivered by the decoupling of support payments from market prices, although with less certainty.

The windfall payments outlined by the Freedom to Farm Act appealed to the chair of the House Agriculture Committee for yet another reason. Rising market prices in the summer of 1995 were forcing some of his constituents to send back to the government cash advances they had received on expected deficiency payments for wheat—at a time when weather damage to their crops prevented them from profiting from the price increases. For these Kansas wheat growers, the traditional deficiency payments were not working well as a safety net in 1995. The prospect of having to repay advance deficiency payments (that they had already spent) to the government angered these farmers and set off alarm bells for Roberts. If a decoupled payment scheme had been in effect in the summer of 1995, rising market prices would not have meant shrinking government payments and revenue losses for the crop-damaged wheat growers in Kansas.

By decoupling support payments from market prices, the Freedom to Farm Act also finessed a budget-related obstacle to eliminating the annual ARP set-aside requirements. Republicans had long suspected ARP land diversions of cutting profits for the most productive farm operators; hurting input, transport, and processing industries; and compromising the competitive position of U.S. farm exporters in world markets. Agribusiness efforts to end ARPs under several previous farm bills had failed, but by the outset of the 1995 debate, the use of ARPs primarily to limit deficiency payment expenditures (instead of to raise market prices) and the uneven application of ARPs across commodities had fueled growing opposition to these annual supply-control programs among farmers as well.[6] Elimination of ARPs was advocated in 1995 by the National Corn Growers Association (NCGA) and by a newly formed coalition of agricultural processors, the Coalition for a Competitive Food and Agricultural System (CCFAS). With the 104th Congress more sympathetic toward full-production agriculture and agribusiness interests than any previous Congress had been, the Republican agricultural leadership set as one of its key objectives the elimination of unpaid annual land diversion under ARPs.

The CBO's February 1995 baseline budget projections assumed ARPs would continue for corn and cotton. If farm support payments remained tied to production and market prices, the CBO estimated that

6. Once deficiency payments were legislated in the 1985 and 1990 farm bills, imposition of ARPs inevitably lowered budget exposure, but farmers only benefited if the supply restrictions raised market prices enough that revenue gains on incremental output (not eligible for deficiency payments) exceeded the opportunity cost of the lost production from the idled land. Farmers found this trade-off unattractive in the 1990s. (See Fatseas 1996 for the proposals to end ARPs and various other recommendations of farm lobby groups at the outset of the 1995 debate.)

set-aside elimination would increase costs by nearly $6.5 billion—because more acres would become eligible for payments and increased output would cause market prices to fall, raising per-unit subsidies. Most analysts considered the CBO's February 1995 ARP projections unrealistic given the strong market outlook that had developed by June. But under congressional budget rules, the estimated additional cost of ARP elimination based on the February CBO projections—an additional 50 percent beyond the savings required from farm programs by the congressional budget resolution—would have to be offset by other savings if the set asides were eliminated with existing support payment instruments. The Freedom to Farm Act finessed this budget-process constraint to ARP elimination by decoupling subsidy payments.

For all these reasons, the unsigned Freedom to Farm outline of June 1995 attracted immediate interest when it was circulated, despite its radical break with past farm support policies. The outline was recognized as having been crafted by a House Republican policy group that included Roberts. Perhaps just a trial balloon at first, Freedom to Farm had demonstrated staying power by late July, and Roberts formally introduced a legislative version of the proposal in early August, cosponsored by Republicans Boehner, Bill Barrett (Nebraska), John Hostettler (Indiana), and Bill Smith (Michigan). The August version of the Freedom to Farm Act stipulated that the fixed decoupled payments to farmers would be distributed under transferable individual contracts that presumably were insulated from future budget cuts by Congress.[7] Roberts indicated that he would spend the August congressional recess advocating his proposal and gauging the reactions of producers, then hold a formal markup session of the Agriculture Committee when Congress reconvened in September. Farm lobby groups withheld judgment on the radical decoupling proposal for the most part, even though many favored eliminating ARPs.

In the Senate, agricultural policy proposals were moving in quite a

7. The payments would be proportioned among the program commodities on the basis of past expenditure shares and made to individual farmers based on their 1995 program yields and base acreage. The traditional program commodities grown on land subject to a contract would be eligible for nonrecourse CCC loans, as would oilseeds and rye grown by any producer. The August Freedom to Farm Act ended the voluntary annual set-aside programs (0,/50/85–92), limited payments to $50,0000 per person, terminated the authority for the cotton and rice programs that had been extended through 1997 in the 1993 budget reconciliation legislation, and suspended relevant sections of the 1938 and 1949 agricultural acts for the 1996–2002 period. No provisions were included for the CRP, nor were provisions included for dairy, sugar, or peanuts.

different direction during the summer of 1995. After the budget resolution was adopted, Lugar did not reissue his early reform proposals, and he began to hint that the Senate might endorse only modest changes to existing programs. While he hedged, Republican Senator Thad Cochran (Mississippi) and fourteen cosponsors—including Republicans Jesse Helms (North Carolina), John Warner (Virginia), and Larry Craig (Indiana) and Democrat David Pryor (Arkansas) from the Agriculture Committee—introduced a traditional farm bill titled the Agricultural Competitiveness Act of 1995. Supporters of the Cochran bill (as it came to be known) characterized policy as being at a crossroads of "whether the U.S. agricultural economy will be offered up to satisfy ideology, leaving U.S. farmers to compete on their own against the treasuries of foreign governments" (Cochran 1995, 3). Its sponsors nevertheless acknowledged, with reluctance, the necessity to reduce spending on agriculture.

In most ways, the Cochran bill extended existing farm programs in the manner he had proposed in the 1994 Uruguay Round implementing legislation debate. Deficiency payments remained uncapped entitlements tied to production of specific crops on established base acreages, and the support prices for sugar and peanuts were maintained at their 1995 levels. To achieve budget savings, the Cochran bill increased nonpayment acres for feed grains, wheat, cotton, and rice from 15 percent to 25 percent. Modest reforms were imposed for sugar and peanuts as minimal steps these industries considered necessary to forestall support-price reductions and more dramatic reforms.[8]

The Cochran bill became a rallying point for producers of the southern commodities (cotton, rice, sugar, and peanuts) and others in agriculture who sought to maintain the traditional policy instruments. The

8. For deficiency payment crops, the Cochran bill increased planting flexibility by allowing farmers to plant alternative crops on up to 100 percent of their base acres and to plant program crops on as much as 25 percent of their historic soybean acres. Farmers would not receive deficiency payments for the crops produced under these planting options, but they would not be penalized by a reduction in their base acreage considered eligible for the support programs in the future. All output of program crops would be eligible for nonrecourse CCC loans. Sugar producers were required to implement a surplus stock program in place of existing marketing allotments (quotas on market sales) to ensure that the U.S. minimum import commitments under the Uruguay Round agreement were met and domestic prices were supported at no cost to taxpayers. For peanuts, the secretary of agriculture was given latitude to lower the national production quota eligible for high price supports to maintain that price level without direct government outlays. The Cochran bill did not include policies for the CRP or dairy products.

budget savings it provided were estimated to be less than $5 billion over seven years. The sponsors acknowledged that agricultural programs might need to be further modified to comply with applicable budget reconciliation instructions. But they hoped to shift some of the remaining budget cuts that might be required of agriculture to nutrition programs.

Senate Democrats on the Agriculture Committee, led by the new minority leader Tom Daschle also outlined a farm policy proposal before the August 1995 congressional recess. Their Farm Security Act of 1995 reverted to the interventionist supply-control and price-support policy instruments favored by relatively high-cost farmers in the Northern Plains. A two-tier payment mechanism was established for feed grains and wheat, with the quantity of output eligible for deficiency payments limited so support payments targeted midsized farms. In conjunction with these payments, the price floor maintained by CCC loan rates was raised to 95 percent of the five-year Olympic moving average of past market prices. Raising CCC loan rate levels under the Senate Democrats' proposal implied renewed government interference with market price fluctuations—in effect a retreat from the cash out. This policy change—endorsed by the National Farmers Union—ran in direct opposition to the Freedom to Farm Act. If market prices fell, higher loan rates could lead to unanticipated CCC expenditures for marketing loans, or even to old-fashioned stock accumulations in government storage. The Senate Democrats capped anticipated total expenditures on farm programs at $7 billion per year, and claimed net savings of $4 billion from the CBO baseline projections. Their proposal increased planting flexibility (by combining separate commodity base acreages into a single farm program base) but gave the secretary of agriculture broad authority to use ARP supply controls, or to otherwise modify program interventions, if expenditures were projected to exceed the authorized levels.[9]

The farm policy proposal of the Senate Democrats, with its emphasis on targeted income support and higher loan rate guarantees, differed from the policy recommendations of the Clinton administration, which more closely extended the existing 1990 law (in keeping with its 1994 Uruguay Round implementing legislation commitments). The presi-

---

9. This Democratic alternative to the Republican decoupling proposal in 1995 was reminiscent of the Democratic Harkin-Gephardt alternative to the (nominally bipartisan) Boschwitz-Boren decoupling proposal of 1985.

dent revised his budget proposals in June, increasing fiscal discipline to counter public support for the agenda of the Republican Congress. The president's June budget endorsed savings of $4 billion from agricultural programs below the projections by the OMB, which were already lower than those of the CBO. The OMB was also more optimistic about lower future aggregate federal budget deficits. Compared to the CBO, the OMB projected that as much as $400 billion less in total spending reductions or new revenue would be required to balance the federal budget over a seven-year period.

Partisan Budget Politics and Rising Commodity Prices

When Congress left Washington for its August recess, the partisanship of the looming budget debate cast a dark shadow on farm bill deliberations. Despite differences in their farm policy prescriptions, House and Senate Democrats positioned themselves squarely behind the Clinton administration's gradualist approach to reducing the budget deficit. This unity required Republican leaders to pass a new federal budget without any Democratic support and face the possibility of a presidential veto. So long as farm program legislation went forward in 1995 as part of this budget process, it too would have to be passed in committee by Republicans alone. In the House Agriculture Committee, the Republicans held a 27 to 22 advantage, but their Senate Agriculture Committee majority was only 10 to 8, so unanimity among Republicans would be required even within committee to pass a bill over Democratic opposition.

Resistance to Change on the Agriculture Committees

Roberts had hoped to return to Washington at the end of August with momentum in support of the Freedom to Farm Act. He won praise from national and regional newspapers and an endorsement from the Kansas Farm Bureau, but other farm organizations remained noncommittal. Neither the American Farm Bureau Federation nor any of the national commodity associations endorsed his decoupling proposal.

Roberts also met with stiff opposition from cotton and rice producers and processors, who feared damage to their industries from the full planting flexibility allowed under the Freedom to Farm Act. On September 15, Bill Emerson (Missouri), the vice chair of the House Agriculture Committee, introduced an alternative farm bill with fellow Republican Larry Combest (Texas). Modeled closely on the Cochran bill in the Senate, Emerson and Combest retained existing support mechanisms for the deficiency payment crops, included the slight program modifications accepted by sugar and peanut producers, and extended the regional milk marketing orders that set formula-driven regional price differentials. To achieve the $13.4 billion budget savings the House Agriculture Committee had been assigned in the budget resolution, Emerson and Combest proposed raising nonpayment acres from 15 to 30 percent, achieving savings of $8.9 billion. Additional savings of $2.5 billion were claimed from reforms to voluntary annual set-aside programs, the peanut program, and dairy supports. A final savings of $2.1 billion was to come from changes to the EEP, the CRP, and federal crop insurance similar to proposals expected from Roberts.

Introduction of the Emerson-Combest bill gave an advantage to proponents of the existing commodity-support programs. The farm bill guidelines from the Clinton administration, the Cochran bill in the Senate, and the Emerson-Combest bill in the House all maintained the existing support mechanisms, albeit with different levels of budget savings. These three traditional proposals also had similar provisions for sugar and peanuts, essentially precluding substantial market deregulation.

To counter this momentum for maintaining status quo programs, Roberts fell back on support from the new House Republican leadership. He argued that the leadership was unwilling to reauthorize farm programs without significant reforms—particularly a cap on future payments (intended to avoid the costly budget overruns that had occurred under the 1985 and 1990 farm bills) and some deregulation of production. Just days before the House Agriculture Committee convened, Roberts played his leadership card. He circulated a letter from Speaker Newt Gingrich (Georgia), Majority Leader Richard Armey (Texas), and Majority Whip Tom DeLay (Texas) indicating that unless the Agriculture Committee reported sweeping reforms, agricultural policy might be changed through the leadership's control of the budget process. The threat implied by Roberts, Gingrich, Armey, and DeLay rested on a rarely invoked provision of the Congressional Budget Act of 1974, which permitted amendments to budget legislation from the House floor whenever an authorizing committee failed to offer a bill achieving the savings specified in a budget resolution. In the twenty years prior to the 1995 budget debate, the Democratic leadership had intervened using this rule only once.

When the House Agriculture Committee met in September, Roberts introduced a new version of his August Freedom to Farm Act, with four main subtitles. The first subtitle suspended the permanent law from 1949 until 2002, and authorized decoupled payments for the feed grains, wheat, cotton, and rice. A total of $38.4 billion was allocated to these payments over seven fiscal years (declining from $6.0 billion in 1996 to $4.4 billion in 2002). The language of the bill was rewritten to strengthen protection of "the interests of operators who were tenants and sharecroppers" but other provisions of the earlier Freedom to Farm Act were essentially unchanged in this subtitle.

The second subtitle of Roberts's bill deregulated the dairy industry. Marketing orders and the dairy price-support program were eliminated. Decoupled ("freedom to milk") contractual payments would be paid to dairy farmers based on their historical production levels. A recourse CCC loan program was established, with loan rates at 90 percent of market prices. The dairy subtitle of Roberts's bill was drafted by Republican Representative Steve Gunderson (Wisconsin) after he failed to gain interregional backing for a complicated scheme to retain marketing orders but provide transfer payments among producers as compensation for regional fluid milk price differentials.[10]

The third subtitle of Roberts's bill extended the sugar and peanut programs through 2002. Roberts had largely conceded there would be no substantial reforms for these import-competing commodities.[11] His concessions were made in an attempt to win Agriculture Committee approval for the decoupled Freedom to Farm payments over the objections of the rice and cotton industries, by enticing some southern committee members into a coalition with midwesterners and policy reform advocates among the Republican majority.

The fourth subtitle of Roberts's bill addressed some of the remaining aspects of farm support programs. Long-term land retirements through

10. The dairy subtitle of Roberts's bill also granted maximum Uruguay Round funding levels to the DEIP, sanctioned a new dairy re-export program, and authorized the secretary of agriculture to help establish an export trading company for dairy products.

11. For sugar, Roberts proposed that support prices be maintained at 1995 levels. Marketing quotas and allotments were repealed and assessments raised to 2 percent of the loan rate for cane processors and 2.2 percent for beet processors. Loans were provided on a recourse basis when imports were below the average of three previous years, but reverted to a nonrecourse basis at higher levels of imports. For peanuts, the support price was lowered from $673 to $610 beginning with the 1996 crop, and an automatic cost-of-production adjustment to the support level was eliminated. The minimum national production quota was also eliminated, some restrictions were relaxed on the sale or lease of quotas across county lines within a state, and a system of priorities was established for allocating quota reductions.

the CRP were reauthorized at the existing level of 36.4 million acres, but annual rental rates on contract extensions were restricted to 75 percent of previous values. EEP authority was reduced below the Uruguay Round limits for the years 1996–2000, but restored to maximum levels in 2001 and 2002.[12]

The question that arose in September 1995 was whether Roberts had brought together the pieces that were needed to pass his fairly comprehensive bill out of the House Agriculture Committee. His most serious challenge came from Emerson and Combest.[13] Emerson argued that his substitute bill was fiscally responsible, gave farmers desirable flexibility, and avoided sending "shock waves" through agriculture by decoupling support payments from market prices and production. The Emerson bill met the committee's budget obligations and, if adopted, would thwart the more radical shift toward decoupling. Democrats on the committee fell in behind the Emerson-Combest bill in an effort to embarrass Roberts. Charles Stenholm (Texas) a leader among these Democrats, indicated he would vote for the Emerson bill, despite his opposition to the deep budget cuts. The substitute was, he said, "a better way [than Roberts] to proceed."

Although the committee debate raged mostly over supply controls and deficiency payments versus planting flexibility and decoupled income support, the fate of the Emerson bill rested as much on Roberts's generous provisions for sugar and inclusion by Emerson of dairy provisions opposed in the Midwest. Gunderson argued that by lowering support prices for manufactured milk products (on which midwestern producers were relatively dependent) the Emerson substitute was a "declaration of war" that had caused the collapse of his earlier attempts to build a dairy consensus. Democrat Collin Peterson (Minnesota), who

12. Holding EEP expenditures below Uruguay Round maximum levels was counted by the CBO as saving $2.9 billion of anticipated expenditures, even though EEP appropriations for 1995 were already less than these maximums and EEP subsidies had been suspended by midyear due to high market prices. Roberts's bill achieved budget savings by ending mandatory participation in the federal crop insurance program as an eligibility criterion for support payments, with the condition that farmers who did not take crop insurance waived eligibility for emergency crop loss assistance. A national commission on the role of government in agriculture was also retained.

13. The September debate in the House Agriculture Committee included an alternative Democratic traditional bill that achieved less than one-third of the Republicans' budget-reduction target. It was doomed to defeat on a party line vote, but the Democrats used the occasion to defend ARP supply controls as a tool of farm policy, and to hammer Roberts for destroying the safety net that traditional farm programs had provided against market price instability.

had worked closely with Gunderson on behalf of midwestern dairy interests, indicated he would oppose Emerson because of the dairy provisions.

When the committee roll call was taken on the Emerson bill, three more southern Republicans (Richard Baker [Louisiana], Ed Bryant [Tennessee], and Saxby Chambliss [Georgia]) abandoned Roberts and cast their votes with Emerson and Combest. Had only Peterson defected from the Democrats' support for Emerson-Combest, Roberts would have been defeated. But Peterson was joined in voting against the Emerson bill by three other Democrats—Tim Johnson (South Dakota), David Minge (Minnesota), and Earl Pomeroy (North Dakota). These last three populist Democrats from the Northern Plains attributed their opposition to the deep budget cuts proposed by Emerson, but acknowledged the influence on their votes of direct lobbying by sugar beet and dairy interests in their districts.

With the Emerson substitute thus narrowly defeated, the Agriculture Committee turned to Roberts's bill. This time, the Democrats—lamenting (in Stenholm's words) that the committee was being forced to have "policy written by Mr. Gingrich or none at all"—voted en masse against Roberts. Emerson and Combest also opposed Roberts, as expected, and when Republicans Baker and Chambliss again broke party ranks, Roberts lacked the majority he needed. Facing defeat, he banged down his gavel and announced suspension of the markup session. A few moments later the gavel resounded again, and Roberts pulled his party into caucus, only to return later to announce tersely that the members had not been able to resolve their differences.

At the time the House markup session broke up in deadlock, the negotiations in the Senate were again taking a different turn. As the deadline for the budget reconciliation bill approached in late September, Lugar announced that he would insist on just four reforms: that budget savings on agriculture reach a minimum level of $13.4 billion, that the authority for ARPs be eliminated, that increased planting flexibility be provided, and that support reductions for sugar and peanuts be commensurate with those faced by other commodities. Lugar failed to obtain unanimous Republican support for a bill that included Freedom to Farm payments for feed grains and wheat while extending traditional support programs for cotton and rice, but a further Republican compromise was being crafted.

The bill Lugar offered in the end included further concessions to supporters of the traditional farm programs. Deficiency payments and crop-specific acreage bases were retained for all crops, with nonpayment acres increased to 30 percent to achieve budget savings. The authority for annual set asides was eliminated and feed grain and wheat producers gained increased planting flexibility, while for cotton and rice the traditional restrictive acreage base planting requirements were maintained. To help offset the projected budget cost of ending ARPs, maximum per-unit deficiency payments were capped at the levels projected for each year from 1996 to 2002 in the February 1995 CBO budget baseline. Loan rates were retained at 85 percent of the Olympic moving average of past prices, and the existing minimum nominal loan rates and marketing loan authorities were retained for cotton and rice. Lugar's bill included generous provisions along Cochran's lines for sugar and peanuts. It also included a cap on CRP expenditures, and provisions to maintain milk marketing orders and regional price differentials. The support-price mechanism was retained for cheese, but price supports on milk powder and butter were eliminated, a gimmick dairy lobbyists hoped would circumvent WTO rules and allow these dairy products to enter world markets as though unsubsidized.

Lugar had done his political work behind the scenes, and the Senate Agriculture Committee approved his new bill on a party line vote.[14] This gave proponents of traditional commodity-support programs another strategic boost; they now had a bill endorsed by at least one of the authorizing Agriculture Committees in Congress. Lugar announced that the Agriculture Committee's decisions met the four criteria he had outlined. Within the constraint of the budget resolution, it offered traditional agriculturalists much of what they sought.

Circumventing House Republican Gridlock

In the House of Representatives, renewed maneuvering to pass the Agriculture Committee part of the Republicans' omnibus budget reconciliation bill began after the defeat Roberts suffered. The four Republican defectors defended their stance, arguing that the farm support programs tied to market prices were working well, and questioning the merits of decoupled Freedom to Farm "welfare" payments for farmers. When Emerson and Combest sought a hearing with the leadership, re-

---

14. The only publicly expressed opposition to Lugar's bill by Agriculture Committee Republicans was voiced by Rick Santorum (Pennsylvania), who objected to the sugar and peanut price support levels on behalf of industrial users seeking lower input prices. His objections delayed approval when the committee first met, but with modest changes a revised bill was adopted on a party line vote with Santorum abstaining.

form-minded members of the Agriculture Committee also mobilized. Led by Republican John Hostettler, freshman members circulated a letter to the Speaker imploring him to "present the task of writing agricultural reconciliation to the House Budget Committee" in order to avoid the bill being "watered down to appease certain commodity groups opposed to reform."

The issue for the House Republican leadership was whether to use its power to force consent to the Roberts bill by the Agriculture Committee dissidents. The internal negotiations became public through a leaked staff memo from the office of Majority Whip DeLay. The memo described a meeting at which the leadership gave Roberts "carte blanche to do what he needs to do." The memo also suggested that there would be nothing to gain from being too hard on the House "Aggies" because "you will get no real reform through the Senate" (Hellman 1995).

Roberts took an unprecedented step when the Republicans on the Agriculture Committee failed to resolve their differences after more than a week of additional negotiations. He announced that his committee would abrogate its budget responsibility. He would hand over decisions about farm policy for the budget reconciliation bill to the leadership of the House of Representatives, as threatened in the letter he had circulated before the committee vote. Roberts asserted that he would win inclusion of his own Freedom to Farm proposal with House leadership backing. Emerson and Combest also made their case to House Speaker Gingrich, but only won assurance there would be no reprisals for their opposition to Roberts.

The Republicans were far behind schedule on the budget reconciliation legislation by late September, and with the 1996 fiscal year about to begin the leadership feared accusations that it had lost control of the congressional calendar. Floor votes on the budget were scheduled for late October and important pieces of the budget reconciliation bill fell into place as House and Senate committees passed proposals on Medicaid, Medicare, and taxes—mostly on strict party line votes. Meanwhile, behind-the-scenes maneuvering continued on the House agriculture provisions. Republican Conference Chair Boehner, a cosponsor of the Roberts bill, acknowledged that a compromise might be necessary in light of the "fragile" Republican majority in the House and eventual need to "deal with the Senate" (*Congressional Quarterly Weekly Report,* 9 September 1995).

In the continuing agricultural negotiations, dairy policy remained one of the pivotal issues. Gunderson's characterization of the dairy policies in the Emerson bill as a declaration of war proved right, but his own proposal for deregulation split regional interests just as badly. A group of thirty dairy-state members pressed for legislation along the lines proposed by Emerson and Combest.[15] Within the House leadership, support for retention of milk marketing orders came from the chair of the Rules Committee, Gerald Solomon, who represented an upstate New York dairy district.[16]

As the House moved toward a floor vote, it became inevitable that whatever concessions were needed would be made by the Republican leadership to their own agriculturalists in order to secure passage of the budget reconciliation bill. Republican farm advocates sensed their advantage; as Roberts dryly observed, the leadership was afforded the "joy" of listening to every commodity group. Emerson and Combest rallied fourteen rural southerners who indicated they would have trouble supporting the budget legislation if it contained the Freedom to Farm Act. They were joined by opponents to Gunderson's dairy deregulation. Unable to satisfy or unify these Republican agriculturalists, Gingrich acknowledged that he lacked the votes he needed for reconciliation. David Hobson (Ohio), a member of the Republican leadership group, told the press that "the big thing" was getting the farm issues resolved (Pianin and Gugliotta 1995, A7).

The afternoon before the floor vote, Gingrich met with the Republican agriculturalists with a proposal to bridge their differences. Roberts's Freedom to Farm Act and the other subtitles of his committee bill would be incorporated in the House budget reconciliation legislation. The cotton, rice, and dairy interests opposed to the Roberts bill were assured that their concerns would be addressed when House and Senate negotiators met in a budget conference committee. With this nebulous assurance, the fourteen rural southern Republicans orga-

15. In the Senate, Republican Jim Jeffords (Vermont), representing the northeastern dairy industry, obtained a ruling that the Gunderson proposal to eliminate milk marketing orders violated the Byrd rule, which excludes extraneous measures lacking spending or revenue implications from budget reconciliation legislation. This essentially precluded consideration of the deregulation of domestic milk markets in the Senate, since a sixty-vote majority would be required to overcome a rules objection.

16. Solomon's role on dairy policy showed the dichotomies that were arising between rhetoric and constituent interests among the new Republican congressional majority. Just weeks before taking on the dairy cause, Solomon had espoused the view that the "historical" changes the Republicans were attempting to bring about required that the leadership "pick up the slack" from committees that fell "behind the revolutionary curve" (*The Washington Post*, October 8, 1995, A4).

nized by Emerson, and the thirty Republicans opposed to deregulation of the dairy industry, joined the House majority to pass the budget reconciliation bill, by a 227 to 203 vote. Emerson insisted that no final deal on farm programs had yet been struck. Some observers concluded that Roberts had conceded the House would accept to the Senate provisions on farm policy in the budget conference committee, while others insisted that he remained committed to moving forward with Freedom to Farm.

The Democrats' "Safety Net" Alternative

As the Republicans labored to conclude the budget reconciliation process, congressional Democrats kept up their attacks on the size of the proposed agricultural budget cuts and any possible shift to decoupled payments. In late October, four Democratic congressmen (Johnson, Minge, Peterson, and Pomeroy) introduced a bill similar to the Senate Democrats' Farm Security Act. These four Democrats had provided the crucial votes to defeat the Emerson substitute in the Agriculture Committee, but their Family Empowerment Act moved in the opposite direction from Roberts's Freedom to Farm legislation. Loan rates were raised to 115 percent of the moving average of past prices in the House Democrats' bill, with budget savings still claimed of $4.4 billion. Criticizing the Freedom to Farm Act again for doling out "welfare payments for seven years" then leaving farmers "without any safety net," Representative Peterson argued that "After the president vetoes the budget—which he's going to do—we'll be players at the table."

Democrats in the House and Senate could weigh various strategies in anticipation of budget negotiations between congressional leaders and the president, but a final negotiating position on agriculture could not be formulated until the Republicans completed their budget reconciliation bill. If the Senate provisions for reduced acreage eligibility for traditional deficiency payments prevailed in conference, then the Democrats could pursue the argument that the budget cuts were too deep and try to negotiate for more payment acres. If the budget conference agreed to the Freedom to Farm Act, the Democrats could still argue the spending cuts were too deep, but they would be caught on the horns of a dilemma created by the clever use Roberts had made of the budget process. With rising prices, farmers and their lobbyists could see that anticipated spending on farm programs would be *less* under Democratic proposals than under Freedom to Farm Act decoupling. The Democrats could attack the Republicans rhetorically for "smoke and mirrors" in balancing the budget, but with high market prices rendering decoupling more generous to farmers than traditional programs, a claim that the Republicans' spending cuts were too deep would ring hollow.

A second strategy for the Democrats was to seek higher loan rates, as had been proposed in the Senate and the House, and then argue that the Republican policies weakened (the Senate bill) or devastated (the House bill) the safety net against falling prices traditionally provided to farmers. Yet many Democrats opposed recoupling price supports to production through higher loan rates. They worried that higher loan rates would potentially lead to large CCC expenditures or distortionary effects on production in years when market prices fell, even if CCC stock accumulation was avoided when loan rates were too high by use of supply controls or marketing loans repaid at lower world prices. Higher loan rates might be subject to international trade sanctions, possibly through bilateral antidumping penalties abroad. Moreover, whatever the outcome of the budget reconciliation conference, it was unlikely that enough Republicans could be persuaded to pass a Democratic policy based on higher loan rates over whatever farm policies their party eventually recommended.

A third negotiating strategy for the Democrats was to seek increased funding for conservation programs and other popular agricultural priorities that they could argue were underfunded in the Republican budget. If the Republicans put forward the Senate bill, this would mean arguing for additional funds, in light of the fact that deficiency payments were going to be less than originally projected. If the Republicans put forward the Freedom to Farm Act, the Democrats might press for additional spending, or they might argue that some of the windfall Roberts had directed into payments to farmers should be directed toward these other conservation and rural uses. The problem with the latter strategy for the Democrats, once again, was that they would have to abandon their assertion that the Republican proposals cut too deeply into farm-support spending.

Capturing the Baseline

The different agricultural provisions in the House and Senate budget reconciliation bills left room for wide-ranging negotiations by the conference committee in early November, even as the year-end deadline for extension of the 1990 farm bill drew closer. One compromise option for Republicans was to revive the proposal Lugar had floated earlier, offering planting flexibility and decoupled contractual payments for feed grains and wheat, while retaining traditional deficiency payments linked to production and prices for cotton and rice. An alternative of allowing individual farmers to choose between the two support programs had also been considered and could be resurrected.

In the end, recognition of the short-run windfall farmers would receive under the Freedom to Farm Act came to dominate the discussion of farm support policy as the House-Senate budget reconciliation conference convened. Market prices had continued to rise, and by November exceeded the existing levels of target prices, as shown in figure 10. A study for Congress by the Food and Agricultural Policy Research Institute (FAPRI) at Iowa State University concluded that payments to farmers would be $5.6 billion greater in 1996 and $2.0 billion greater in 1997 under the decoupling of the House bill than under the traditional payments of the Senate bill (FAPRI 1995a). To agricultural insiders, Roberts described this as "capturing the baseline," and to outsiders he justified the windfall as an "investment in agriculture." In conference budget negotiations, his staff made the case that *only* the fixed contractual Freedom to Farm payments would ensure that the expenditures projected in the February 1995 CBO baseline were captured by agricultural programs. Roberts himself made this telling point in an impassioned defense of his Freedom to Farm approach, which he delivered personally at an unusual USDA hearing hosted by Secretary Glickman. At this hearing Roberts could scarcely have been more candid. Referring to Freedom to Farm, he said, "It captures the remaining baseline at the highest level we can expect. That baseline is delivered to producers on a guaranteed basis. All of the other plans being considered by Congress do not capture the baseline. Instead, because they leave the existing program structure in place, next year's CBO snapshot, when Dan [Glickman] provides the CBO in February what he expects to happen in agriculture, will show we have about $11 billion less to spend" (1995).

As these realities became clear, the idea of decoupling became sufficiently attractive—first to southern Republican agriculturalists and eventually even to a sufficient number of Democrats—to ensure its eventual passage. Cotton and rice interests were encouraged by Freedom to Farm proponents to "do the math," and subsequently moderated their opposition to decoupled payments. One by one, the alternative commodity-support payment schemes were rejected by the negotiators as less beneficial to farmers than the approach Roberts championed, and the conference committee adopted policies much closer to the Freedom to Farm Act than many observers expected.

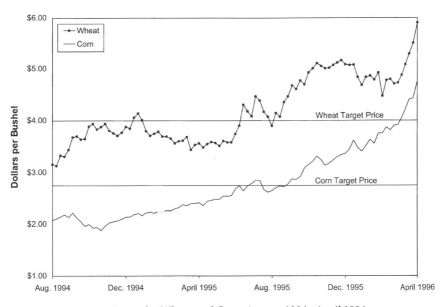

Figure 10.   Rising Prices for Wheat and Corn, August 1994–April 1996
Source: Wall Street Journal, various issues.

The final agricultural title of the conference budget reconciliation bill authorized annual Freedom to Farm contract payments of $5.5 billion in 1996 and $5.8 billion in 1997, then payments declined to $4 billion by 2002. Planting flexibility was provided for feed grains and wheat, and for cotton and rice, and was extended to allow production of fruits and vegetables on 15 percent of contract base acreage. Authority for mandatory and voluntary annual set asides was eliminated, and in a step with potentially important long-term implications, the Agricultural Act of 1949 was repealed as the permanent legislation for farm programs.

Cotton and rice interests won several key concessions in the conference budget reconciliation bill. Restrictions that had strengthened payment limitations on individual farmers in the earlier Freedom to Farm Act were eliminated, and marketing loans were retained. Loan rates were kept at 85 percent of the five-year Olympic moving average of past market prices, with minimum nominal rates retained for cotton and rice. These various deals reduced the pool of money available for contractual Freedom to Farm payments, mostly for the benefit of the cotton and rice sectors. To offset the budgetary cost projected by the CBO for these support measures, the maximum levels of loan rates were capped for seven years at their 1995 nominal values. Other producers also sought compensation for the concessions to cotton and rice by changing the base for calculating the percentage of the contractual payments received by each commodity from the historic payments during 1990–1995 to the projected payments for 1996–2000. This reduced the share of Freedom to Farm payments going to cotton from 17.8 percent to 11.7 percent.[17]

The most difficult area for the conference negotiations was on dairy policy, which was still torn by regional differences.[18] A deadlock between Gunderson and the midwestern producers, and Solomon and the northeastern producers, forced the conferees to drop both the deregulation proposal and the Senate dairy provisions. This left the budget conference without an agreement to achieve savings on dairy. Roberts warned that the intransigence of the dairy interests would bring "trouble down the road," and House Speaker Gingrich railed that "It is unfair for one part of agriculture to block reform in its programs as we are pursuing change across the rest." Nevertheless, to resolve this impasse, budget discipline was further relaxed on behalf of agriculture. The House and Senate leadership agreed to lower the budget savings mandated from agricultural programs from the original $13.4 billion to $12.2 billion, largely because $800 million anticipated from dairy reform had not materialized.

High-Stakes Budget Politics

The Republican majorities in the House and Senate approved the conference budget reconciliation bill in mid-November, again with the

17. Among other provisions, the budget conference committee resolved CRP policy along the lines of the House bill. Cotton retained special "Step-2 payments" for processors with an aggregate spending cap of $701 million over 1996–2002, and a new livestock environment assistance program sought by Lugar was included with funding authorized up to $100 million per year. The peanut program was reauthorized through 2002 (in contrast to a limited reauthorization through 2000 that had been agreed to in the Senate), with the support price reduced to $610 per ton, the cost-of-production adjustment formula for price supports eliminated, and no minimum required on the national quota eligible for support.

18. The conference negotiations over sugar were also contentious. Lugar pressed for a tax on Florida producers to pay for restoration of the Everglades, and a broader tax on domestic and imported sugar was also proposed. Defenders of the sugar program eventually beat back these challenges. Sugar support prices were maintained at the 1995 levels, sugar marketing allotments were eliminated, and marketing assessments paid by processors were dropped to the levels specified in the Senate bill (less than proposed by the House). Modest concessions to critics of the sugar program were to keep the level of imports triggering nonrecourse loans at 1.5 million metric tons and to retain a $0.01 per pound forfeiture penalty negotiated in the Senate bill.

vote essentially along party lines. By this late date, failure of Congress and the administration to agree on even temporary budget authority for the new fiscal year had resulted in an unprecedented six-day shutdown of some government services. A short-term compromise to end the government shutdown was reached by Republican and Democratic negotiators on November 19, restoring funding for government operations through mid-December. In this compromise, the president agreed to negotiate legislation to balance the budget in seven years based on CBO projections with their larger future deficits than projected by the OMB. In exchange, the Republicans agreed that the budget would provide "adequate funding" for programs in the president's priority areas of Medicare, welfare, Medicaid, education, agriculture, national defense, veterans, and the environment. Interpretation of these commitments was disputed as soon as the budget negotiations resumed.[19] Then, on December 7, the president vetoed the congressional budget reconciliation bill. This set the stage for a more protracted government shutdown, and a final political showdown between the president and Republican congressional leadership—a showdown that effectively brought the Republicans' self-proclaimed revolution to an end.

As the administration and the Republican congressional leaders jockeyed for position in the budget negotiations, both sides awaited the results of updated CBO budget projections. When the new projections were released, fiscal deficits were estimated to be $135 billion smaller over seven years than had been anticipated by the CBO ten months earlier. The revised CBO projections significantly narrowed the $400 billion gap between what the administration claimed was necessary to balance the budget, based on OMB projections, and what the Republican congressional leadership had previously claimed was needed, as determined by the CBO. The Republicans therefore modified their budget, using the smaller gap from the revised projections to expand spending plans in hopes of striking a deal with the president.

The December CBO baseline projected lower spending on agriculture under continuation of the 1990 farm bill, as widely anticipated. Projected CCC expenditures on commodity and export programs fell over seven years through 2002 from $56.6 billion to $48.8 billion (see table 13).

19. The Republican leadership claimed that the president reneged on commitments to a balanced budget in seven years, and demanded that he provide a precise plan around which negotiations could proceed. The administration argued that protecting the president's priorities was equally important to the November 19 agreement, and called on the Republicans to be forthcoming with concessions on Medicare and other spending.

Table 13.   Projected Agriculture Spending (in Billions of Dollars), 1996–2002

Fiscal Year	1995 CBO Baseline Projections		Decoupled Payments	
			Compared to February 1995 CBO Baseline	Compared to December 1995 CBO Baseline
	February 1995	December 1995		
1996	8.6	3.8	−1.3	+2.8
1997	8.5	5.6	−1.5	+1.1
1998	8.4	8.1	−1.4	−1.0
1999	8.2	8.2	−1.5	−1.4
2000	7.9	7.8	−1.6	−1.5
2001	7.5	7.7	−2.5	−2.2
2002	7.5	7.6	−2.4	−2.4
Total	56.6	48.8	−12.2	−4.6

Note: Baseline spending projected by CBO includes CCC spending for price supports and related programs (primarily the Export Enhancement Program) assuming continuation of 1990 law as modified through 1995. Budget changes with decoupled payments include savings in non-CCC agricultural programs of nearly $1.0 billion.

The farm-program savings in the new CBO baseline were derived primarily from higher market price expectations, and hence lower deficiency payments, during 1996 and 1997. With these lower projected deficiency payments, spending on agriculture proposed in the budget reconciliation bill (with decoupled Freedom to Farm payments) exceeded projected expenditures under extension of the 1990 law by $3.9 billion. This again demonstrated the appeal of decoupled payment contracts to Roberts and other Freedom to Farm proponents.

With the new budget figures, a continued Republican commitment to policy changes that would save $12.2 billion from agriculture would leave room for expenditures of only $36.6 billion. Such a drastic cut would allow the savings on agricultural programs from rising market prices between the February and December CBO budget baselines to offset nonagricultural spending or tax cuts. This possible loss of nearly $8 billion from the CBO agricultural budget baseline alarmed Republican agriculturalists. They quickly convinced the House and Senate leadership to give agriculture credit for the budget savings derived from rising market prices—a decision that allowed the spending levels carefully negotiated among agricultural interests in the budget process to be retained, despite the new CBO projections. Behind the smoke and mirrors, the Republicans' farm bill now gave an estimated budget savings of only $4.6 billion over seven years, compared to the budget conference agreement of $12.2 billion.

The level of anticipated spending on agriculture was thus becoming acceptable to many Democrats, but there remained substantial structural differences between the Republican and Democratic farm bill proposals.[20] The administration used the December veto of the budget legislation to list various arguments against Freedom to Farm decoupling. The president asserted that the Republican agricultural proposal "eliminates the safety net that farm programs provide for U.S. agriculture, provides windfall payments to producers when prices are high but does not protect family farm income when prices are low, slashes spending for agricultural export assistance, and reduces the environmental benefits of the Conservation Reserve Program (White House 1995)." Whereas most presidents had viewed (Democratic) congressional farm bill proposals as too generous, President Clinton still tried to reject the Republicans' bill in 1995 as not generous enough. An administration budget released in mid-December included no changes in policies affecting projected farm spending, thus topping its own previous recommendations, and allowing the Democrats to resurrect their argument that the Republicans were cutting agricultural spending by too much. The year that had begun with efforts to cut farm spending had ended in a partisan bidding war to boost farm spending instead.

The Republicans' budget initiative in Congress had brought the president closer than at the beginning of the year to endorsing fiscal balance, and the revised CBO projections had closed the gap even further. Still, the Republican Congress lost political standing when the budget battle led to the second disruption of government services in mid-December. Yielding to the unpopularity of the shutdown, for which they were blamed in public opinion polls, the Republicans reached agreement with the president for another temporary spending resolution in early January 1996. Resolutions approved by large bi-

---

20. In early December, the administration had released a farm bill proposal that called for increasing nonpayment acres to 21 percent to achieve budget savings, as well as increased planting flexibility, elimination of minimum nominal loan rates for cotton and rice, and continued ARP set-aside authority. The OMB projected farm program expenditures at $42.4 billion during 1996–2002 under existing law, and credited the administration's proposals with a savings of $5.0 billion. The administration quickly backed away from this proposal, suggesting fewer spending cuts were required. Even so, seemingly no irreconcilable differences existed in the *budget* implications of the Democratic and Republican farm policy proposals at this point. The OMB projections implied less spending under the administration's proposal than the Republicans were recommending under the conference budget reconciliation bill, while congressional Democrats continued to call for cuts of $4 billion using CBO projections—the same level of cuts proposed by the Republicans.

partisan majorities a few weeks later extended spending authorities through March, diffusing any sense of immediate budget crisis.

Emergence of a Bipartisan Coalition

With farm legislation entangled in the collapsing budget negotiations throughout December 1995, the 104th Congress failed to replace (or extend) the 1990 farm bill before it expired. Technically, the support programs for feed grains and wheat reverted back to the permanent legislation from 1949 at the end of the year. This untenable reversion to permanent law kept pressure on Congress for a new farm policy. Farmers needed to know before the spring crop planting season what programs would be in effect, and the proponents of farm-support legislation could decry the dire consequences of failure to enact a new law.[21] Adding to the agriculturalists' sense of urgency was the prospect that a fully updated CBO budget baseline, often released in February, was likely to project even less spending under the recent (but now expired) farm programs. A way out of the impasse had to be found, and the sooner the better.

Cohesion among Republicans

In anticipation of the possibility that the budget talks would fail, by January 1996 Roberts had introduced his Freedom to Farm policies as freestanding legislation, titled the Agricultural Market Transition Act. Much of the initial resistance Roberts had faced among commodity groups had been quieted by the lucrative decoupled payments anticipated under the Freedom to Farm contracts, or by the concessions that had been made as the farm bill title had been worked through the budget process. Cotton producers and processors had withdrawn their once adamant opposition and Roberts's bill was now cosponsored by the two former dissident Republican Agriculture Committee members, Emerson and Combest. The American Farm Bureau Federation had endorsed decoupled farm payments as part of the Republican budget package. The National Corn Growers Association had also endorsed decoupled payments but opposed the caps on loan rates that were part of the legislation.[22]

21. Under the permanent law, the USDA was required to offer loan rates for crops to be produced in 1996 from $6.52 to $7.82 per bushel for wheat and up to $5.30 per bushel for corn to farmers holding required production allotments.

22. The Farm Bureau endorsed decoupled payments in conjunction with other components of the Republican budget—in particular, tax relief on capital gains, inheritance,

Opposition to the decoupled payments continued to be voiced by Democrats early in 1996, but no cohesive alternative crystallized. Minority Leader Daschle and his supporters remained opposed to the elimination of a market-related farm safety net, and they pressed for higher loan rates. Daschle had insisted that the Roberts proposals were a deal breaker in the budget talks, but this proposition was never tested because the budget negotiations broke down over many other issues. The administration and House Democrats continued to object to large cash payments to farmers when market prices were high, and the secretary of agriculture suggested extending the 1990 farm bill for one or two years as an alternative. Democrats also argued that permanent legislation had to be retained to ensure a safety net for farmers and to keep pressure on Congress to maintain farm programs in the future, and sought funds more immediately for their rural constituents. They proposed that some of the money designated for contract payments—or some additional funds—be directed to purposes ranging from higher loan rates to agricultural research and spending for environmental protection, conservation, or rural development. Supporters of these various programs coalesced around the "Fund for Rural America" concept to augment Freedom to Farm, but no consensus formed for a comprehensive Democratic alternative.

By mid-January, with the Republican budget legislation doomed, Roberts considered other means to expedite farm policy action. Citing the pressure created by reversion to permanent law for the forthcoming spring planting season, he proposed that the farm commodity title from the budget reconciliation bill be attached to the continuing resolution enacted to keep the government operational through March. This pressure tactic was rejected by Daschle, who essentially held veto power once the Republicans conceded that they wanted to avoid a third government shutdown. Roberts then expected to wait until after a February congressional recess to move his bill forward, but when the Senate

---

and health insurance premiums. The corn growers, while endorsing Freedom to Farm payments, called for removal of the loan rate caps, for marketing loans as a new permanent law, and for additional funding for export and conservation programs. Rice processors continued to object to the elimination of crop-specific acreage bases and planting requirements, fearing that rice production would fall and processing capacity in some parts of the country would be underutilized. The NFU and the National Association of Wheat Growers continued to oppose Roberts's elimination of the safety net for farmers, and the American Soybean Association opposed the decoupling of payments from production without higher loan rates to protect soybean producers.

scheduled a farm bill floor debate just days before the recess was to begin, Roberts reversed himself and with the backing of the House leadership called his Agriculture Committee into session.

By the time the House Agriculture Committee met in late January 1996, negotiations had renewed among regional dairy interests, and a complicated scheme similar to the regulatory package initially sought by Gunderson had been agreed upon. Gunderson argued this new agreement would eventually lead to deregulation of the dairy industry, but he acknowledged that its many provisions were also designed to raise the incomes of dairy producers.[23] Other negotiations had also proceeded among the agriculturalists. Planting flexibility under Freedom to Farm was reduced slightly at the behest of fruit and vegetable producers. An agribusiness effort to allow early termination of CRP contracts—so planted crop acreage could be expanded while prices were high—was turned back when a congressional caucus voiced opposition. Roberts's new bill included nullification of the 1949 permanent law and reintroduced his National Commission on the Future of Production Agriculture. With these modifications in place, Roberts had lined up unanimous if begrudging support among the Republican committee majority, ensuring that this time around he would not fail to report out a farm bill.

Roberts had also hoped to logroll support from some Democrats in negotiations that preceded the Agriculture Committee meeting. This attempt was thwarted when the House Republican leadership refused to endorse funding for the Democrats' priorities outside the framework of a broad budget deal. Roberts was forced to withdraw a tentative offer of support for the Fund for Rural America at the eleventh hour, which led to another acrimonious committee session.[24] Nonetheless, the Agricul-

23. Under the complicated dairy agreement, a floor would be set under fluid milk prices, higher standards for nonfat milk solids used in California would be imposed nationally, and support prices would be retained for cheese but withdrawn from butter and powdered milk. Marketing-order price differentials would be maintained, but part of the differential revenue would be pooled among the regions over a two-year transition period. Revenue for processed products would also be pooled, with each farmer receiving an average of these returns. Within two years, the secretary of agriculture would be required to amend the marketing orders, reducing the number from thirty-four to no more than thirteen. Failure to revise the marketing-order system would trigger a cessation of all federal dairy programs.

24. To gain the Democrats' allegiance, Roberts sought to make as much as $2.5 billion available for the Fund for Rural America. The possibility of adding these funds had originated in earlier compromise discussions around an overall budget package with conservative (and often rural) Democrats known as "Blue Dogs." As late as the night before the

tural Market Transition Act was approved by the committee with unanimous Republican support. Roberts's bill received three Democratic committee votes, but his bid for a floor debate before the House recessed failed when the Democratic minority refused to cooperate.

The new farm bill also faced pockets of strong opposition within the Republican Party. Dan Miller circulated a letter indicating he expected Roberts to keep the earlier promise to allow critics of the sugar and peanut programs to offer amendments from the House floor. Dairy policy remained as contentious as ever. Solomon and other Republicans protecting upstate New York interests opposed the Gunderson compromise, which also drew strong opposition from dairy processors and consumer groups. The dairy processors gained national attention when CBS news anchor Dan Rather warned after the Agriculture Committee vote that he had been alerted by a major Republican financial contributor to a secret deal that would raise milk prices.

Bipartisan Senate Compromise

The farm policy debate in the Senate had all along been less partisan than in the House of Representatives, and was less subject to disciplined Agriculture Committee or leadership control. In late January, Lugar introduced the Freedom to Farm bill, essentially unchanged from the vetoed budget reconciliation legislation. Lugar was engaged in a longshot campaign for the Republican presidential nomination in 1996 and thus had an interest in the Senate approving some farm bill before the Iowa Republican caucuses in early February. His interest was shared by Senate Majority Leader Robert Dole, the primary campaign front-runner and eventual Republican presidential nominee. At the opposite extreme, Daschle was threatening a filibuster against legislation incorporating any form of Freedom to Farm contracts. To move a bill through the Senate, Lugar and Dole were willing to accept options that ranged from extension of the existing farm programs to redirecting part of the Freedom to Farm contract payments to other uses.

Lugar was unable to move his initial bill forward in late January, but he had anticipated this outcome and had cosponsored a bipartisan substitute bill with Democratic Senator Leahy, the former Agriculture Committee chair, who was willing to break ranks with Daschle and

---

Agriculture Committee meeting, the Democrats thought these funds could be utilized in Roberts's farm bill, for which budget savings relative to the December 1995 CBO baseline of about $2 billion could then still be claimed.

other Democratic leaders. The Lugar-Leahy bill retained Freedom to Farm payments and ended ARP authority, but had a broader scope, including both conservation titles and reauthorization of the food stamp program. At Leahy's insistence, the Senate bill also included the "Northeast Dairy Compact," a controversial authority to raise regional milk prices above the level authorized by the existing federal marketing order in six New England states.[25]

When the Lugar bill was taken up on the Senate floor, Democrats tried to draft an alternative to Freedom to Farm payments that Daschle might support. What they proposed was splitting the contract payments, with 40 percent guaranteed to farmers and the remaining 60 percent retained to fund other policies. Lugar and Dole might have been willing to accept a scheme to split the payments among various uses, perhaps based on a calculation that such provisions would eventually be dropped in a House-Senate conference (just as similar alternatives had been abandoned during earlier negotiations of the budget reconciliation conference committee). In any case, bipartisan agreement on such a scheme failed when fourteen Republicans signaled their objections to scaling back the direct payments going to farmers. The Senate then approved a bill along Lugar-Leahy lines by a nearly veto-proof 64 to 32 majority. To gain this bipartisan support, the Republicans allowed retention of the 1949 permanent law, a concession that Daschle and other Democrats claimed was a key victory for maintaining a safety net for farmers. Leahy's Northeast Dairy Compact was voted down on a floor amendment.[26]

Posturing in the House

The Lugar-Leahy alliance preserved decoupled Freedom to Farm payments but also broadened the scope of the farm bill beyond the narrow commodity focus of Roberts. This was in the logrolling tradition of parlaying farm, conservation, and nutrition programs in a single package to ensure bipartisan support for farm policies on the floor, just as

25. An increase in the contract payments to rice producers of more than $200 million also had been added to the Lugar-Leahy bill to secure the support of Louisiana's Democratic senators.

26. Other provisions that had been added to ensure bipartisan support for the Senate bill included higher loan rates for soybeans, and authorization of expenditures of $200 million for preservation of the Everglades and $300 million for the Fund for Rural America. Research, trade, rural development, and credit provisions passed earlier in the year by the Agriculture Committee were also incorporated in the Senate bill.

when Democrats had controlled Congress. With the Republicans in control in 1996, however, traditional logrolling for the farm bill opened potentially divisive fissures within the majority party. For one thing, the level of expenditures in the Senate bill was likely to be opposed by House Republican budget hawks.

Views of some Republicans on reform of the federal nutrition programs also led to opposition to the Lugar-Leahy bill. Their efforts to limit eligibility and cut the costs of nutrition assistance programs were an integral part of pending Republican proposals to change federal welfare entitlements. Welfare reform proposals had been included in the omnibus budget reconciliation bill, with reduced expenditures on the nutrition programs accounting for $34 billion of the planned budget savings. After the collapse of the budget legislation, Republicans were looking for another way to pass a welfare reform bill that the president would sign into law. Reauthorization of the existing nutrition programs in a stand-alone farm bill was a symbolic blow to their welfare reform commitments, especially since the farm bill was being trumpeted as having a certain urgency, while efforts to pass a welfare reform bill, though eventually to succeed, were for the moment bogged down in partisan dispute.

Conservation provisions in the Lugar-Leahy bill were also potentially problematic because they exacerbated differences between Republicans who were calling for fewer mandates and less government intervention—as espoused by Roberts in his earlier policy ledger—and those who sought an expanded government role in protecting the environment. The deregulators had prevailed in the House in the spring of 1995, but their momentum had withered under adverse fallout from the budget debate. By February 1996, extreme environmental deregulation was clearly out of public favor. More narrowly, some provisions of the Senate bill, especially an explicit emphasis on using the CRP to protect water quality, brought regional disputes among agriculturalists to a head. The new CRP authorization potentially shifted future eligibility from the western wheat regions that included Roberts's Kansas district to the more heavily populated midwestern states.

The strategy Roberts had followed from the time that funding for the farm-support programs had become immersed in the budget reconciliation process had been to focus on decoupled payments and other commodity issues, while holding other aspects of policy for later consideration in a separate bill. This second farm bill was to deliver on some of the promises made to farmers in the policy ledger to offset lower support payments under the Republican fiscal agenda. The Lugar-Leahy Senate compromise forced Roberts to abandon this strategy. He announced that he would quickly introduce the Agricultural Regulatory Relief and Trade Act in the House, conceding that it would strengthen the negotiating position of the House Republicans in dealing with the Senate, even if it failed to keep the two farm bills separated.

The Agricultural Regulatory Relief and Trade Act unveiled by Roberts after the congressional recess rhetorically promised to reduce the government's involvement in farmers' lives. Among its provisions, the bill allowed farmers more flexibility in their choices of conservation compliance practices, exempted wetlands of less than one acre from regulation, and extended authority for the CRP. Paralleling the coverage of the Lugar-Leahy legislation, Roberts included titles on reform of federal agricultural credit programs; block grants of rural development funds to the states; and reauthorizations of international food aid programs, research, and public information programs. Food stamps and other nutrition programs were not reauthorized in the House bill, in contrast to the pending legislation from the Senate.

Movement toward Convergence

During the February congressional recess, negotiations had also continued over rules under which the Agricultural Market Transition Act would be debated on the House floor. Roberts obtained a modified closed rule to limit floor debate, and at the start it was widely acknowledged that the basic argument over decoupling of farm-support payments from market prices had been settled. As Stenholm put it, the advocates of Freedom to Farm Act contracts, now titled production flexibility contracts (PFCs), had carried the day.[27] Long-awaited votes on amendments to end the sugar and peanut programs were anticlimactic. The beneficiaries of the sugar and peanut programs had expressed confidence about retaining their program structures, even though a well-financed and broad coalition of industries, market-oriented reformers, consumer groups, and environmentalists had advocated market deregulation throughout the farm bill debate. The producers' confidence proved well-founded, with the Republican leadership working behind

27. Democrats continued to assail the fixed PFC payments as a needless windfall in the short run that left farmers without a safety net in the long run. But few of the alternatives that had been under discussion were offered as amendments. One such alternative, a last-ditch Democratic attempt to reduce the contract payments to farmers by shifting almost $2 billion to agricultural research, was defeated.

the scenes to ensure the final outcomes (Ingersoll 1996). The recorded votes showed the peanut amendment failing by 209 to 212 and the sugar amendment defeated by 208 to 217.[28] Roberts, who had made his accommodation with the producers much earlier, turned and gave the victory "thumbs up" to sugar producer lobbyists seated in the House gallery.

The outcome was different when it came to an amendment on dairy policy, although the result was hardly liberal reform. The chair of the Rules Committee used his power to thwart Gunderson's plan. Solomon's sole dairy amendment maintained marketing orders (with the number of regions to be reduced to between ten and fourteen) but phased out the price-support programs for all manufactured milk products over five years.[29] The Solomon amendment passed overwhelmingly after Gunderson conceded on the House floor that it would save taxpayers and consumers nearly $4 billion, while his own plan, caught up in trying to raise producer incomes and then achieve deregulation, would raise their costs by more than $3 billion.

The Agriculture Committee was also unsuccessful in keeping a narrow commodity focus to the House bill. On various amendments, the provisions for reauthorization of the CRP were broadened; annual expenditures on cost-sharing programs for environmental practices and facilities were doubled from $100 million to $200 million; another $200 million was added for restoration of the Everglades; and international food aid authorities were adopted. These measures all had the support of the Republican leadership. When the chair of the Appropriations Committee, Republican Robert Livingston (Louisiana), dissented and opposed the creation of new mandatory conservation programs, Speaker Gingrich made an unusual floor appearance to reply that circumstances dictated an exception to budget restraint for the sake of environmental objectives. Budget hawks lost the vote on the main conservation amendment 373 to 37.

The final floor challenge to the House farm bill came from Agriculture Committee Democrats who proposed increased funding for rural development, higher soybean loan rates, and an extension of perma-

---

28. The outcomes of these two votes were not as close as recorded—several token votes were shifted in favor of each amendment once it was clear it would not pass.

29. Under the modified closed rules of debate obtained by Roberts, midwestern opponents of the marketing orders were denied a chance to offer an amendment for full deregulation as an alternative to Gunderson.

nent law. Roberts had supported more conservation spending but turned a budget argument against the Democrats, and their amendment was defeated. The House passed the farm bill, still without reauthorizing food stamps and other nutrition programs, by 270 to 155. The logrolling process had increased the cost of the bill by $3.5 billion, but had won over the votes of fifty-four Democrats.

End Game on the Farm Bill

Despite the remaining differences in scope and detail between the House and Senate farm bills, the wild uncertainty that had characterized the debate in the previous year had dissipated in the winter of 1996. A palpable sense of convergence settled on the farm policy process once the House had passed its version of new legislation. There was now widespread support, given high market prices, for shifting the commodity programs into decoupled PFC payments. Issuing sizable government payments to their farm constituents prior to the general November elections appealed to a wide circle of incumbents in both parties. Secretary Glickman announced that the president would not veto the farm bill because of the decoupling policy *alone,* but reiterated the administration's concerns for a strengthened safety net for farmers, and for conservation, nutrition, and rural development programs.

Reaching a final compromise on the farm bill rested on a decision by House and Senate Republicans to forgo the opportunity to press other aspects of their political agenda in favor of a victory on farm support programs. With billions of dollars of PFC payments for farm constituent groups at stake, with spring planting already underway in most parts of the country, and with their party badly in need of a legislative success more than a year after its historic 1994 election victory, the Republicans accommodated enough Democratic demands to ensure enactment of the new farm bill. With prices high, farm policy reformers defeated a last-ditch proposal by commodity groups and the administration to remove the caps imposed on loan rates for corn and wheat, but the compromise abandoned Roberts's plans for a second farm bill, and made room for conservation and nutrition titles that thwarted the most controversial Republican proposals for deregulation and budget restraint.[30] The farm bill conference committee agreed to reauthorize the

30. The wheat and corn commodity groups had concluded that CBO was miscalculating the expected savings from imposing the loan-rate caps. They were willing to forgo almost $500 million of guaranteed contract payments in exchange for higher loan rates that

CRP with an early-out option for some acreage, but rejected the radical departure from previous wetlands policy of exempting areas of less than one acre from regulation. Agreement was reached to reauthorize the food stamp program for two years while the welfare reform debate proceeded—a compromise that Democrats accepted. The Fund for Rural America was authorized at $300 million over three years. With these agreements, common ground was found to ensure bipartisan support from the breadth of the legislation.[31]

The last issues faced by the conference committee were dairy policy and the retention of the permanent farm program law. Leahy had indicated throughout that he would insist on authority for the Northeast Dairy Compact, and opponents of decoupling continued to argue the permanent law provided an essential safety net for farmers. Roberts was willing to accept retention of permanent law, with its implication that follow-up legislation would have to be enacted by Congress when the 1996 farm bill expired in 2002. His opposition to retaining permanent law had only been a temporary concession to reform advocates in the House of Representatives; he had not included nullification of the permanent law in his original Freedom to Farm Act the previous August. In the final negotiations, he offered an extension of the PFC contracts through 2003 or continuation of the 1949 Act through 2004 in lieu of the permanent farm bill authority. Neither offer was acceptable to proponents of retaining the 1949 legislation. A short note from the secretary of agriculture stated simply that Democrats needed the Senate version of permanent law, and Roberts conceded. Leahy accepted authority in the legislation for the secretary of agriculture to establish the Northeast Dairy Compact if there was a compelling public interest in the region.[32]

---

they calculated—correctly it later turned out—would be much more valuable if prices fell in future years.

31. There also remained a long list of other details to be settled about the commodity programs. Proponents of reform scored two small victories on planting flexibility in last-hour bargaining. A proposal to allow the secretary of agriculture to require that 50 percent of historical rice acreage of PFC contract recipients be retained in rice production was rejected. Planting flexibility was enhanced when a decision was made to allow haying and grazing on all contract acreage. Market conditions again were key in determining this latter outcome. High crop prices were putting upward pressure on hay prices, ameliorating some of the initial opposition by cattlemen to use of the contract land for production of livestock feed.

32. The secretary of agriculture subsequently approved establishment of the Northeast Dairy Compact, a setback for reform advocates.

The conference farm bill was titled the Federal Agriculture Improvement and Reform (FAIR) Act. The FAIR Act was scored as saving $2 billion from the December CBO budget baseline. The Republican leadership claimed that they had imposed budget discipline. The final bill passed in the House of Representatives by an overwhelming 318 to 89 majority and in the Senate by 74 to 26. The president signed it into law in a low-key ceremony on April 4, 1996. Yet even as the new law was taking effect, President Clinton promised he would introduce subsequent legislation in 1997 to improve the safety net for farmers.

Chapter Five

The Political Economy of the FAIR Act

IN CHAPTER 4, WE DESCRIBED THE SEQUENCE of policy proposals and political negotiations that led to unexpected domestic farm policy reforms in the 1996 FAIR Act. In this chapter, we step back from the political process to address two fundamental analytical questions about these reforms. First, what were the economic impacts of the FAIR Act on U.S. agriculture? Second, what fundamental economic and political forces drove Congress and the president to adopt the originally rejected Freedom to Farm approach?

At the outset of the farm bill debate, economic analysis suggested that elimination of the existing farm programs in 1995 would result in more efficient resource use and an increase in income derived directly from markets. When the FAIR Act passed, it was thus acclaimed by farm policy proponents and critics alike for freeing agriculture from many of the distorting production incentives spawned by the traditional programs. Yet the higher market prices that helped produce the FAIR Act would have led to fewer production distortions even under those programs, and smaller initial budget outlays as well.

Without a change in party control of Congress, and without an unexpected interlude of rising farm prices in 1995–96, the most important reforms in the FAIR Act would not have been undertaken. Prior to the November 1994 Republican midterm election victory, and prior to the 1995 run-up in commodity prices, few participants in the farm policy process expected radical change, and those that did expect change were not anticipating decoupled support payments. A number of proposals were advanced for eliminating unpaid ARP set asides, and the ascendancy of the Republican Party in Congress heightened the prospects for this reform move. But it was not foreseen that a combination of Republican control of Congress and high commodity prices would eventually trigger an important restructuring of the deficiency payment mechanism for providing support to farmers. We examine the importance of these two coincident events in producing the FAIR Act in 1996 and compare them to a number of other sources of change often considered conducive to reform, which had much smaller impacts at the time. These include the content of the Uruguay Round Agreement on Agriculture and related international negotiations, federal budget pressure, the cumulative structural modernization in agriculture, a diminished potency of the farm lobby, and the emergence of newly dominant ideas favoring a smaller role of the government in the domestic economy (including the farm economy). These other policy-driving forces may prove influential in future years, but they did not prompt the surprising policy changes embraced by Congress in the 1996 FAIR Act.

Economic Impacts of the FAIR Act Reforms

If the FAIR Act is preserved for its scheduled duration from 1996 to 2002, it will deserve to be classified in some important respects as a policy reform victory, certainly as a substantial extension of the limited cash-out reforms previously undertaken. Unlike earlier cash outs, the FAIR Act sought to decouple direct support payments almost entirely from market conditions and farm production decisions. This nearly complete decoupling of payments was the step that had eluded market-oriented reformers on at least two prior occasions—first in 1985, with congressional rejection of the Boschwitz-Boren proposal, then once more in the late 1980s, when international negotiators rejected the zero option proposal in the GATT Uruguay Round. Congress had only partially decoupled support payments from planting decisions and crop yields in the 1985 and 1990 farm bills. The FAIR Act not only fully decoupled support for the former deficiency payment crops, it also eliminated all authority for annual acreage reductions.

Reform Gains from the FAIR Act

From a market-oriented perspective, the main reform features of the FAIR Act provide numerous advantages compared to previous cash outs. In the past, the commodity programs had offered farmers a conflicting mix of incentives, which drove up costs and generated market distortions. Deficiency payments tied to base-acreage production of specific crops created uneconomic incentives for supply expansion and distorted land values, particularly in regions for which the payments constituted a large proportion of net farm income. Simultaneously, supply was constrained by ARPs and, in some cases, by restrictions on planting flexibility on the program acreage bases. Provisions for partial deficiency payments on voluntarily idled land created a further disincentive for efficient production.

The distorting effects of the traditional farm support programs were substantially reduced under the FAIR Act because of the ending of deficiency payments, the decoupling of cash support from production decisions, and the elimination of acreage bases and annual supply controls. Efficiency gains from the decoupling of support and the end to ARPs yield economic benefits for producers and consumers. Earlier limited cash-out reforms had kept some market-distorting program incentives in place, particularly by leaving government policy makers with little means to control expenditure other than by a lapse into damaging production controls. The FAIR Act eliminated this incentive for policy distortion, made the income transfers to farmers explicit and transparent, and allowed low-cost farmers to escape the inefficiency and opportunity cost of idling portions of their land.

Under its production flexibility contracts, the FAIR Act also sought to move closer to the elusive goal of budget certainty, replacing the open-ended deficiency payment entitlements from the 1985 and 1990 farm bills with an explicit cap on most farm support expenditures. Cost overruns had been an embarrassment to past cash-out reforms of farm policy. The FAIR Act not only fixed planned support payments but seemed to offer some increased budget discipline compared to previous years. The total seven-year federal expenditure of $35.4 billion originally authorized for decoupled payments in the FAIR Act implied annual support outlays below the average expenditures under either the 1985 or 1990 farm bill. By this comparison, at least, farm support payments were reduced by the 1996 FAIR Act, and the prospects for more efficient resource allocations within the sector were increased.

Another important reform feature under the FAIR Act was the capping of nominal loan rates at seemingly nonintrusive levels. This would ensure that the period of high farm commodity prices during the mid-1990s did not lead automatically to market-distorting price-support levels and growth in entitlement claims if prices fell. Farm programs had become highly distorting and costly after price supports ratcheted up during the 1970s commodity boom (and general inflation) proved too high in the 1980s. The FAIR Act insulated farm policy from such an automatic growth of intrusive support.

The full decoupling of support payments from prices and production under the FAIR Act also potentially enhanced the bargaining position of the United States for future international trade negotiations. It never made sense from the standpoint of economic efficiency for the United States to engage in supply control, when the European Union (a somewhat higher-cost producer) was going ahead with full production.

By unilaterally abandoning its annual supply-control measures for export crops under the FAIR Act, the United States strengthened its position as a low-cost supplier of grains to world markets. This could indirectly pressure international competitors into parallel reforms.

Having unilaterally adopted fully decoupled support payments in the FAIR Act, the United States also became more persuasive in arguing that its trade partners and competitors abroad—especially the European Union—should do the same, in order to eliminate remaining distortions affecting trade volumes and market prices. Thanks to the FAIR Act, the United States no longer needs the blue box exemption built into the final Uruguay Round Agreement on Agriculture. This might allow U.S. negotiators to argue for repeal of the blue box exemption across the board, and thus perhaps pressure the European Union, which has consistently remained behind the United States in moving toward farm policy reform, into accepting fully decoupled payments as well. Under the MacSharry plan, the European Union finally moved *toward* a cash out in 1992, reducing its intervention price guarantees and compensating farmers with cash payments, while embracing acreage set-aside requirements. When the 1996 FAIR Act ended U.S. set asides, it completed a reversal of the longstanding policy stances of the United States and European Union on annual production controls. With less competitive policies, the Europeans could find themselves more inclined to undertake further reforms.[1]

Limitations of the FAIR Act Reforms

Despite the important accomplishments of eliminating annual supply controls and decoupling support for the former deficiency payment crops from production decisions and market prices, the reform gains made in the 1996 FAIR Act were limited. The FAIR Act is certainly not a cutout of farm programs, because federal government payments to farmers will continue; payments were decoupled, but not terminated.[2]

---

1. In July 1997, the European Commission made such a reform proposal (called its "Agenda 2000") for decoupled payments. The commission argued that lowering domestic prices to world levels, eliminating export subsidies and acreage set asides, and providing direct compensatory payments to the beneficiaries of the CAP were steps necessary to manage budget costs, avoid surplus accumulations, and pave the way for enlargement of the European Union.

2. One minor exception was that the price-support program for honey was terminated in 1996. This was a clean cutout, but CCC expenditures on the honey program had averaged only $43 million annually since 1985, and government receipts had exceeded outlays in fiscal years 1994 and 1995. Earlier (in 1993) the small wool and mohair support program

Nor is the FAIR Act a guaranteed buyout of farm programs, even though some proponents described it as such.[3] The FAIR Act maintains a baseline of farm program spending for at least seven years and does not repeal the permanent legislation that will automatically trigger a reversion to high price supports and supply controls if Congress fails to take further action in 2002. This almost guarantees new legislation on farm programs. Thus, the institutions and the institutional incentives remain in place to extend decoupled payments, or even to re-implement some of the more intrusive programs and policy instruments that the FAIR Act sought to eliminate.

The FAIR Act also fails to squeeze farmers out of their traditional acceptance of government support. The former deficiency payment programs entailed some restrictions on farmers' production decisions, and participation rates varied among commodities depending on market conditions. The FAIR Act PFC payments, in contrast, are sufficiently generous and free of significant compliance costs—and so easy to claim relative to previous farm program payments—that essentially all of those eligible have opted to take advantage of the offer. As a consequence, rates of participation in the farm support program actually rose under the FAIR Act compared to preceding years.[4] An *enlarged* constituency of beneficiaries thus has become associated with the FAIR Act payments. These beneficiaries may now be more likely to expend political resources to sustain future payments, or to seek some other equivalent support, when the FAIR Act expires.

The FAIR Act that finally emerged from Congress in April 1996 was not as market-oriented a measure as the Freedom to Farm Act originally proposed in August 1995. The floor under market prices set by CCC loan rates was kept at 85 percent of a moving average of past price lev-

---

had also been ended without compensation to farmers, just as support programs for other minor commodities had disappeared in the decades after the Second World War. Wool and mohair support payments had averaged about $100 million from 1985–90, but jumped to nearly twice that level in 1991–93, making them a target for which agriculturalists eventually made a concession in budget negotiations.

3. When the FAIR Act was completed, Terry Francl of the Farm Bureau called it "a $36 billion buyout" (Ingersoll 1996). As we earlier pointed out, a *New York Times* headline on April 5, 1996, read, "Clinton Signs Farm Bill Ending Subsidies." See also Stinson, Coggins, and Ramezani 1998.

4. Under deficiency payments, participation rates for wheat, for example, averaged 87 percent from 1993–95, while for corn the participation rates averaged 81 percent. The USDA ensured that all farmers who were eligible for the new FAIR Act payments were notified of the sign-up criteria, and the participation rate reached nearly 100 percent.

els, although subject to nominal caps, and marketing loans were retained in the final legislation. These price-support interventions constitute supply-enhancing incentives by reducing downward price risk, especially for producers of cotton and rice. The FAIR Act also retained the "three entity" rule, which allows some wealthy farmers to circumvent program payment limitations by establishing eligibility for ostensibly separate operations. Retention of this rule demonstrates how little the FAIR Act did to address equity issues, either through an effective means test or an individual entitlement cap. The PFC payments were calculated for each farm on the basis of past output levels, leaving payments concentrated, as before, among large-scale producers.

As with earlier reform efforts, the FAIR Act did not significantly extend the principle of market deregulation beyond the export-oriented deficiency payment crops. There was no cash out for commodities such as dairy, sugar, and peanuts (and also tobacco, although this crop is handled in separate legislation). The support programs for these commodities escaped convincing reform. Marketing order regulation of regional prices of fluid milk was extended, and TRQs that limit imports of dairy products remain in place. The number of regional milk marketing orders was to be reduced, and price supports for dairy products were scheduled to be phased out by the end of 1999, but the FAIR Act authorized a new Northeast Dairy Compact that increased regional price disparities. Sugar price supports well above world price levels were maintained under the FAIR Act, enforced by TRQs to limit imports. The domestic support price of peanuts was lowered, but also remained well above world price levels—with production quotas still in use and limited options for sale, lease, or transfer of the quotas even among counties within a state.

Changes to U.S. agricultural export policies were also modest under the FAIR Act. The EEP and DEIP were reauthorized with the full funding permitted under the Uruguay Round agreement in 2000–2002.[5] The use of public funds to help agribusiness promote U.S. products in foreign markets was continued, although at a somewhat reduced level.

The FAIR Act also provided authority for some entirely new spending in agriculture, most of it tied nominally to environmental policies.

5. For 1996–99, EEP expenditures were capped below the maximum levels permitted by the Uruguay Round Agreement on Agriculture, but during these years it was expected that high international market prices would make export subsidy spending unnecessary.

The federal role in farm credit markets was reaffirmed, although somewhat tighter rules were written governing the provision of subsidized loans. New "pilot" revenue insurance programs were also authorized—programs that have potentially large production-stimulating consequences and create uncertain budget exposure.

Through renewal of long-term paid land diversions in the CRP, a significant supply-control instrument was extended by the FAIR Act. While supply controls through unpaid annual acreage set asides were eliminated, the total acreage authority for paid CRP contracts was held at its 1995 level of 36.4 million acres—despite strong farm commodity demand and favorable prices for producers at the time. The voluntary nature of the CRP ensures that idling land will continue to be expensive for taxpayers; farmers must forgo the newly decoupled PFC payments on CRP land enrollments, so the commodity programs and the CRP will still be bidding against each other. The secretary of agriculture was given wide discretion in determining the location of future CRP enrollments as existing contracts expired. This did not satisfy the concerns of many environmentalists, who wanted a stronger guarantee that land fragility and off-farm pollution issues would be given priority in the secretary's enrollment decisions. However, because the secretary had made known his intention to maintain the size of the CRP, commodity groups worried about low prices were reassured.[6]

Finally, it was the short-term budget expenditures under the FAIR Act that made it seem least like a bold reform in 1996. When the FAIR Act became law, it increased farm program costs compared to an extension of the 1990 farm bill. As we have described, before market prices increased, the CBO projected that the farm bill title in the 1995 budget reconciliation legislation (essentially the same proposals as the FAIR Act for the defi-

6. While paid acreage idling under the CRP remained intrusive under the FAIR Act, some modest reform gains could be claimed. The 1990 farm bill increased the CRP emphasis on water quality as an environmental consideration, added wildlife habitat, and established a continuous signup program for small areas devoted to practices designated as valuable by the Environmental Protection Agency. CRP enrollments had fallen to 32.8 million acres by spring of 1997, and contracts on 21.4 million acres were due to expire. The USDA enrolled 16.8 million acres in May 1997 (including reenrollments of 11.7 million acres formerly under contract). This was the largest single signup ever. Yet with prices still relatively high, and despite the secretary's assurance, this signup only maintained the CRP at just over 28 million acres—8 million less than the maximum authorized by the FAIR Act. A second signup was conducted in late 1997, increasing the CRP acreage slightly. The distribution of enrolled acres changed only a little among regions as a result of these two post–FAIR Act signups, with the largest change an increase from 27 to 31 percent in the Northern Plains.

ciency payment commodities) would reduce expected budget costs compared to continuation of existing policies by $2.8 billion during fiscal years 1996 and 1997, and by $12.2 billion over seven years. After market prices increased, this calculation had to be redone. In December 1995, the CBO projected that the same farm bill proposals would increase expenditures compared to the 1990 law by $3.9 billion in 1996 and 1997, and would produce a net savings over seven years of just $4.6 billion. These calculations were then redone (by the USDA) once again in mid-1996. Using the high price projections then prevalent, the new calculations showed not only an increase in costs in the short run, but a net increase over the whole seven-year life of the FAIR Act. In mid-1996, USDA calculated that the seven-year cost of the FAIR Act would be a full $25 billion higher than if deficiency payments under the 1990 law had simply been extended (Young and Westcott 1996). Thus, the FAIR Act was perceived at the time as providing a substantial windfall gain to farmers.

Measuring the Efficiency Gains

Along with increased income transfers to farmers, the FAIR Act provided only modest short-run efficiency gains within the U.S. farm sector. Proponents of the FAIR Act emphasized that ending ARPs and decoupling support payments gave farmers greater freedom to respond to market signals, and greater incentives to plant for the market rather than to try to "farm the government programs." For the deficiency payment programs that were reformed most by the FAIR Act, this would have been a measurable benefit at the levels of prices anticipated in February 1995. But the flexibility gains were actually quite small when the FAIR Act came into effect in 1996. With the relatively high farm commodity prices then prevailing, the traditional deficiency payment programs would have provided almost as much freedom to farm.

Prior to the rise in market prices in 1995–96, the CBO projected (in February 1995) that continuation of ARPs under extension of the 1990 farm bill would idle between three and six million acres of corn and cotton base acreage annually during the 1996–2002 period. A larger aggregate acreage was projected to be idled each year under the voluntary set-aside programs, through which farmers could receive deficiency payments even if they didn't produce crops. The voluntarily idled area was expected to exceed twelve million acres annually across all commodities. The CBO made the assumption that CRP land diversions would not extend beyond the termination of the ten-year contracts authorized under the 1985 and 1990 farm bills. Thus, the acreage enrolled in the CRP was projected to decline from nearly thirty-five million acres to less than twenty million.

Various estimates of the economic efficiency gains that could be achieved by eliminating farm program interventions circulated during the 1995–96 farm bill debate. These estimates rested on different assumptions about the amount of ARP and voluntarily idled land that would go into production, the productivity of the previously idled land, and the substitution decisions by producers among commodities— given the expected market prices and the absence of deficiency payments and base-acreage restrictions. A Heritage Foundation study suggested that 95 percent of ARP land and 60 percent of voluntarily idled land would be utilized for program crops if the traditional policies were eliminated (Frydenlund 1995). Analysis by FAPRI noted that ARP acres tended to have below-average productivity and concluded that only 50 to 60 percent would return to production if price expectations remained at the prevailing trend levels. FAPRI also concluded that only 25 percent of voluntarily idled land would return to production at these prices, because producing crops on the voluntarily idled acreage had always been possible (without loss of government payments) if farmers considered it to be profitable.

In an April 1995 analysis, FAPRI provided detailed estimates of the economic effects of an elimination of traditional price-support and supply-control interventions (FAPRI 1995a).[7] In terms of specific commodities, projected acreage of corn increased when ARPs were eliminated, driving prices down slightly. The elimination of acreage controls was projected to allow soybean plantings to rise by several million acres (2 to 4 percent), causing prices to drop by over 5 percent. Wheat acreage, in contrast, was projected to fall by about 3 percent (over two million acres) without the production incentives from deficiency payments, pushing market prices up. Elimination of the traditional programs had more pronounced effects for rice and cotton. Without deficiency payments, rice acreage was projected to fall by 20 percent (about 500,000 acres) despite an increase of more than 10 percent in market prices. Although projected cotton ARPs of 10 percent were eliminated, planted cotton acreage was projected to fall, as farmers switched to alternative crops.

At the aggregate level, FAPRI estimated in April 1995 that total mar-

7. This study was completed before Roberts made his Freedom to Farm proposal, but included analysis of a hypothetical "no program" scenario in which deficiency payments, base acreages, and ARPs were eliminated.

ket receipts for crops and livestock would decline slightly from 1996 to 2002 as a result of eliminating the traditional support programs. The decline in receipts was more than offset, however, by lower production costs. The resulting change in net income (omitting the government payments usually reported in farm income statistics) provides an estimate of the aggregate economic efficiency gains that can be attributed to eliminating the disincentives, restrictions, and incentives associated with the traditional support programs—and to the adoption instead of the input usage, acreages planted, and crop mix that maximized market returns. A gain of $818 million was projected, on average, over the seven years from 1996 to 2002, an increase in net farm income of 4.4 percent.

By the time the FAIR Act was signed into law in April 1996, market prices had risen compared to expectations from the year before. At these higher prices, ARPs would almost certainly have been set to zero for all commodities under the deficiency payment programs. The efficiency gains from eliminating the traditional programs would thus be lower than estimated by FAPRI at least in the short run, because an important part of these estimated gains came from bringing ARP acreage back into production. Higher prices also might have induced more land into production from the voluntary set-aside programs, but this effect cannot be attributed to a change in policy. Under the high prices of 1996–97, few income gains in agriculture could be attributed to the freeing up of production potential because of the shift to FAIR Act decoupled payments.

An important remaining land-use policy issue affecting production efficiency under the FAIR Act is size of the CRP. Here, the limited reach of the FAIR Act in restraining supply-control measures becomes apparent. The 36.4 million acre maximum-enrollment target amounts to continuation of a substantial land diversion under CRP contracts. Maintaining this level of enrollment affects the efficiency of production and, all else equal, puts upward pressure on market prices. FAPRI, for example, raised its assumption about acreage enrolled in the CRP from nineteen million by 2002 in its April 1995 analysis (before Congress extended CRP authority) to thirty million acres by 2002 in a May 1996 assessment of the FAIR Act—even though commodity prices were by then at the highest level in twenty years (FAPRI 1996).[8] Thus, the CRP

8. For wheat alone, CRP acreage that had been projected in the April 1995 FAPRI analysis to fall from 10.8 million acres in 1994 to 4.5 million acres in 2002 instead was projected in May 1996 to remain above 9 million acres, nearly 15 percent of anticipated planted wheat acreage. This FAPRI forecast proved accurate through 1998 when the first two post–FAIR Act CRP signups were completed.

continues to serve as a significant supply-control instrument under the FAIR Act.

Explaining the Politics of the FAIR Act

The policy changes made in the 1996 FAIR Act are relatively straightforward to assess in economic terms, but somewhat more difficult to account for in political terms. Most analyses of U.S. farm politics predating the FAIR Act were geared to an explanation of continuity in U.S. farm policy, not policy change. Some scholars had been willing to consider significant change prior to the FAIR Act, but the legislative politics of 1995–96 did not conform well to their expectations about how that change would occur. With continuous Democratic control of at least one branch of Congress since 1954, Cochrane and Runge argued in 1992, for example, that farm policy change would be extremely difficult without strong presidential leadership determined to "break through the special-interest, legislative bargaining process" (248). But in 1996, the most important policy reforms contained in the FAIR Act came from Congress, and were enacted despite considerable resistance from the president.

Party Control as a Determinant of Farm Policy

Prior to the 1996 FAIR Act, most policy analysts neglected the influence of party control in Congress on the content of U.S. farm policy. B. Delworth Gardner's account of the politics of U.S. agriculture emphasizes changing structures in Congress that had "diminished the role of political parties" and "weakened the influence of party leadership" (1995, 186). Likewise, Browne (1988) acknowledges an early history of party influence in U.S. farm policy debates, but concludes that the influence of party within the Agricultural Committees of Congress had long since been replaced by the influence of bipartisan coalition building, based largely on commodity-by-commodity "issue expertise."

Our review shows Browne was correct to recognize the historical importance for farm policy of party control in Congress. Republicans resisted farm program enactment in the 1920s, before Democratic ascendancy helped pass the Agricultural Adjustment Act of 1933. After the Second World War, the Republican capture of Congress in the midterm elections of 1946 helped facilitate passage of Title II of the 1948 Agricultural Act, a measure that—if it had survived—was designed to put postwar U.S. farm policy on a market-oriented track by lowering support prices. The Democratic recapture of Congress in the November

1948 election then led, by late 1949, to an extension of high price supports fixed at 90 percent of parity. When the Republicans regained control of Congress in the 1952 election, they successfully replaced these high price supports with a lower minimum parity level. In the 1954 midterm elections, the Democratic Party recaptured Congress once again, and farm programs reverted to heavier dependence on supply controls. Thus, during this important early period, the fluctuating fortunes of market-oriented reform efforts corresponded closely to changes of party control in Congress.

After 1954, Democratic control of the House of Representatives was maintained for the next four decades, from January 1955 through December 1994. Because it did not change, the latent importance of party control in Congress was neglected during this period. Most policy analysis *assumed* continuous Democratic control, then focused their attention on other variables within the context of this established majority regime.[9] Party control of Congress only came back into play as a more visible determinant of policy after the November 1994 election.

Party control has a noticeable role in shaping policy because of the powerful legislative assets institutionally provided to leaders of the majority, particularly within the House of Representatives. More than just voting majorities within all committees and on the House or Senate floor, these assets also include committee chair control over the legislative agenda. When the November 1994 midterm election produced Republican Party majorities in both houses of Congress, this powerful agenda-setting authority shifted from Democratic to Republican Party control.[10]

For a shift in party control to produce a significant change in legislative outcomes, two additional conditions are required. Rank-and-file

9. See Shepsle and Weingast 1994 for a discussion of the tendency for political science during these years to underemphasize the party control variable.

10. In the Senate, it is more difficult for the majority party leadership to control the agenda, particularly on the floor, than in the House of Representatives. The still powerful House Rules Committee, which functions in practice as an arm of the majority party leadership, performs a unique gatekeeping role by determining the terms under which bills can be considered for floor debate and final votes. The most important deliberations of the House Rules Committee frequently take place not in the committee room on the third floor of the Capitol, but in the speaker's suite of offices on the second floor, where the speaker, the majority leader, and the majority whip try to bring rank-and-file members into line before the committee meets to adopt a rule for a controversial bill. Minority party members of the Rules Committee can express their objections to a rule, and hope for favorable press attention, but not much more.

party members in Congress must first comply with the preferences expressed by their party leaders. At the outset of the 104th session of Congress in 1995–96, at the moment at which the Republicans savored majority control for the first time in four decades, average rank-and-file Republican members in the House were strongly united behind the party leadership. Republican House members voted in lockstep with one another and with the party leadership over 90 percent of the time. This was the highest level of support within a majority party in the House in more than a dozen years.

Not only must parties vote in a disciplined fashion for a shift in party control to produce a change in legislative outcomes; preferences regarding policy content must also differ between the parties on the key issues in question. In the election campaign of 1994, the Republican House candidates used unified support for their campaign platform, the Contract with America, as a device to drive home where they differed *as a party* from the Democrats. But party differences on agricultural policy were not presented in this 1994 House Republican manifesto, leaving open the question of whether there were such differences, and if so, whether the new Republican majority would make them an issue in 1995–96.

Arguments can be made that party does not matter anymore for farm policy. Inside the Agriculture Committees of Congress, whenever narrow commodity issues are at stake, party differences tend to be trumped by regional loyalties. Members will often be identified as advocates for certain commodities, rather than as Republicans or Democrats. This commodity identity partly reflects personal background, but more often it reflects regional constituent interests.[11]

The durable strength of commodity-based and regional preferences separate from the party label is vividly illustrated by radically changed party control in what used to be called the "solid Democratic South." The Deep South is now a more solid region for Republicans than for Democrats, and a key part of their party power base. Yet, House and Senate Agriculture Committee endorsement for highly protective policies for southern commodities has scarcely been altered by this shift in party alliance. What matters most about the South for agricultural pol-

---

11. Senator Richard Lugar of Indiana owns a family farm that produces corn, for example, while Representative Charles Stenholm of Texas is himself a cotton farmer. Democratic Senator Kent Conrad of North Dakota speaks for wheat, Republican Senator Jesse Helms of North Carolina for tobacco, Democratic Senator Patrick Leahy of Vermont for the dairy industry in his state, and so on across commodities and regions.

icy is that it still produces cotton, rice, sugar, peanuts, and tobacco—all commodities for which there is a long history of heavy market intervention.

The apparent power of commodity and regional loyalties over party differences also reflects successful recruitment and cultivation of Congress members by narrow commodity-based political action committees (PACs). Across all issues (not just agriculture), members of the House of Representatives tend to rely heavily on PACs for campaign funding; those that win elections receive on average more than 40 percent of their campaign funds from PACs (B. Delworth Gardner 1995). Agricultural PACs gave a total of $15.5 million to members of Congress in 1993–94, making them the nation's third-largest source of PAC money overall. Sugar, dairy, and peanut organizations stood out as especially large contributors, giving $4.1 million. These three commodity PAC groups gave House Agriculture Committee members an average of $18,341 each in 1993–94, and Senate Agriculture Committee members an average of $45,604 (Center for Responsive Politics 1995).

B. Delworth Gardner (1995) describes the differing campaign contribution strategies of various farm-commodity PACs, and finds those that make the largest contributions per million dollars of output sales (in rank order these are sugar, tobacco, cotton, peanuts, and dairy) tend to receive the highest levels of farm program support from Congress. Commodity PACs secure these benefits not by favoring one party over another, but by favoring whichever candidate seems most likely to get elected—which usually means incumbents. As a general rule, contributions to incumbents tend to exceed those to challengers by more than five to one.[12]

And yet, party control still influences farm policy. Party loyalties do not dominate in debates among producer groups, but they emerge as important when the enactment of legislation comes at issue. Farm commodity PACs and lobby groups alone lack the political resources to deliver floor majorities in the House and Senate.[13] Commodity-based

12. Thus, prior to November 1994 more agricultural PAC money went to Democrats than to Republicans, and after the Republican capture of Congress more agricultural PAC money went to the new majority party. During the first six months of 1995, for example, Republicans received 55 percent of sugar industry PAC donations from eighteen different organizations (which gave a total of $660,000), whereas in 1993 Democrats received 62 percent of sugar PAC money.

13. In the Senate, the geographic dispersion of American agriculture still gives farm interests alone surprising political clout. There are few "farm dependent" states, but there remain a large number of states with enough agriculture to be important. B. Delworth

agricultural interests are salient only to a small fraction of the members of Congress, well short of a minimum winning floor coalition. To be enacted, farm bills must be attractive, or at least acceptable, to a mix of constituencies with broader interests. These supporters are drawn from various constituencies, among them farm organizations that are not commodity based, agribusiness, environmentalists, food consumers, and advocates for the rural and urban poor. When this larger set of non-commodity-based farm bill constituencies is surveyed, policy preferences do divide sharply along party lines.

In broad terms across most issues, the Democratic Party still tends to support a significant domestic policy role for the federal government, while the Republican Party tends to favor less government and more of a role for the private sector. These basic differences in party preferences are carried into questions of agricultural policy. On issues of commodity programs, Democrats will often be more comfortable with higher price supports and more intrusive supply controls; this is also the traditional position of the NFU, which claims to represent the smaller-sized, higher-cost farmers who tend to identify themselves as Democrats. Republicans will more often be comfortable with farm income supports that do not constrain full-production agriculture; this is the traditional position of the Farm Bureau, which generally represents larger-sized commercial farmers and export interests. On issues of environmental policy affecting agriculture, Democrats are more likely to welcome land-idling conservation programs and environmental regulation, while Republicans are more likely to favor full production and to object to government environmental regulations, especially those that inconvenience commercial farm operations. On issues of nutrition and consumer protection, Democrats are more likely to argue for well-funded federal nutrition-assistance programs and extensive food safety regulations. Republicans are more likely to argue that business reputations for safety earned in free markets, balanced assessments of regulatory risks and benefits, and allowing crop prices to fall are the best ways to help consumers.

A measure of such divergent party leanings between Republicans and Democrats in Congress can be derived by comparing the "favora-

---

Gardner has listed the "top producing states" for seven different groups of farm program commodities: wheat, feed grains, and soybeans; sugar; cotton; rice; peanuts; tobacco; and dairy products. When these lists are combined, they include thirty-five out of the fifty states.

bility ratings" assigned to key members of Congress by a sample of constituency-linked advocacy groups. Consider the favorability ratings (from 0 to 100) made by six different groups: the AFBF, the NFU, the League of Conservation Voters (LCV), the Libertarian Party (LP), the National Taxpayers Union (NTU), and Bread for the World (BFW). For each of these six lobby groups, the ratings given to Republicans tend to differ sharply from ratings given to Democrats. Republicans tend to be rated high by the AFBF, the LP, and the NTU; and low by the NFU, the LCV, and BFW. Democrats are rated just the opposite: they receive high ratings from the NFU, the LCV, and BFW; and low ratings from the AFBF, the LP, and the NTU.

Table 14 shows the average ratings given to House and Senate committee chairs by these six lobby groups for three different Congresses: the 101st Congress of 1989–90 (the Congress that passed the 1990 farm bill, when all committee chairs were Democrats), the 103rd Congress of 1993–94 (the Congress that passed the Uruguay Round implementing legislation, when all committee chairs were still Democrats), and the 104th Congress of 1995 (the Congress that passed the 1996 FAIR Act, after all committee chairs became Republicans). From these ratings, it is clear that the Republican committee chairs who took over in the 104th Congress were viewed as ideologically distinct from the Democratic

Table 14. Advocacy Group Ratings of House and Senate Committee Chairs

	101st Congress: 1989–90 (Democratic Majority)		103rd Congress: 1993–94 (Democratic Majority)		104th Congress: 1995–96 (Republican Majority)	
	House	Senate	House	Senate	House	Senate
American Farm Bureau Federation	28.7	44.3	21.6	41.6	89.5	92.0
National Farmers Union	79.4	78.3	73.3	85.7	29.2	30.8
League of Conservation Voters	68.5	58.5	73.3	72.1	12.4	16.3
Libertarian Party	11.6	—	9.6	9.4	64.8	74.0
National Taxpayers Union	18.0	28.7	18.5	20.8	82.5	83.6
Bread for the World	74.9	82.7	62.6	79.2	12.9	18.6

Note: Derived from authors' calculations, based on favorability ratings (1–100) periodically published in newsletters by groups listed. Ratings shown are averages for all House and Senate majority party committee chairs. Rankings for 104th Congress are based on 1995 only.

chairs they replaced along every dimension. Key farm bill constituencies thus perceive highly significant differences between Republicans and Democrats.

These significant differences between Republicans and Democrats on farm policy issues do not mean one party is more favorably inclined toward farmers than the other. Both parties have traditionally advocated helping farmers, and in the end both parties tend to support generous farm bills. The capture of Congress by Republicans in November 1994 did not mean farm programs were soon going to disappear. Republicans in Congress had joined Democrats in rejecting the Reagan administration's call to cut out farm programs in 1981 and 1985, and a decade later Pat Roberts used the fact that thirty-three freshman Republicans were dependent on agriculture in their districts to convince the House leadership once again not to cut farm program budgets too severely. Still, the shift in party control did bring a significant movement in congressional preferences away from market-intrusive support programs and toward policies that did not constrain farm production or agribusiness marketing activities.

The Republican Congress Ends Annual Supply Controls

Because the Republican-controlled 104th Congress was more inclined than any Democratic Congress had been toward full production agriculture and agribusiness interests, the new Republican agricultural leadership set as one of its key objectives the elimination of unpaid annual land diversions under ARPs. In the early stage of the farm bill debate, however, another set of preferences brought to Congress by the Republican leadership first had to be addressed. This was the Republican preference (clearly visible in the NTU ratings shown in table 14) for greater federal budget discipline. A few Republican agriculturalists, led by Lugar, wanted this party preference for budget discipline to be applied to farm programs, but a much larger number, led by Roberts, opposed cutting farm program spending sharply. Roberts battled successfully on behalf of agriculturalists (when he broke with the Republican move toward devolution of power back to the states to defend food stamps as a federal entitlement) and emerged as the clear winner in the farm program budget battle.

What forces allowed Roberts and other Republican proponents of farm programs to prevail in this way, over the announced preferences of their own party leadership? The agriculturalists made good rhetorical use of their argument that farm program spending had already been cut disproportionately since 1985. But it was the relatively large number of House Republicans who still cared about farm programs, together with the relatively small savings that agricultural cuts could provide, that finally persuaded the House leadership to yield (including even Majority Leader Dick Armey, earlier the most vocal opponent of farm programs in the entire Congress). House Republican leaders knew the real budget battle of 1995 would take place over the much larger issues of tax cuts, welfare, and health care entitlements. To win this larger partisan battle, every single rank-and-file Republican vote would count. This gave Roberts and the farm district Republicans that he rallied the leverage needed to face down the Budget Committee and save farm programs (plus a variety of agribusiness subsidy programs) from the cuts for which Lugar was calling in the Senate.

Once Roberts and the other Republican agriculturalists had contained the threat of excessive budget cuts, they were faced with the next step in the process: trying to build a unified majority coalition, from their members on the Agriculture Committee, for specific policies affordable within the budget space they had worked so hard to win. Over most of the summer of 1995 this presented itself as a nearly insurmountable political problem. Because of virtually unanimous partisan Democratic opposition to the Republican budget agenda, Roberts knew he needed to craft a farm bill that could win the support of almost every Republican on his committee. A consensus would have to be reached among old-style agriculturalists and new-style budget hawks, and include not only his own midwestern grain constituents—who wanted ARP elimination and greater planting flexibility—but also the southern crop advocates on the committee who were generally opposed to any radical policy change.

In effect, Roberts never solved this coalition-building problem in the summer of 1995. His Freedom to Farm Act was attractive to some of his constituents, solved the budget problem, and made the elimination of ARPs affordable under the CBO rules, but it was blocked by Representatives Emerson, Combest, Baker, and Chambliss. When these Republicans balked, the Freedom to Farm proposal seemed dead. Lugar had likewise failed in the Senate to gain southern Republican support for a much weaker version of reform, one that continued traditional programs for cotton and rice.

Republican control of Congress was therefore not enough, by itself, to go beyond ARP elimination and generate a consensus for decoupled Freedom to Farm payments. Decoupling became politically acceptable only after a second enabling condition emerged in the summer and fall of 1995—the sudden and rapid increase in farm commodity prices. If this commodity price boom had not taken place, the Freedom to Farm Act would not have moved forward. The Republican 104th Congress most likely would have embraced something similar to the bill that actually passed the Senate Agriculture Committee in September 1995, a far more cautious measure that eliminated ARP authority and gave increased planting flexibility to feed grain and wheat producers, but maintained restrictive planting requirements for cotton and rice. This bill retained deficiency payments tied to production and market prices, and met budget requirements by increasing nonpayment acreage to 30 percent.

High Commodity Prices Induce Decoupled Subsidy Payments

Without steadily rising commodity prices in late 1995, Congress would never have been persuaded to embrace Freedom to Farm decoupled payments. Without above-trend prices, in fact, Roberts never would have proposed this approach in the first place.

When the idea of full decoupling had been presented ten years earlier, as the 1985 Boschwitz-Boren plan to replace traditional programs with fixed transition payments, it was firmly rejected by Republicans and Democrats alike. To Republican agriculturalists in Congress, the Boschwitz-Boren decoupling proposal too closely resembled a degrading form of welfare; and to prairie populist Democrats, it had seemed too much like a farm program designed by export-oriented agribusiness firms seeking low inputs costs. Farm commodity prices were also low in 1985, and were falling, making fixed decoupled payments less attractive to farmers as the legislative debate progressed.

Full decoupling of support payments from market prices or production decisions was not considered seriously by Congress as an option when it rewrote farm policy in 1990, and it remained essentially off the table when the 1995 farm bill debate began. In late 1994, Senator Lugar had solicited advice from knowledgeable participants in the farm policy process, and then promulgated a provocative list of fifty-three critical questions to guide hearings on the farm bill. Not one of these questions raised the option of decoupled payments (Lugar 1994).

Numerous experts had been arguing for increased planting flexibility prior to the 1995 farm bill debate, but through the winter and spring almost none advocated decoupling. The privately funded National Center for Food and Agriculture Policy (NCFAP) convened an extensive working group of academicians and leaders of farm organizations early in 1995, hoping to push U.S. farm policy reform. The NCFAP recommendations proposed a budgetary "capping" of farm program entitlements, but did not suggest decoupling (NCFAP 1995). A market-oriented proposal prepared for the Democratic Leadership Council also endorsed a budgetary cap, yet this paper explicitly rejected decoupling as an option, arguing instead for safety net payments that would be made "only when farm revenues fell below levels set by new federal standards" (Runge, Schnittker, and Penny 1995, 39). Fully decoupled payments ("payments to farmers *for being farmers*") were also rejected as a policy "disaster" at a conference of the market-oriented American Enterprise Institute (Wright 1995, 23).

Farm lobby groups were generating new policy ideas of their own just prior to the 1995 debate, but the new concept attracting the greatest attention, an idea pushed by a coalition of Iowa corn growers, was a plan for revenue assurance that would guarantee farmers 70 percent of normal crop income. This "Iowa Plan" represented a sharp break from the traditional method of sending payments to farmers, but it was not decoupling. It was still essentially a deficiency payment scheme, with annual payment guarantees coupled to production levels on individual farms and to market price outcomes. The flexibility contained in the Iowa plan was not especially valued by grain farmers in the more marginal regions of the Midwest where planting options were not so abundant; for this reason, the Iowa plan was resisted by wheat farmers in western Kansas, and hence also by Roberts (Kilman 1994).

Throughout the spring of 1995, as he fought to protect agriculture's portion of the CBO budget baseline, Roberts himself fought almost as hard to defend the reputation of traditional farm policies. He took credit for having earlier helped to devise the deficiency payment programs and was viewed by his colleagues in the House as a "fierce protector of the status quo in agriculture" (Penny 1994). There was no hint before mid-1995 that he was about to advocate a radical decoupling option. Roberts only came to the idea of decoupling in the summer of 1995 because it appeared to solve two problems for him—it neutralized the $6.5 billion in additional program expenditures that the CBO estimated were required for ARP elimination, and it offered aid to his Kansas constituents who had suffered crop damage.

Roberts was not successful at first in his effort to sell the radical idea of fully decoupled payments to his colleagues in Congress. His early advocacy effort revolved too much around a speculative and exaggerated warning of how vulnerable farm spending might be to budget cuts in the future, unless the moneys recently negotiated into the 1995 budget resolution were locked in through fixed payment contracts. This early argument for using decoupling to protect agriculture from future budget cuts was powerful at the time, but it was still not enough to persuade cotton and rice interests in the South, who remained firmly attached to payments tied to existing base acreages and market prices. Thus, when Roberts tried to rally a majority for the Freedom to Farm Act from his committee, internal Republican defections blocked his initiative.

It was not until later, after crop prices continued their sharp rise, that the idea of decoupling became sufficiently attractive, first to southern Republicans in Congress and eventually even to a significant number of Democrats, ensuring its final passage. By November 1995, market prices had risen well above the target price levels set by the 1990 farm bill. At this point it became clear that the Freedom to Farm Act would not just protect farm spending from future budget cuts; it would also bring an immediate *increase* in cash payments to farmers compared to existing law. Once Roberts was able to advocate Freedom to Farm as a way to increase spending on farmers in the short run, he received a more positive response. In just six months' time, a farm bill debate that had begun by making no reference at all to decoupled payments was able to coalesce around the desirability of this radical new plan. An unacceptable option had been transformed into an irresistible choice by rising market prices.

Alternative Explanations for the FAIR Act Outcomes

On the eve of the 1995 farm bill debate, few experienced insiders expected radical policy change. Those that expected change focused not on the variables we have stressed as decisive—party control of Congress and changing market conditions—but instead concentrated on a variety of other circumstances inside and outside the farm sector: the Uruguay Round agreement, federal budget pressure, the cumulative structural modernization in agriculture, the diminished potency of the farm lobby, and the emergence of newly dominant ideas about the appropriate role of the government in the farm sector. These other sources of change may help in future years to strengthen and extend policy reforms, but they had surprisingly little influence upon the 1996 FAIR Act.

The Uruguay Round Agreement on Agriculture

The final 1993 Uruguay Round Agreement on Agriculture does not provide a convincing explanation for U.S. farm policy change in 1995–

96, because the terms of the agreement were carefully written to require no support-level reductions beyond those already undertaken in the 1985 and 1990 farm bills. A reassurance that the Uruguay Round would require no immediate changes in U.S. farm policy was also built into the implementing legislation negotiations in 1994 between the congressional farm lobby and the Clinton administration. The Uruguay Round did have some influence on the pace and direction of policy reform in the European Union, but in the United States the international negotiation functioned more as a source of farm policy continuity than as a force for policy change.

More specifically, the elimination of ARP authority and the switch to decoupled payments achieved in the FAIR Act cannot be represented as a response to the Uruguay Round, because the international agreement was explicitly written to permit payments that were partly coupled to production and prices. The blue box agreement that emerged from the Blair House meeting in 1992 effectively exempted both U.S. deficiency payments and similar EU compensation payments from any Uruguay Round disciplines, on a condition that production-limiting programs such as acreage reductions would accompany those payments. Partly coupled deficiency payments and ARPs thus emerged from the Uruguay Round as privileged policy instruments. When the United States subsequently gave up these instruments in the 1996 FAIR Act, it was not in response to any international obligation or pressure.

In the course of the 1995–96 congressional farm bill debate, the Uruguay Round agreement was almost never mentioned, except in reference to export subsidies, partly because the farm lobby felt it had already secured most of what it could get from the Uruguay Round in the congressional debate of 1994. Reform advocates did occasionally represent the recent Uruguay Round outcome as a reason for U.S. farmers to have new faith in open world markets, but U.S. farm groups demonstrated, in the end, only limited faith in greater market orientation. Under the FAIR Act, the USDA retained its full authority for use of export subsidies up to the Uruguay Round limits, and import-competing commodities remained almost as heavily protected as ever.

Federal Budget Pressure

Federal budget pressures are also unconvincing as an explanation for the key reforms in the FAIR Act. Congressional budget rules certainly helped to drive the outcome, but these rules mostly functioned as a source of opportunity and advantage, not as a constraint, for agriculturalists in Congress.

When the farm bill debate began, Republicans in Congress thought they had a mandate from their 1994 midterm election victory to balance the federal budget by cutting government spending sharply. They learned the limits of that mandate as the year progressed. In agriculture, they first encountered effective resistance from their own internal farm block, led by Roberts. The House leadership eventually accepted less budget discipline in the small area of agricultural programs, in part to ensure the support it needed from farm district members in the much larger budget battle that was looming over tax cuts and federal spending levels. When the House Republican leadership subsequently over-reached its mandate on these larger budget issues and lost the budget showdown with the president, fiscal discipline on agriculture was further relaxed. In the Senate, farm program proponents sweetened a bipartisan bill with expanded spending for conservation, nutrition, and other purposes. The allure of spending more through the farm bill eventually became too great, in an election year, for even the House Republican leadership to resist.

Actual budget disciplines thus proved relatively weak in the end, but the budget *rules* used by Congress were highly influential to the final FAIR Act outcome. Without the pay-as-you-go rule (which put a high budget cost on the option of ARP elimination, assuming traditional deficiency payments) and without the constantly obsolescent CBO budget baseline projections (making it possible to capture higher spending with decoupled payments, once market prices started to go up), there would have been no compelling reason for the Republicans to move toward decoupling in 1995. Pay-as-you-go rules alone would probably not have been enough to compel decoupling, even with a Republican Congress.[14] Once prices started rising, however, the baseline capture opportunity made decoupling attractive among Republicans.

The switch to decoupled income support allowed Congress to give farmers larger payments at a time of unexpected high prices, yet it was

14. Again, the compromise proposal forged by Lugar in the Senate offset the cost of ending ARP authority and generated the additional budget savings then being called for (at that point, roughly $13.4 billion over seven years) by placing maximum caps on per-unit deficiency payments and increasing nonpayment (flex) acres from 15 to 30 percent. Had prices been low, or had they been falling during 1995, the final farm bill probably would have adopted these more traditional instruments.

depicted within congressional budget rules as costing the taxpayer less than continuation of the previous programs. The surprising emergence of a lucrative baseline capture opportunity in 1995–96 provided by the rise in world prices meant that real budget discipline was not an influential force behind the 1996 FAIR Act.

The rise of market prices probably would have been enough to alter the final farm bill outcome, but in different ways, had Democrats controlled Congress in 1995–96. By late October 1995, rising prices had given House Democrats an opportunity to put forward their Family Empowerment Act, which raised loan rates to 115 percent of the five-year moving average of past prices, while promising as much budget savings (against the outdated CBO baseline projection) as the Republicans finally settled upon. Other Democrats backed the Fund for Rural America as a means to direct the baseline capture opportunity into expansion of traditional activist and intrusive policies. Democrats in a congressional majority would have found a way to make these expenditures fit into budget constraints, perhaps by pressuring the CBO to count higher loan rates and other generous short-term changes as having no effect on expenditures, because projected market prices were so high. Had these policies been enacted, they would have proven costly later when prices fell, but it was not budget pressure that determined the alternative choice of Freedom to Farm decoupling.

The Cumulative Structural Modernization of Agriculture

The unexpected shift toward decoupled payments under the FAIR Act cannot be attributed to the structural modernization that was continuing in the agricultural sector. The modernization of agricultural production since the Second World War has continuously improved U.S. competitiveness, and led an increasing percentage of farmers to favor cash payments and lessened market intervention over supply controls and high price supports. This systemic change does help explain the progressive movement toward a cash out of farm programs for export crops since the mid-1960s, and the impetus to eliminate remaining annual acreage set asides in 1995–96, a move that enjoyed wide (though not universal) support among farm groups. But the structural transformation that had occurred in agriculture had not led to widespread calls for decoupling when Congress took up the farm bill debate early in 1995. Indeed, outside of the rhetoric of GATT negotiators and a few academic reform advocates, decoupling continued to be held in disrepute.

Diminished Potency of the Farm Lobby

Perhaps the FAIR Act grew out of a long-term systemic change in the demography of the farm sector in a different sense. Honma and Hayami (1986), who use theories of collective action to explain rising levels of farm support despite falling numbers of farmers, posit a limit to this paradoxical result. Their analysis suggests that once farmers represent less than 5 percent of the total population, the political marketplace may start supplying decreasing levels of protection. When the 1995–96 farm bill debate began, farmers numbered under 2 percent of the total U.S. population. For years, it had been commonplace for reform advocates to hope for a policy change based upon "the long, slow erosion of farmers' political clout in Washington" (*New York Times*, 25 July 1994, 1). Reform advocates had in the past consistently overrated the influence of this demographic factor. But were the farm policy changes incorporated in the 1996 FAIR Act a reflection at last of demography-driven farm lobby weakness?

Despite a continued reduction in the number of farmers, the 1996 FAIR Act outcome suggests little in the way of a diminished political clout for farm organizations. For the deficiency payment crops, the most important policy changes in the FAIR Act—the end to unpaid land diversions and decoupling of income payments—provided more, not less, taxpayer money to farmers. For import-competing commodities (sugar and peanuts), farm organizations continued to win head-on battles against well-funded and widely publicized reform initiatives, and dairy policy changes in the FAIR Act added protection for high-cost producers in New England by imposing higher market prices on consumers.

The process through which the FAIR Act was enacted likewise provides evidence of continued farm lobby strength. The original Freedom to Farm proposal did not come from reform-minded crusaders within the new Republican leadership, or from urban-based farm program critics, or even from budget hawks. Freedom to Farm was an idea that came originally from the chair of the House Agriculture Committee, recognized at the time as one of the strongest Republican proponents of traditional farm programs.

The farm bill passage process has traditionally been explained by political scientists as a committee-based logroll. House and Senate agriculturalists use their initial control over the legislation-drafting process to assemble a multifaceted policy package sufficiently generous to a wide enough variety of constituencies to guarantee the minimum winning coalition needed for passage on the floor. This traditional process was somewhat weakened by fiscal pressures in the 1990 farm bill debate, when the reauthorization of farm legislation was ultimately constrained late in the year by a budget reconciliation process that the Agriculture Committees did not completely control, leading to the introduction of nonpayment flex acres as a cost-saving step. Compared to 1990, budget pressures appeared even stronger early in 1995, but a loss of Agriculture Committee control never took place. When Roberts failed in September 1995 to muster a majority within the House Agriculture Committee for a farm title to the Republican budget legislation, he was forced to turn to the House leadership for support, and it seemed the traditional process had been disrupted. Yet, even at this juncture, Roberts and the Republican agriculturalists retained the upper hand. To get the farm-bloc support needed in its larger budget battle, the House leadership backed Roberts in the drafting of a budget reconciliation bill that contained generous provisions for agriculture.

When President Clinton vetoed the budget reconciliation legislation, an even more generous stand-alone farm bill was prepared and quickly passed early in 1996. The bipartisan process used to enact this stand-alone bill conforms closely to the tradition of the committee-based logroll. Thus, the 1996 farm bill process, in its final stages, was closer to the tradition of secure farm lobby control than either the budget reconciliation battle of late 1995, or the budget-driven farm bill process late in 1990. The final legislative outcomes in the 1996 FAIR Act are different from the bipartisan logroll result that would have emerged had Democrats controlled Congress, but a similar logrolling process remains recognizable.

Emergence of Newly Dominant Ideas

A final alternative explanation for the FAIR Act is one based on the power of ideas. Perhaps the move made in the 1996 FAIR Act toward ARP elimination and decoupled payments was a product of more than just clashing interests; perhaps it represented a victory for market-oriented ideas and the notion, expressed even by a Democratic president, that the era of "big government" was over. Hall (1993) has argued that a growing discrepancy between policy outcomes and objectives can trigger either a first-order change (in policy instrument settings), a second-order change (in instruments), or a third-order change (in ideas, goals, and objectives). As the original New Deal idea that the agricultural sector needed help gradually became obsolete, from the Second World War onward the New Deal–era farm programs that were the institutional embodiment of that idea increasingly began to malfunction. Various first-order and second-order policy changes followed accordingly. Was the 1996 FAIR Act at last a third-order change, one that emerged from a larger contestation over fundamental goals and objectives, and one that brought with it a new set of dominant policy ideas?

Some scholars have identified the FAIR Act outcome as part of a larger idea-driven process. Coleman, Skogstad, and Atkinson (1997) argue that the FAIR Act reforms in the United States (and simultaneous farm policy reforms in Canada and Australia) resulted from such a change of ideas. Tweeten and Zulauf (1997) likewise argue that the FAIR Act reflects the emergence of a "new public policy paradigm for agriculture," one that is distinctive because it assumes that a long-term economic equilibrium has very nearly been achieved in the sector, and because it stresses the importance of economic efficiency and off-farm income in place of governmental interventions to boost prices by controlling supply.[15] Yet, it was not the rise to dominance of market-oriented ideas that drove the FAIR Act outcome.

Several features of the 1995–96 farm bill debate indicate that ideas such as small government, market orientation, and an end to supports for agriculture were not yet being embraced within U.S. farm policy. First, if the idea of market orientation had been driving the outcome, reform would have been felt by all crops, not just by the deficiency payment crops, where the budget baseline capture option existed. Second, if (as Hall argues) third-order changes are unlikely to occur without some kind of society-wide contestation and engagement, then there is little to suggest such a fundamental change in 1995–96.[16] There was actually far more social contestation and engagement over agricultural policy at the peak of the inflationary commodity boom of the 1970s (when labor and consumer interests were mobilized against high food prices), or at the depths of the farm crisis of the 1980s (when populist

15. The usage by Tweeten and Zulauf and also by Coleman, Skogstad, and Atkinson of the word *paradigm* is potentially confusing: most natural scientists prefer to use the word more narrowly—to identify new and purely descriptive understandings of unchanging natural realities—rather than broadly to describe a set of ideas, both descriptive and prescriptive, regarding constantly changing social conditions, institutions, and phenomena. See Kuhn 1962 for the etymology of *paradigm* in science.

16. Coleman, Skogstad, and Atkinson argue that their paradigm shift in agriculture was accomplished in 1995–96 through negotiations between state actors and group representatives, rather than through society-wide contestation.

farm groups were mobilized against high debts and low crop prices) than there was during the 1995–96 farm bill debate.

The capture of control of both houses of Congress by the Republican Party, after four decades in the minority, seemed at the time to signal a broad shift toward the idea of smaller government and the culmination of a steady erosion of support for New Deal interventionist approaches. But the Republicans learned the limits to their mandate for change, in their unsuccessful 1995–96 battles with the president over the budget and over entitlement program cutbacks.

If the 1995 Republican mandate had been somewhat stronger, and if a corresponding third-order change had taken place in U.S. farm policy, we can imagine what it might have looked like by recalling the policy ledger briefly touted by Roberts early in 1995. This ledger surfaced at a time when ideas of budget discipline and free market fundamentalism did seem to reign, just after the Republican election victory. The policy ledger, which the Agriculture Committee chair offered as common ground on which both Republican agriculturalists and the new House leadership could stand, promised to lower federal support expenditures and reduce market interventions. Beyond this, farmers were to benefit from elimination of ARPs and greater planting flexibility, from deficit reductions and lower taxes that the Republican Party would champion, from specific tax breaks, from lessening of burdensome regulations, and from strengthening of private property rights. If the market-oriented, small government Republican "revolution" (as the leaders themselves called it) had not been so easily turned back (by Roberts and his supporters for agriculture, among others), this ledger might have emerged as the essential outline of a new American farm policy: a loss of traditional producer supports, compensated by tax breaks and deregulation. This would have been a sharp break from the fundamental assumptions of the New Deal regarding both the role of government and the vulnerability of the farm sector to market forces. Farmers would no longer be protected from the dangers of the market by a benevolent government; they would be protected not from the market but from the regulators and tax collectors of the government itself, and they would be protected not as farmers but as citizens with property rights. The farm bill that passed in 1996 incorporated no such bold reformulation of basic assumptions.[17]

17. When the 105th Congress convened in 1997, short-term budget deficit projections fell mainly due to unexpected tax revenue from a continued robust economy. This allowed the Republican Congress and Democratic president to reach a deal on budget leg-

Outside of the agriculturalists in the Republican Party, the tone of the congressional debate over the 1996 FAIR Act also indicates that old ideas were alive and well. Most Democrats who voted for the FAIR Act did not like decoupling on principle, and many did not vote for the act because it incorporated this objectionable idea. Senator Wendell H. Ford of Kentucky, the minority whip, predicted a "taxpayer revolt" once it became clear that farmers would be paid money whether they planted a crop or not. Senator Tom Daschle, the minority leader, echoed Ford's view, arguing that "it won't take long for journalists to see farmers getting $300,000 for doing nothing" (*Congressional Record* 1996, S868). And Democrat Kent Conrad heaped abuse on the idea of moving toward decoupled payments. On the floor of the Senate, he likened the decoupled payments that the FAIR Act would provide in 1996 and 1997 to the poison-spiked Kool-Aid served by Jim Jones to his deluded followers at their mass suicide in Guyana: "It tastes good on the way down, but when you drink it you're dead" (S728).[18]

Nor was it only the populist wing of the Democratic Party in the Senate that continued to reject decoupled payments. Secretary of Agriculture Glickman remained a champion for traditional policy instruments; he derided the decoupled payments approach both as a dangerous shredding of the traditional safety net, and as a move toward a form of welfare. President Clinton was a steady advocate of the status quo. Throughout the farm bill debate, the president stressed that U.S. agriculture was on an "even footing" and needed no major policy changes. When he finally signed the FAIR Act, he hedged his endorsement with a promise to introduce legislation the following year to recouple some farm programs and payments to the market, to ensure that farmers once

---

islation that cut some tax rates and raised spending for some social programs—the deal that had eluded congressional leaders in 1995–96. The 1997 budget deal reflected a windfall capture opportunity on a grand scale not unlike the one that rising market prices had made possible in agriculture the previous year: because of increased revenue projections, Congress could claim to be passing legislation to balance the budget while simultaneously changing tax and spending policies in ways that slowed the speed at which that balance would be reached. In the 1997 budget legislation, Republicans were able to deliver some of the reduced estate, capital gains, and health insurance taxes promised in Roberts's 1995 policy ledger. The Republicans remained less successful on their stated objective of providing wide-ranging regulatory relief to farmers.

18. Populist Democrats from the Northern Plains states continued to have good political reasons to resist consolidation of any new ideas that would eventually take farm payments away from their constituents. In the northern plains, farm payments make up a significant share of net farm income, and the idea of unfettered market competition still has limited appeal.

again had a strong safety net. The policy debate in 1995–96 thus reflected a shift in party control and in market conditions much more than an emergence of newly dominant ideas about policy.

The Reform Problem after the 1996 FAIR Act

It required both the Republican recapture of Congress and unexpected high market prices to produce the surprising FAIR Act policy reforms of 1996. The combination of reforms that were passed (ending ARPs and embracing decoupling) and those that failed (retaining export subsidies and market interventions for import-competing crops) reflect the orientation of the new Republican majority and the opportunity created by favorable market conditions, but not a more fundamental shift in dominant policy ideas. Farm lobby groups retained control of the legislative process, offsetting a demographic loss with the usual investments in organization, attention to process, and financial campaign contributions. Federal budget pressure and commitments made by the United States in the Uruguay Round and other international negotiations offered little constraint on domestic policy.

Our earlier review of policy reform efforts in the 1970s and 1980s reinforces the conclusion that the combination of a change in party control of Congress and rising prices was key to determining the farm bill legislative outcome in 1995–96. The early 1970s were also marked by high prices, but market-oriented reforms were frustrated, in part due to continued Democratic control of Congress. Republicans controlled the executive branch of government during these years, and a Republican secretary of agriculture hailed high prices as an opportunity to shed government constraints and plant "fence row to fence row." It would have been relatively painless due to high prices to implement a full cutout of farm program supports in the 1970s, but Democratic control in Congress ensured a different outcome. The Democratic Congress opted to stick with traditional support policies, partly because of the unprecedented rates of inflation at the time. They used the high farm price interlude not to reduce government involvement in agriculture, but to lock in a safety net of target prices and loan rates that ultimately increased budget exposure and required intrusive supply controls when commodity prices subsequently fell.

The farm policy experience of the 1980s is also consistent with the conclusion we have drawn about the importance of party control and market prices. Republicans controlled the executive branch of government in the 1980s, and for a time the Senate as well. The administration pushed for bold policy reforms in 1985, and Senators Boschwitz and Boren introduced their radical scheme to end supply controls and switch to decoupled payments. These reform attempts were blocked in 1985 partly because Democrats still controlled the House, and partly because prices were low (and falling) as the debate proceeded. Falling commodity prices had likewise blocked durable market-oriented reforms much earlier, when a tentative move toward flexible price supports in 1953–54 by the 83rd Congress (Republican by a scant margin), was followed by a reversion to supply controls after Democrats recaptured control of Congress.

Not until forty years later, in 1995–96, was another farm bill written under a Republican House and Senate, this time with the help of the highest prices in two decades. It did not seem to matter, on this occasion, that the executive branch was under Democratic control, and that the president opposed the Freedom to Farm Act. A stand-pat Democratic president could not block a congressional embrace of change in 1995–96, any more than the reform-minded Republican presidents of the 1970s and 1980s could produce policy changes in their day over the objections of a Democratic Congress. Since the original AAA of 1933, in fact, change in U.S. agricultural policy has yet to be determined by the executive rather than the legislative branch of government.

Republican control of Congress without high prices in 1995–96 would have led to a result quite different from the FAIR Act. With Republican control but low prices, the choice, in all likelihood, would have been a cautious budget-cutting version of existing programs (something like the bill that passed the Senate late in 1995). Some Republicans might have championed a wider-ranging agenda for legislative change (along the lines of Roberts's policy ledger), but would have found their mandate limited. Even eliminating ARP supply-control authority would have been much harder for the Republicans had prices been low. Only high prices and a budget baseline capture opportunity enabled the new majority party to deliver more flexibility to their farm sector constituents, simultaneously with more subsidies, through decoupling. This deepened the slow cash out that had long been underway but did not put farm policy on a new strategic path of either a squeeze out, a buyout, or a cutout.

Chapter Six

The Uncertain Future of Farm Policy

IN THE PREVIOUS CHAPTER we concluded that without a combination of unforeseen circumstances, including the first full switch in party control in four decades and the highest commodity prices in two decades, Congress would not have embraced the most significant farm policy reforms contained in the 1996 FAIR Act. In this chapter, we examine the resilience of the FAIR Act during a subsequent period when farm prices fell sharply. We also look ahead to the farm bill Congress will have to write by 2002, when the FAIR Act expires. Will its key reforms—planting flexibility, termination of annual ARP authority, capping of loan rates at nonintrusive levels, and decoupling of support payments for export crops—be continued? Will these reforms be improved upon and extended to other commodities? Or will the reform gains won at substantial budget cost in 1996 be reversed in the next farm bill?

The 1996 FAIR Act fully decoupled the partial cash out previously undertaken for export crops, but it did not fully reform farm policy or even put policy on a new strategic path toward such full reform. The cash-out component of the FAIR Act was incomplete, because protection of import-competing commodities was still provided through market restrictions—not direct payments. Nor did the FAIR Act provide a cutout, or a squeeze out, even for export crops, because cash payments were enlarged and perpetuated, and because participation by farmers increased. With permanent legislation and a budget baseline still in place, the FAIR Act was not a convincing buyout for export crops either; whether it will function as the first step of a buyout will not be known at least until the next farm bill is written.

Approaching 2002 and beyond, will any new policy reform paths be followed? Judging from the experiences of the past, the outcome will depend upon the combination of a number of policy-driving factors, including short-term as well as long-term factors, both within and outside the farm sector. One entirely new consideration will be the operation and performance of the FAIR Act itself. If policy-driving factors align in the right fashion, U.S. farm programs could be moved much further along a reform path—perhaps all the way to a comprehensive elimination of both market interventions and direct support payments. The generous cash outlays made under the FAIR Act then might be credited as the early part of an effective buyout of farm subsidies. But should the most important policy-driving factors combine in an adverse way, further reform progress could become impossible. Some of the more innovative features of the 1996 FAIR Act could be discredited and reversed. Falling farm prices in 1998 were enough to severely challenge the reform gains from the FAIR Act. Republicans still controlled Congress, and most of these gains were retained, but large unanticipated increases in farm program spending amounted to de facto abandonment of the decoupling of support payment levels from market prices.

The payment adjustments made in 1998 and the wide range of possible policy outcomes in the years ahead demonstrate that the FAIR Act debate was just one more episode in a continuing political struggle over agricultural policy reform. Politics in the United States tends to favor incremental change; significant policy shifts are seldom made all at once, or once and for all. Reform advocates who hope to consolidate and extend the market-liberalizing gains or budget certainty sought by the FAIR Act in 1996 will face a formidable challenge when the next farm bill is written. Within agriculture, reformers will need to consolidate their support among producers of export crops and agribusiness processors and suppliers, broaden their support among other beneficiaries of open markets (such as producers of poultry and livestock who gain from abundant feed inputs), and weaken or isolate those seeking reintervention or continuation of unreformed programs. Reform advocates will also require help, not hindrance, from larger sources of change in the policy environment—sources that are not under their control but will mostly determine the direction of farm policy. The environment for reform was much less favorable by the end of 1998 than it had been when the FAIR Act was endorsed, and the future of farm policy remains uncertain.

Determinants of Future Farm Policy

In assessing the prospects for further farm policy reform, it is unrealistic to attempt a single prediction of future outcomes. More useful is a structured framework of alternative contingencies under which future farm policies might be made, assessing the influence of the most important factors driving policy under each contingency.

Our historical review identifies at least six somewhat independent policy-driving factors that are likely to shape the outcome when Con-

gress writes the next farm bill. First is the continuing structural transformation of U.S. agriculture. This source of change comes from long-
term developments in agricultural technology, the evolution of the
nonfarm economy in which agriculture competes for resources, demographic shifts, and evolving institutional arrangements. These tend to
be slow and incremental transformations, but they must be considered
even when examining near-term policy outcomes.

A second factor of proven significance to U.S. farm policy is the condition and structure of international markets. The growth of export
markets for U.S. farm products has tended to sustain liberalizing policy
reforms in the past, just as the loss of such markets has tended to encourage illiberal domestic market interventions. Market conditions can
change quickly, and our historical analysis confirms the substantial impact of such changes on the policy process. International market structures evolve more slowly, but our analysis also establishes a link
between this evolution and farm policy reform.

A third demonstrated influence upon farm policy is party control in
Congress. Our analysis shows party control was important to the original AAA of 1933, to various farm policy battles fought subsequently,
and to the 1996 FAIR Act. The future of farm policy reform remains uncertain as long as there is uncertainty about which political party controls Congress.

Federal budget pressure is a fourth factor of significance for farm policy reform. Budget constraints can prove illusory, and budget rules can
be exploited in unexpected ways, but federal budget considerations are
likely to influence the outcome of the next farm bill.

A fifth determinant in future farm policy reform is the political feedback generated by earlier policy change. Since the New Deal, farm
programs have tended to strengthen the process establishment of governmental institutions and advocacy groups that benefit from legislated interventions. The FAIR Act stands some chance of breaking this
pattern, by generating a new kind of political feedback that will weaken
rather than strengthen the reform-blocking influence of the process establishment in U.S. agriculture.

There is also some possibility that future change in policy will be driven forward by a sixth factor: the dominance of new policy ideas. The
FAIR Act did not represent a clear victory for ideas favoring market orientation and a smaller government role in farm policy. Yet looking to the
future, circumstances can be imagined in which such ideas strengthen

their hold on policy makers or conversely in which such ideas lose credibility.

The Structural Transformation of Agriculture

The remarkable structural transformation that agriculture in the United States has undergone since the Second World War has dramatically altered what constitutes good farm policy. The structural transformation of American agriculture can be expected to continue in the future, led in part by productivity gains arising from new applications of biotechnology and information management. The United States has recently emerged as the world leader in the area of transgenic crops, accounting in 1997 for nearly two-thirds of world production. The area planted to genetically modified crops—led by soybeans and cotton—had risen to 34 million acres (from essentially none in the early 1990s), and was projected to rise to as much as 150 million acres by 2000. Farmers planting new transgenic soybeans could limit herbicide treatments to a single application, cutting chemical input costs by 10 to 40 percent and lessening environmental degradation. Acquisitions, mergers, and alliances designed to facilitate development and marketing of new bioengineered products swept through the input-supply, processing, and marketing sectors that served production agriculture in the 1990s.[1] Likewise, the information revolution that occurred throughout the economy brought to agriculture precision applications of fertilizers and other purchased inputs, and innovations in farm management and production practices. Complementing these new technologies and institutional changes, off-farm employment opportunities created by the strong U.S. economy increased the returns to labor and capital resources for which the agricultural sector had to compete. This robust economic growth added further to the agricultural modernization process, continuing and potentially accelerating the structural change we have described as long underway.[2]

1. Typifying the biotechnology-induced restructuring of the mid-1990s were purchases by the agricultural chemical company Monsanto of numerous small research firms and a merger of DuPont and the seed company Pioneer. Such acquisitions and mergers were designed to allow integrated firms to capture the property rights to biotechnological innovations and exploit synergies across stages of the production process—from basic research through final product marketing.

2. In a recent reevaluation of productivity growth rates in agriculture, Ball, Bureau, Nehring, and Somwaru (1997) estimate that total factor productivity growth rates increased in the periods 1979–89 and 1989–94 compared to earlier years.

Continued structural change augers well for reform of farm policy in the long run. The highly competitive farmers that emerge from the transformation process will increasingly prefer to use modern market instruments rather than government interventions to manage risks.[3] For this group of farmers, the opportunity to make flexible planting decisions in response to market forces has become a more important source of income growth than the projected rents from government commodity programs. This increasingly powerful farm constituency, and the agribusiness firms that serve it, will become a growing voice in support of planting flexibility. In the long run, these commercial farmers will favor the additional freedom to farm built into the design of policy by the FAIR Act. But in the short term, even for this group, slow structural change may matter less than potentially rapid changes in world market conditions, or the operation of the new law itself. The differential pressure of structural change on the policy outcome in the next farm bill is likely to be small compared to the pressure already felt at the time of the 1996 FAIR Act.

In spite of continuing structural transformations, some segments of the U.S. farm sector may not grow more comfortable with market liberalization in the years ahead. On the Northern Plains, for example, where alternatives to growing wheat are fewer than in many other parts of the country, farmers remain particularly sensitive to drought and single-crop disease and price shocks. The value of farm assets, and even the survival of some small towns, remains dependent upon continued federal support, either in the form of FAIR Act decoupled payments; subsidized crop, revenue, or income insurance; or perhaps a return to more traditional policy instruments. Similarly, the policies that have been used to support sugar and peanut producers have artificially held land and labor in the production of these crops. Investments continue to be made in production capacity, and those who make these new investments can be expected in future years to defend the programs that keep their investments profitable.

In other cases, it may be the very speed of agriculture's structural transformation that perpetuates demands for government programs from some producers. The application of modern biotechnology to dairy production—specifically the introduction in the 1990s of an output-enhancing growth hormone known as BST—raised calls for protec-

---

3. Among these instruments are forward contracting and hedging, futures markets, yield futures and options, and hybrid cash contracts.

tion from some high-cost dairy producers both regionally (among states) and nationally. Where the identity of small rural communities continues to revolve around relatively high-cost operations, the adjustments implied by the biotechnology revolution could increase—rather than diminish—the importance of government support and safety net programs to politically organized farm groups.

Some of the most immediate effects of structural transformation are occurring in parts of the U.S. farm sector that are not directly dependent on government programs. One type of change comes not from new technology but from new institutional arrangements, including the growing use of production and marketing contracts. The contractor typically owns the commodity being produced and supplies most of the inputs, while farmers receive payments for the production services they provide. Use of these new contracting practices has grown most rapidly in such areas as poultry, eggs, hogs, and some specialty crops, but similar practices are also showing up in export crop production, where price premiums are paid for specialized corn and soybeans with specific quality traits. These new types of contracts weaken the link between market prices of homogeneous bulk commodities and farm income. If the use of these contracting practices were to spread more widely among crop producers, farmer attachment to intrusive commodity support policies might diminish. So far, however, the impact of new contracting arrangements on political advocacy, either for or against the traditional crop programs, has been small.

One reason the new contracting practices have had little effect on farm policy is that even with these innovations, and despite much talk about the rapid industrialization of agriculture, nonfamily corporations continue to constitute only a small share of the total farm sector. Input supply industries and processing industries are increasingly integrated and concentrated, but producer interests continue to drive the farm policy process, and most production, especially of the traditionally supported crops, continues to take place on family-owned farms.[4]

Even the most competitive commercial farmers are not above seek-

4. Sole proprietorships constituted 86 percent of all U.S. farms in 1992, and still generated 54 percent of all farm sales. Nonfamily corporations accounted for only 0.4 percent of farms, and 6 percent of farm product sales (USDA 1996). Large farm units have for some time dominated certain areas of production, particularly beef cattle feedlots, poultry, and commercial vegetable production. Again, these tend to be areas in which direct intervention has been minimal.

ing support through government programs. Export-oriented wheat farmers may not like ARPs, but many still favor the EEP. Commercial corn farmers also oppose ARPs and want more planting flexibility, but they still lobby for ethanol subsidies and support the restrictions on sugar imports that increase demand for corn-based sweeteners. Expensive acreage diversion programs like the CRP remain popular among large landowners, in part because the rental rates offered are often higher than the prevailing local market rates. Owners of large as well as small farms receiving cash payments under the FAIR Act will probably want payments of some kind to continue after 2002, if only to protect their asset values.

For all of these reasons, the continuing structural transformation of agriculture is unlikely to provide a decisive impetus for further farm policy reform in the near term. Other policy-driving factors will have a greater impact on the policy outcomes that emerge when the FAIR Act expires.

The Dynamics of International Markets

The condition and structure of markets are important factors in determining future farm policy—especially international markets for export crops for which domestic farm programs have been cashed out, along with some high-value commodities (such as livestock products) that utilize these crops as inputs. The reform gains secured in the FAIR Act are only likely to be continued and extended to other commodities if market conditions are strong and if international market structures become more open. Conversely, the climate for continued liberalizing reform will sour if world market conditions deteriorate or if market barriers proliferate. It was a loss of access to markets abroad (after the First World War and especially during the Great Depression) that originally pushed the U.S. government to intervene in domestic agriculture. And it was only with the gradual regaining of access to growing foreign markets in the 1960s and 1970s (for a time in Russia, but also in Japan and then in other high-growth countries across the Pacific) that U.S. policy for export crops was propelled along the path of a cash out. If international markets provide a strong source of demand growth for farm products in the years ahead, the prospects for consolidating the cash-out reforms for export crops—and perhaps for moving next to a reduction in cash payments—could remain strong as well.

At the time the FAIR Act was passed in 1996, buoyant agricultural forecasts suggested that a number of powerful events would continue to generate relatively high crop prices into the near-term future. Reduced worldwide levels of grain stocks; a tapering off of global yield trends; an increase in world population; and income growth in China, India, and other populous developing countries were all cited as pointing toward continued high prices. The USDA and other forecasters projected much stronger price trends in 1997 and early in 1998 than they had at the outset of the farm bill debate in February 1995. Some policy analysts predicted that a new era of relatively strong commodity prices was likely to continue for several decades (Tweeten 1998). But projections for strong farm prices based on the short-term market boom in 1995–96 soon proved erroneous.

Export crop prices fell sharply from their spring peak by late 1996, and they moved persistently downward again in the spring and summer of 1998, as shown in figure 11. Prices were driven down by a recovery of U.S. production from low 1996 levels, by worldwide supply responses induced by the high prices of the previous years, by appreciation of the U.S. dollar (of nearly 25 percent) between 1995 and 1998, and by slowed growth and recession in Asia. With prices *falling* from strong forecast levels in 1997–98, the traditional deficiency payment

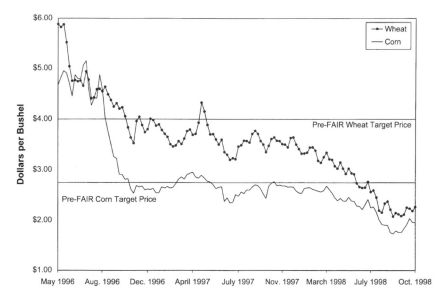

Figure 11.   Falling Prices for Wheat and Corn, May 1996–October 1998
Source: Wall Street Journal, various issues.

programs—not decoupling—would have provided the opportunity to attain larger outlays for farmers. Had deficiency payments still been in effect, falling prices also would have undermined arguments to abandon annual supply-control authority. The most important reforms in the FAIR Act simply would not have been legislated had the farm bill debate taken place in 1997–98 instead of 1995–96.

Whether international demand and market price levels will recover and become relatively strong again by the time the FAIR Act expires in 2002 is subject to uncertainty. Price levels were projected to recover modestly from low 1998 levels in subsequent years, but a variety of developments could cause prices to remain weakened. One such development would be consecutive years of weather favorable for extensive acreage plantings and high yields, either domestically or in temperate zone regions of competitor countries beyond the United States. Moreover, long-term estimates for growth of per-capita world food supply at constant real prices remained in the range of 1.7 to 2.6 percent annually, while estimates of growth in per-capita food demand ranged from 1.6 to 1.9 percent. These estimates suggest continuation of the downward real price trend of the period since the Second World War.

The most threatening short-term market scenario would be a sustained adverse shift in macroeconomic conditions—as occurred in the 1930s when farm commodity prices were driven downward by world depression, and again in the 1980s when deflationary policies and high interest rates brought a collapse of farm exports and prices. The possibility of such a sustained macroeconomic downturn had emerged in the late 1990s, from the largely unpredicted financial crisis that spread quickly across the developing countries of East Asia—including Thailand, Malaysia, Indonesia, and South Korea—then later to Russia and Brazil. Sales of farm products to these countries suffered (falling by one-third in value from 1996 to 1998), as sharp currency devaluations made imports from the United States more costly, and as their national incomes fell. The Japanese economy, which had stagnated even prior to the 1997–98 regional crisis, remained weak and threatened to drag down income growth even more widely in the Asian region, perhaps causing currency values there to depreciate further against the U.S. dollar. Such an outcome would continue to damage export markets for U.S. farm commodities, and would weaken congressional support for extending the market-oriented FAIR Act approach.

A threat to strong international markets might also come from a fal-

tering of policy reform progress in the European Union. If EU membership grows to include central and east European countries such as
Poland, Hungary, the Czech Republic, and Slovakia, and these countries respond to the strong production incentives (and consumption
disincentives) still contained in the CAP, burdensome new farm surpluses could be the result. If the European Union were then tempted to
resume aggressive direct export subsidization by exploiting the loophole it claims in the Uruguay Round agreement (to accumulate unused
subsidy allowances from early years for later use), world market prices
for cereals, dairy products, and sugar might drop more sharply,
prompting a reassessment in the United States of the market-oriented
FAIR Act. Further reform of the CAP along the lines of the 1997 European Commission Agenda 2000 proposal—which advocated both lower
intervention prices and a switch to decoupled compensation payments
in the cereals and oilseeds sectors—prior to enlargement could avoid
this outcome. If the European Union completed such a reform, it could
then afford to adopt a more forthcoming posture in the WTO negotiations on agriculture beginning in 1999, and momentum for a negotiated
liberalization worldwide might ensue.[5] If the EU enlargement issue
paralyzes the next WTO round of agricultural negotiations, however, or
if regional trade initiatives(planned through extension of NAFTA into
the broader Free Trade Area of the Americas [FTAA] or through trade
venues such as the Asian Pacific Economic Cooperation [APEC] forum)
lose momentum, any optimism about export market outlets for U.S.
farm products could fade—again dampening enthusiasm for extending the FAIR Act approach to farm policy.

Party Control of Congress

Our historical analysis shows that changes in party control, particularly in Congress, often produce changes in farm policy direction. Shifts
in party control help explain enactment of the original AAA in 1933, the
vacillation over reduced price-support levels versus reliance on supply
controls during 1946–54, and decoupling and other reform features of
the FAIR Act in 1996. The importance of party-based farm policy differ-

5. See Coleman and Tangermann 1997; and Josling 1998. Even with the Agenda 2000
reforms, modernization of agricultural production in central and eastern Europe could
subject U.S agriculture to increased competitive pressure in world markets and amplify
calls for domestic support.

ences was evident once again when market prices fell in 1998. During the summer, congressional Democrats called for a virtual rewriting of the 1996 FAIR Act to "restore the safety net," particularly through higher loan rates and off-budget emergency assistance to farmers facing crop or income losses. Republicans argued for "staying the course" with the FAIR Act, and offered help in the form of measures to boost foreign demand for U.S. farm products, plus tax relief targeted toward farmers.

As prices continued to drop through the autumn of 1998, an election year bidding war ensued between Democratic and Republican agriculturalists over the granting of new benefits to farmers, and in this process the budget discipline features of the FAIR Act were ignored. Congressional Democrats again failed to win endorsement for higher loan rates from the Clinton administration, but the president supported emergency crop disaster relief expenditures of $500 million (not subject to pay-as-you-go budget rules and circumventing the 1994 crop insurance reform law). The president also instructed his secretary of agriculture to use existing CCC authority to buy $250 million of wheat for food aid donations. Republicans countered with calls for even higher emergency disaster relief and an acceleration of scheduled tax breaks. Bipartisan support arose for various indirect aids to farmers: augmentation of export credit guarantees, exemption of farm products from economic embargoes imposed after India and Pakistan carried out underground nuclear weapon testing, and an allowance permitting farmers to receive one-half of their scheduled 1999 decoupled PFC payments in advance.

With prices still low, the bidding over more generous farm programs heightened by September 1998. Senate Minority Leader Daschle continued to press for higher loan rates—despite being rebuffed by Senate floor votes. Removing the FAIR Act loan rate caps would have raised the price-support levels (per bushel) from $1.89 to $2.19 for corn, and from $2.58 to $3.18 for wheat, at a cost of between $4 and 8 billion for one year, depending on whether market prices settled at the high or low end of a range of projected values. Republicans in their own way sought to be equally generous; they unveiled an alternative plan for special decoupled "market loss payments" to supplement the income support provided under the FAIR Act. Yet when they sent the president an agricultural appropriations bill authorizing $3.9 billion in disaster relief and new decoupled payments, he vetoed it as not generous enough. Only when the new aid was pushed up to nearly $7 billion were the Democrats willing to abandon their effort to raise loan rates and agree to the farm spending package.[6]

Thus with low prices in 1998 Congress and the administration delivered unbudgeted new support to farmers in numerous ways, enough to keep net cash farm income near its 1996 level, despite low prices.[7] With Republicans still holding a twenty-two-seat majority in the House of Representatives and control of the Senate, the basic structural components of the FAIR Act reforms were mostly maintained: planting flexibility continued, annual supply controls were not reimposed, the loan rate caps held, and cash payments remained decoupled from planting decisions and nominally from market prices. But the budget discipline once touted by Republicans as a virtue of the fixed payments adopted under the FAIR Act failed its first serious test with the deal brokered in 1998, and the increased payments in compensation for lower prices were a de facto abandonment of full decoupling.

With congressional Democrats having drawn the battle lines for renewed farm-sector interventions by their attacks on the FAIR Act in 1998, future legislative prospects for farm policy reform will depend in important ways on whether or not the Republicans continue to maintain a majority in Congress.[8] If the Democrats were to regain control of Congress in 2000 or beyond, the new leadership would feel an obligation to act on its persistent criticisms and restore some form of a more traditional safety net for export crop producers. Particularly in 2000–2002, if market prices are low at the same time that decoupled payments are scheduled to decline, a Democratic majority in Congress could be tempted to formally reverse some FAIR Act reforms. Under these circumstances, Northern Plains Democrats almost surely would seek authority to raise loan rates, and perhaps also to recouple income support payments to market conditions, or even to revive short-term supply controls—if not through ARPs then perhaps through new CRP options, or a voluntary paid land diversion. Antipoverty Democrats, under these circumstances, might also make appropriations for a more

6. The 1998 farm spending package included $3.1 billion in direct payments, $2.4 billion to compensate farmers for crop disaster losses, and $1 billion in accelerated tax relief. Marketing loan payments estimated at over $2 billion were also incurred, as even the capped loan rates became intrusive.

7. Net cash income was $56.6 billion in 1996, peaked at a record $60.8 billion in 1997, and was projected to be $56.4 billion in 1998.

8. Following the 1998 election the Republican margin in the Senate was unchanged (55 Republicans, 45 Democrats), but the Republican majority in the House decreased by five seats (223 Republicans, 210 Democrats, 1 independent).

substantial Fund for Rural America, and environmentalist Democrats would be tempted to promote payments or services to farmers as compensation for mandated management activities. They might advocate an enlarged CRP, or an expensive new "green payment" income support scheme nominally tied to farmers' adoption of conservation practices.

Conversely, if the Republican Party retains control of Congress, and if a Republican captures the presidency as well in 2000, the prospects for consolidation and extension of the FAIR Act become more favorable. Under Republican majorities in the future, farm support policies are more likely to take the form of tax breaks or protection from government regulations, rather than intrusive commodity programs, at least for export crops. Republicans have an underlying policy aversion to supply controls for these crops, a viewpoint unlikely to change so long as they receive political backing from large-scale farmers and agribusiness interests. This preference was an important factor in the elimination of annual ARP authority under the FAIR Act, and will continue to find expression, barring a prolonged period of very low prices, if Republicans remain in the majority in Congress.

Because Republicans can easily be identified as the original authors of the FAIR Act, they have a partisan reason to argue that the freedom to farm experiment is worth building upon when the next farm bill is written. Republican retention of control in Congress could also help sustain the FAIR Act through a simple incumbency effect. Continued Republican control would result in policy stability, entirely apart from party-based policy preferences or party-linked policy authorship. So long as Republicans constitute a majority in Congress, staff changes might be kept to a minimum. The resistance of policy to change that was once associated with forty years of Democratic control could emerge anew under an era of continuous (and increasingly cautious) Republican control. For export crops at least, this would favor extension of the market-oriented FAIR Act approach.

Republican control of Congress is less likely, by itself, to lead to reform for the import-competing commodities that remained protected under the FAIR Act. The strong Republican Party base in the South tends to make incumbent southern Republicans, as much as Democrats once were, the natural defenders of existing programs for sugar, peanuts, and tobacco. Republicans have also shown themselves comfortable with paid long-term land diversions in place of unpaid annual acreage restrictions: Ezra Taft Benson argued in favor of these policies as early as the 1950s, and Pat Roberts repeated the argument during the

FAIR Act debate, stating that continuation of the CRP made ARPs unnecessary.

Republicans seem amenable as well to extending a new safety net to farmers through federally subsidized insurance programs. Two new insurance programs combining price and yield risk protection (the Income Protection [IP] program and the Crop Revenue Coverage [CRC] program) were made available under the FAIR Act starting in 1996. As with traditional federal crop insurance, the USDA intervenes to subsidize and reinsure these new farm revenue and income insurance policies. Federal subsidies and costs associated with various farm-sector insurance programs approached $2.0 billion by 1997, and the newest programs create new kinds of budget exposure, even without unscheduled disaster relief payments, as authorized in 1998. Yet most Republican agriculturalists defend these interventions, arguing that they were needed by farmers facing competitive markets.[9]

If the next farm bill is written on schedule in 2002, it will be during an election year within a new president's first term in office. Were the presidency and Congress controlled by the same party, it would mark the first time since the Carter administration that a farm bill came up for renewal under a unified rather than a divided government. Perhaps a unified government would increase accountability in the policy-making process, and thus reduce the risk of revived farm program spending, but the 1977 farm bill and the election year "emergency" revisions in 1978 are not reassuring precedents. Whether the unified government is Republican or Democratic, in the end the elected members of Congress, and especially the party leaders and Agriculture Committee chairs in the House and Senate, will design the next farm bill and then broker the majorities needed to ensure its passage.

Federal Budget Constraints

Federal budget constraints, plus the pay-as-you-go congressional budget rules that grew out of those constraints, can exert a powerful influence on both the shape and generosity of farm programs. This was certainly the case in 1990, when farm program reauthorization was embedded into a larger budget reconciliation process. It was also the case

9. The new Republican House Agriculture Committee chair following the 1998 election, Larry Combest of Texas, had blocked Roberts's early attempt to pass the Freedom to Farm bill in September 1995. Combest signaled his own views in 1998 by saying, "I just don't see how we can get out of agriculture when it's so important" (Kilman 1998).

in 1995–96, when budget rules created the lucrative baseline capture option, and helped inspire the shift to decoupled payments once market prices started to rise.

The federal budget baseline of anticipated expenditures remaining available for various farm programs is projected around $8.0 billion annually when the FAIR Act expires. Decoupled payments to farmers decline from $6.0 billion in 1997 to $4.0 billion by 2002, then are assumed by the CBO to continue indefinitely at that level. These anticipated decoupled payments will be one source of funds available to the Agriculture Committees when a new farm bill is written. Expenditures for CRP acreage retirements and environmental cost-sharing programs are projected to add about $2.0 billion more in direct payments to farmers. Authorized export subsidies remained around $0.5 billion per year in 2002 under the FAIR Act, and crop, revenue, and income insurance costs and subsidies are projected to be around $1.5 billion per year.

Altogether, anticipated federal support payments directly to farmers are projected to be about 15 percent of net farm income at the end of the FAIR Act in 2002 (USDA 1998). By post–New Deal standards, this is actually a relatively low percentage, but it is not unprecedented: federal support payments earlier declined to less than 20 percent of net farm income from 1973 to 1982 (see table 9). During that earlier period, it was strong market prices—not a limit on federal farm program budget authority—that rendered the proportion of income derived from government payments temporarily low. By 2002, in the absence of supplementary payments, the shrunken CBO baseline for farm program spending could itself constrain farm policy legislative options.

For the export crops for which farm supports were cashed out, a low budget ceiling when the FAIR Act expires could impose more budget discipline than the CBO baseline in 1995–96. Were there pressure for further budget cuts the projected payments available to farmers could shrink to such a low level as to make unattractive the conditions (such as conservation compliance) still required for receiving those payments. Farmers might then cease program participation voluntarily—along the lines of a squeeze out. Anticipating this outcome, the House and Senate Agriculture Committees might at last decide to switch from expensive income support payments (decoupled or otherwise) to something else, perhaps a comprehensive farm income insurance approach. This would bring to an end the direct subsidization of farmers through cashed-out commodity support programs. While some new and untested intervention instruments might supplant direct payments, the long-running cash out of New Deal–era support policies that began in the 1960s would finally be followed by a decisive budget-driven squeeze out.

Tight budget caps will not generate similar reform pressures for import-competing commodities when the FAIR Act expires. The sugar, peanut, and tobacco programs operate at virtually zero cost to taxpayers, and could conceivably remain unthreatened even under federal budget constraints. Likewise, the import restrictions on dairy products, and the new regional dairy pricing regulations mandated by the FAIR Act, are immune to direct budget pressure. Yet budget constraints could threaten the import-competing commodity programs indirectly. With a small and shrinking farm-budget pie to divide, the competing regional and commodity interests that have traditionally joined to promote Agriculture Committee legislation could at last fragment, making farm program renewal on the floor of Congress more difficult. If budget limits were to finally terminate farm programs for export crops, the traditional vote-trading relationships within agriculture might break down, blocking the formation of a coalition strong enough to reauthorize even budget-neutral programs for import-competing commodities.

Spending limits might not only rule out some interventionist policy choices—they conceivably could rule out some market liberalizing options as well. Buyouts, in particular, require high short-run outlays. If Congress wanted to make a final one-time buyout of the FAIR Act decoupled cash payments, budget constraints could be an impediment. Payments of $4 billion per year in perpetuity have a real present value of $57 billion at an interest rate of 7 percent (more at lower interest rates and less at higher interest rates). In the political arena, farm program beneficiaries might view some such present-value calculation as a lower bound on a one-time buyout payment. Reform advocates, if they offered a buyout, would almost certainly argue for spending less. A buyout compromise might be reached only if farm groups perceived themselves as too weak to marshal the political resources necessary to sustain annual payments over the long run, yet strong enough to obtain a lucrative once-only payment in the short run.

Any move by Congress to liberalize markets for import-competing commodities through a cash-out or buyout strategy could also be precluded by budget constraints. One such reform proposal emerged in 1997–98, when public health advocates and the tobacco industry reached a tentative agreement in their long battle over smoking and industry liability for treatment of related diseases and disabilities.

The proposed settlement traded limitations on future liability claims against the tobacco companies for restrictions on tobacco advertising, targets for reduced teenage use of tobacco, and more than $500 billion in industry reimbursement payments for tobacco-related state and federal medical expenditures over twenty-five years. Public health advocates and the industry agreed that the burden of reducing tobacco use should not be borne by tobacco farmers. Had legislation for this settlement gone forward, direct payments would have been made to farmers as compensation for losses due to reduced domestic cigarette consumption, in something of an industry-financed partial buyout.[10] Senator Lugar made a more sweeping buyout proposal to end the entire tobacco production quota system once and for all.[11] The industry payments in the proposed settlement could have funded such buyout measures, but in the end Congress failed to enact such sweeping tobacco legislation.

Several avenues of escape from budget ceilings might emerge by 2002, making room for increased federal spending—either intervention programs or cash-out or buyout payments. A simple budget waiver is one path that might allow higher spending; all that is required is for Congress to declare that the spending is for an emergency, as it did in 1998. This would be likely in the event of a deep farm sector economic crisis, brought on by natural events in agriculture or by a deteriorating macroeconomic situation. Especially in election years, significant new funds always seem to be found for agricultural programs. A less transparent manipulation of budget rules might also be arranged when the FAIR Act expires. The CBO could instantly recharge the farm budget baseline at that point by assessing the spending implications of a return to permanent legislation; Congress could then use this new enlarged

10. The proposed settlement would have raised cigarette prices by as much as $1.50 per pack to reduce domestic sales of U.S.-produced tobacco by about 10 percent. The market price for tobacco quota rentals was approximately $0.42 per pound, and the various buyout proposals offered generous compensation for loss of quota: around $8.00 per pound. At this compensation rate, payments for quota lost due to reduced domestic consumption would have been around $1.4 billion (Womach 1998). After this legislation failed, the tobacco companies negotiated smaller payment packages with a number of states. Tobacco farmers continued to press for substantial compensation for lost production as part of this arrangement.

11. A buyout of the entire tobacco quota program under Lugar's amendment to the proposed 1998 settlement would have cost around $12.2 billion. Had the legislation gone forward, inclusion of Lugar's proposal to end the tobacco supply-control program would have added an ironic twist, because the lower market price of tobacco that would result from elimination of quota rents counteracted the settlement's intent to raise retail cigarette prices in an effort to reduce consumption.

baseline as the standard against which to evaluate proposed farm spending. This admittedly audacious option was rejected in 1990 and 1996, but in neither case was the farm sector facing dire circumstances.

The potential for escape from tight farm program budget constraints is increased by the surprising late-1990s turnaround in overall federal budget balances. The fiscal year 1998 federal budget ended with a $70 billion surplus, the first surplus since 1969 and the largest on record in nominal terms. The federal budget became balanced not so much because of any new consensus that the activities of government should shrink, but because higher tax revenues spurred by economic growth caught up with high government spending levels. With unexpected surpluses, both the president and Congress began to contemplate a variety of new fiscal policy options, from increased spending on highways and mass transit (a successful bipartisan logroll in 1998), to cutting tax rates (mainly a Republican preference), to an expansion of social-service government spending (mostly a Democratic preference). If annual budget surpluses are sustained through 2002, congressional spending is likely to be less disciplined when the next farm bill is written. A new spirit may emerge in Congress (particularly if Democrats regain majority control) to rebuild ties to traditional working-class and middle-class constituents, not only by protecting social security benefits and logrolling increased spending for health and education, but perhaps also by increasing funding for farm programs and rural development.

Political Feedback from the FAIR Act

Our analysis has shown that farm policies themselves can alter farm politics. It was the operation of the original 1933 AAA that helped empower the agricultural process establishment that then marshaled forces to perpetuate the New Deal farm legislation. Political feedback further augmented those policies over time, by strengthening the organizations and institutions that were most heavily vested in them. Arguably, the FAIR Act might provide a break from this historical pattern. Some members of the agricultural process establishment that originally helped draft the FAIR Act, and then organized the coalition needed to push it through Congress, could find themselves weakened rather than strengthened by this legislation.

The single most significant political feedback repercussion from the FAIR Act could be a weakening of the lobby groups that have traditionally promoted support programs for growers of feed grains, wheat, cotton, and rice. With the separate programs that once provided deficiency payments replaced by a common program of decoupled payments, the organizations claiming to represent these commodity interests may have more difficulty channeling specific benefits to their constituencies. Commodity groups cannot lobby for higher target prices for their crops under the FAIR Act, because target prices have been eliminated. They cannot lobby for more planting flexibility, because the FAIR Act already permits complete flexibility. Nor can they lobby for larger or smaller ARPs, because annual ARP authority was abolished. Under the FAIR Act policy regime, without separate programs of market-linked payments and acreage set asides for specific crops, the once powerful interest groups that grew up around those programs could lose their importance as a crucial policy-driving force.

Not all crop-specific lobbying options vanished under the FAIR Act, of course. Farm support payments are still made on a per-unit basis by commodity, are still based on separate cropping histories, and differ among farmers accordingly, despite decoupling of these payments from planting decisions and market prices. Crop-specific loan rates also remain a target for lobbying pressure. The wheat growers still have an incentive to organize to protect the EEP. With their deficiency payment safety net now diminished, wheat growers may actually have a stronger incentive to defend export subsidies (and other price-boosting measures) when crop prices fall. Corn growers still have an incentive to organize to defend ethanol tax exemptions and the sugar price-support program that increases demand for corn-based sweeteners. Again, in the absence of deficiency payments, the motive to exploit these indirect means to attain higher prices are now actually stronger for corn producers. Cotton and rice farmers also have reasons to continue to organize on a crop-specific basis, to defend the distinctive and lucrative three-entity rule that guarantees especially large decoupled payments. Thus, the operation of the FAIR Act can be expected to only marginally diminish the membership and the political visibility of commodity organizations that were originally formed to defend deficiency payment programs. But any weakening of these commodity organizations could diminish their chances of sustaining the support they won for their members in 1996.

While commodity-specific organizations may weaken under the FAIR Act, there may be some compensating revival in the strength of more traditional general farm organizations—such as the Farm Bureau, or perhaps the NFU. This is likely to be a limited revival, however. The

NFU, by opposing the FAIR Act to the end in the 1995–96 debate, momentarily marginalized its own influence inside the process establishment. The farm organization most committed to reversing the FAIR Act will thus be in the worst position to do so, especially if Congress remains under Republican control. The Farm Bureau, while it too was initially opposed to decoupling, was from the start arguing for greater planting flexibility and finally came around to support the FAIR Act. This history gives the Farm Bureau greater political standing to affect subsequent policy, especially if Congress retains a Republican majority.

Political feedback could make the Farm Bureau a stronger supporter of the FAIR Act as time passes. Increased planting flexibility and the elimination of ARPs were initially appreciated by Farm Bureau members; both corn and soybean acreages increased after it was enacted.[12] Commercial farmers who experienced gains from this planting flexibility could oppose even more strongly any return to programs that restrict their planting options. If their influence strengthened, the Farm Bureau could then adhere to the FAIR Act status quo and turn more of its attention to tax and environmental regulation issues—such as those briefly highlighted by Roberts's policy ledger before the market price run-up of 1995–96.[13]

The FAIR Act could also generate political feedback in favor of a continued cash out of farm commodity programs through international competition and negotiation channels. The unilateral U.S. decoupling and elimination of ARPs under the FAIR Act could increase political pressure inside the European Union to follow suit, which in turn might pave the way for elimination of the blue box exemptions for payments still partially coupled to production and market prices. Were Agenda 2000 adopted, in part under these pressures, and if as a consequence the blue box were eliminated, the result would be a useful international lock in, through the WTO, of the decoupling step first taken under the FAIR Act in 1996.[14]

12. Corn and soybean planting acreage increased from 133.8 million in 1995 to 143.7 million in 1996 (under high prices), and then continued to rise even as prices fell: to 150.8 million acres in 1997 and 153.5 million in 1998. Wheat acreage, in contrast, increased from 1995 to 1996, but fell in the following two years.

13. Roberts joined the Senate Agriculture Committee after his senatorial election in November 1996.

14. Josling (1998) advocates the use of international agreements to lock in domestic policy changes in this fashion. Temporarily, however, the European Union increased its wheat acreage set asides from 5 percent in 1997 to 10 percent in 1998.

Other policy reform gains building on the FAIR Act approach are also conceivable under future WTO negotiations, including a similar lock in of reduced export subsidization and greater market liberalization for import-competing commodities. Regional trade agreements could generate pressure on the illiberal import-competing commodity programs for dairy, sugar, and peanuts. Under NAFTA, by 2002 the United States and Mexico will be only six years away from the scheduled full elimination of bilateral agricultural trade barriers, when Mexico will become a potential competitive source of sugar in the U.S. market, placing the U.S. sugar program under greater reform pressure. A move to cash out the sugar or peanut program taken in conjunction with an extension of NAFTA—or through APEC or in conjunction with a renewal of trade relationships with Cuba—could be justified within a larger foreign policy design, just as Agenda 2000 may be adopted in Europe in part to accommodate integration of central and east European countries.

It is uncertain, though, whether any such internationally brokered political feedback gains will come in time to influence a new farm bill when the FAIR Act expires. The WTO negotiations on agriculture scheduled to start in 1999 will probably still be underway three years later, because the most logical deadline for their completion (the expiration of the Uruguay Round peace clause) is 2003. Regional trade negotiations may be on a slower timetable for completion, even under the best of circumstances. A U.S. farm bill that precedes any international agreement could conceivably embrace new reforms in anticipation of WTO or regional bargains about to be struck, but our historical assessment suggests that a bill postponing reforms to preserve U.S. negotiating options is more likely.

The Impact of Ideas

The 1996 FAIR Act did not emerge from a convincing embrace of ideas about small government and market-oriented farm policies—but will these ideas be dominant when the next farm bill is written? The 1996 law was an internally inconsistent policy mix, based more on compromise and convenience than on conviction. It led to larger rather than smaller government outlays for agriculture and was market oriented for some crops but not others. Liberalizing reforms in the FAIR Act were persistently opposed by leaders at the center of the political system, including by the president and the secretary of agriculture in addition to most Democrats in Congress.

Under some future circumstances, the farm policy debate could move more convincingly in the direction of reform ideas, setting the stage for a more complete market-liberalizing policy outcome. If a foreign financial crisis and recession are avoided, if momentum toward trade liberalization is sustained, and if commodity markets regain strength by 2002, then advocates of market-oriented farming will have a stronger basis on which to make the case that markets can be trusted and agriculture no longer needs special help. If Republicans retain their congressional majority in 2000, and if political feedback from the successful operation of the FAIR Act should in the meantime weaken some of the lobby groups within the traditional agricultural process establishment, arguments against freer markets and smaller government programs could also weaken. The continued structural and demographic transformation of agriculture might add still more strength to the idea of market-oriented farming, as older farmers raised on the expectation of government supports continue to retire, and as younger farmers who may have initially prospered under the FAIR Act acquire a louder political voice.

Anticipating a need to debate the future of farm programs, Congress in the FAIR Act mandated the creation of a Commission on 21st Century Production Agriculture, instructing it to report by January 1, 2001, the changes that had taken place in U.S. agriculture, and to recommend specific legislation for future federal involvement in farm programs. Conceivably, the report of this bipartisan commission could provide an important public statement—just before the next farm bill debate— that the idea of reliance on markets and smaller government had at last become dominant within American agriculture.

The dominance of such ideas could equally well fail to materialize. Just as the 1994 peso crisis produced a backlash against NAFTA, the 1997–98 Asian financial crisis could weaken political support for free markets in general. In 1997–98, even Republican support for fast track had waned—and so many Democrats in Congress refused to support their own party's president that renewal of this trade agreement ratification authority was defeated. This suggests a weak rather than strong political consensus for the idea of free trade.

Whether the idea of smaller government is in fact becoming dominant is also open to question. Less federal support may be the new reality for politically weak groups such as welfare recipients, but advocacy organizations speaking for the politically articulate and well-organized middle class (including Medicare and social security recipients, and perhaps also farm groups) might eye the prospect of short-term federal budget surpluses with new hope for gaining more federal support. A Democratic recapture of Congress, or for agriculture a protracted market price slump, could undercut the idea of further movement away from government programs.

Thus, there is reason for skepticism about the power of newly dominant ideas to drive the outcome of the next farm bill debate. The agricultural process establishment remains intact, and within this establishment self-survival still compels an embrace of more traditional thinking. A genuine shift in dominant ideas is certainly possible in U.S. farm policy, as evidenced by the 1933 enactment of the original AAA. In American politics, however, this sort of ideological shift will not ordinarily take place until prevailing ideas have been conclusively defeated through a deep process of society-wide contestation, of the kind that took place during the Great Depression.[15] Even if such a contest of views emerges by the next farm bill, there is no guarantee that reform ideas will come to dominate.

Reform Scenarios for the Next Farm Bill

Taking these six policy-driving factors into account, scenarios of a more complete policy reform victory in the next farm bill can be constructed—but equally plausible are scenarios involving reform setbacks. Thus, it is possible to imagine both a best- and a worst-case scenario for future policy reform.[16]

A Scenario for an End to Farm Programs

Under a best-case scenario for farm policy reform, the market-oriented features of the FAIR Act would be retained when a new farm bill is written, a fixed schedule would be set for ending any remaining transition payments to export crop producers, and the import-competing commodities that escaped reform in 1996 would also be obliged, at last, to face market disciplines. Permanent farm program legislation would be repealed. Under this scenario, the generous FAIR Act payments made in 1996 and 1997 would deserve acknowledgment as components of a successful buyout of the U.S. farm policies that were established during the New Deal. The next farm bill would then become the last farm bill.

---

15. In taking this view of how newly dominant ideas emerge, we find ourselves closer to Hall (1993) than to Tweeten and Zulauf (1997).

16. A preliminary version of this analysis was presented by Paarlberg and Orden (1996).

A number of policy-driving factors would have to combine in the right manner to produce such a best-case scenario for reform. Significant extension of the 1996 reforms most likely will emerge if market conditions and structures combine to restore higher commodity prices; if Republicans retain and widen their control of Congress; if congressional budget rules remain a constraint on agricultural spending (but not so much as to block all future cash-out or buyout options); and if political feedback from the operation of the FAIR Act weakens the traditional agricultural process establishment. Under these conditions, reform-oriented ideas may at last become dominant, adding still more momentum to the reform impulse.

Strong market prices are obviously crucial to a best-case reform scenario. Farmers will be more likely to accept an extension of the FAIR Act approach beyond 2002 if they calculate that they did as well or better receiving decoupled payments between 1996 and 2002 than they would have done under the old deficiency payment programs. With reasonably high market prices expected beyond 2002, Republicans would favor continuing down the FAIR Act path toward market-oriented farming. Even Democrats—while sensitive to complaints from populists about delivering benefits to agribusiness or from environmentalists about land coming out of the CRP if prices are strong enough—would have to admit that the deregulation of crop production accomplished under the FAIR Act in 1996 was the most popular policy option to continue. Republicans, supported by agribusiness insistence on unfettered production, would be able to claim vindication for the market-oriented policies they had championed seven years earlier.

In addition to renewed strength in market prices, reform prospects would be enhanced by a continued and widened Republican control of Congress, a Republican recapture of the White House in the 2000 election, and sufficient federal budget pressures to ensure policy discipline. Reform prospects would also improve with rapid progress in the European Union toward further CAP reform, particularly by no revival of heavy export subsidization. Under these conditions, and assuming Congress would grant the new president the fast-track authority needed to strike trade agreements, renewed WTO agricultural negotiations might secure an early harvest of agreed reforms. The completion of an international agricultural trade agreement might then present options for further domestic reform in the next farm bill; at least it would keep farm groups from using stalled negotiations as a pretext for new subsidies. Liberalization commitments on agriculture under regional trade agreements, both within the Western Hemisphere and across the Atlantic and the Pacific, would add to the reform momentum.

If all these favorable conditions were met, political feedback from the operation of the FAIR Act would probably then also become a strong factor pushing toward still more reform. In a best-case reform scenario, commodity-specific lobby groups for export crops would lose dues-paying members and influence, for lack of a clear mission. Groups representing import-competing commodities would then lack the coalition partners necessary to defend their own programs. Decoupling in the United States would inspire a parallel decoupling by the European Union, leading to an agreement to eliminate the blue box in the WTO and locking in the reform. A preliminary agreement on total elimination of export subsidies might also emerge within the WTO at this point, and a further round of more serious tariff cuts could be scheduled, leading to still more reform pressure on domestic sugar, peanut, and dairy programs. The bipartisan Commission on 21st Century Production Agriculture might report, on the eve of the new farm bill debate, that agriculture was prospering, markets were opening up, and an extension of antiquated New Deal–era farm programs into the next millennium was not necessary.

As the farm bill debate got underway, prices would be strong enough to contain any political pressure in Congress for a larger CRP, and as CRP contracts expired, many would not be renewed. With the CRP freed to operate solely as a resource protection program favored by outdoors enthusiasts and environmentalists, it would still provide some cash benefits to farmers while no longer serving a dual role as a serious supply-control program. Democrats and environmentalists might seek to transform the decoupled payments that remain in the farm policy baseline into a larger flow of payments tied to environmental regulations, but they would be blocked from doing so by the Republican majority in Congress.

Thanks to continued budget discipline, decoupled transition payments would provisionally be scheduled to dwindle over the life of the new farm bill. This would remove opportunities for tough environmental conditioning, which, in turn, could weaken the interest of environmental groups in supporting any farm program extension at all. Farm Bureau–led Republicans might then abandon all cooperation with environmentalists by opting to pursue an unabashed agenda of environmental deregulation and full production, thus weakening the coalition for commodity program renewal. A worthwhile debate might ensue on environmental policy, but with export crop producers in pursuit of an agenda of tax breaks and deregulation, the import-competing producers seeking to hold onto their traditional commodity programs would find themselves isolated and weakened as never before. Regional advocates for dairy, sugar, peanut, and tobacco interests would still strongly defend their traditional programs inside the Agriculture Committees, but the minimum winning coalition needed to block challenges to these programs on the floor of the House of Representatives would have been lost, and the Republican leadership, despite complaints from rural southern constituents, would allow them to be defeated one by one.

So complete is the demise of traditional farm programs under this reform scenario that the permanent 1949 farm legislation would be repealed by Congress in 2002, perhaps replaced only by a noninterventionist minimal safety net consisting of loan rates set far below expected market prices, plus crop or revenue insurance with minimal subsidization. With the effective repeal of the permanent 1949 law, the era of big government in U.S. agriculture would finally be over. The New Deal farm programs that for three generations seemed a permanent fixture of agricultural politics in the United States would no longer exist.

Under this best-case reform scenario, the 1996 FAIR Act would deserve to be remembered as a critical point of change. The decoupled payment windfall that farmers were given under the FAIR Act in 1996 and 1997 would have effectively helped to buy out any claim by agriculture to future farm program extension. At this juncture, with the institutional power of the old agricultural process establishment in demise, the idea of trusting markets would emerge as more clearly dominant. The farm economy would come to be seen as not much different from the rest of the U.S. economy, and for this reason no longer in need of its distinctive support programs. This by no means suggests an end to political efforts to secure policies favorable to agriculture—just that these policies would take the form of tax breaks, regulatory relief, and other interventions more typical of other sectors.

A Setback Scenario for Farm Policy Reform

While a propitious combination of circumstances might greatly advance policy reform in 2002, an opposing mix could just as easily deal a decisive setback to reform. Under a worst-case scenario, Congress might abandon some of the core FAIR Act reforms, deepening the partial setbacks that occurred in 1998. A new farm bill might not only retain permanent legislation and leave import-competing commodity programs unreformed: it could revert to more intrusive or expensive farm support instruments for export crops. This worst-case reform scenario could unfold if market prices remain low; if the Democratic Party regains control of Congress; if federal budget pressures slacken; and if international negotiations to open world markets or to end subsidies fail or become stalled.

A persistence of low commodity prices after 1998 could continue to undercut the appeal of the FAIR Act to U.S. export crop producers—particularly if low prices persist into the years 2000–2002, when decoupled payments are scheduled to decline as well. This would subject the whole concept of decoupling to renewed criticism. The monetary windfall farmers received under the FAIR Act in 1996 and 1997 would be long forgotten. With low prices, the de facto abandonment of decoupling that took place in 1998 might become institutionalized. If Congress writes a new farm bill under so much as the fear of low or falling prices in 2002, it could lack the courage to continue with decoupled payments, and return to market-linked (recoupled) programs.

Particularly if the Democratic Party were to retain the presidency in 2000 and retake control of both houses of Congress at a time when commodity prices were falling, a significant retreat from the FAIR Act approach would become likely. Democrats speaking for marginal farm constituents vowed in 1996 to amend the decoupling component of the FAIR Act as soon as they got their chance. They had only limited success in 1998, but a change in party control would offer them a better opportunity. A return of Democrats to majority control of Congress would mean new committee chairs and new aides in key congressional staff positions. With low crop prices, these reenergized Democratic activists would feel vindicated in their earlier criticisms of the FAIR Act, and would put forward their own vision of a strengthened safety net for farm producers. With Democrats in control, pay-as-you-go budget rules could be relaxed, especially if federal budget surpluses had by then become the norm. If congressional budget rules were relaxed, a number of farm program spending options might be revived.

Two kinds of farm bills might emerge. The first could restore past interventionist programs with higher loan rates, maximum use of EEP and DIEP, expanded green box export programs, CRP expansion, and perhaps even renewed annual ARP authority. An alternative "new age" interventionist farm bill could be constructed around a more heavily subsidized farm revenue or income insurance program, a voluntary paid annual land diversion program, or other generous payments tied to adoption of conservation practices. With low prices, large commercial farmers as well as small marginal farmers would find participation attractive.

If prices are low in 2000–2002, and if Democrats control Congress, the Republican leadership would find it untenable politically to object to budget waivers to spend more on farm programs. Republicans would once again compete with Democrats in an effort to show generosity toward farmers. In the context of a price collapse, not even tight budget disciplines would ensure market-oriented policies, because limits on spending could tempt a Democratic Congress to reinsert authority for crop-specific annual supply controls as a criterion for receiving any program benefits.

A worst-case scenario for reform assumes continued loss of export outlets for U.S. farm products. An extended period of slow growth in Asia, higher dollar exchange rates, continued labor and environmentalist objections to renewed fast track authority, and lack of progress in further policy reform in the European Union could set back domestic policy reform in the United States. Under these worst-case circum-. stances, farmers and their representatives in Congress in the midterm 2002 election year would be clamoring not for more market-oriented reform but for more government assistance to agriculture. Among many southern farm-district Republicans as well as among all farm-district Democrats, a strong urge could arise to "correct the error of the FAIR Act." The rhetoric of debate could shift from exalting the virtues of markets to decrying the risks and disruptions to which farm markets particularly remain prone, and the negative effects on U.S. farmers of continued interventions by competitors abroad.

At a minimum under this worst-case reform scenario, the import-competing commodities that mostly escaped market liberalization in 1996 would continue to escape reform, and any further movement toward open markets for these products would come to a halt. Direct cash payments to farmers would be extended, and perhaps increased. Democrats would take credit for having wisely objected to any proposed repeal of permanent farm program law, which would again be retained, ensuring that this next farm bill would not be the last. The 1996 FAIR Act, rather than being viewed in retrospect as an effective buyout of farm programs, would come to be seen as a short-sighted experiment with decoupling—an experiment that wasted money while prices were high in 1996–97, and then began to fail. In the realm of ideas, the New Deal–era assumption of farm sector entitlement to special government protections would be strengthened rather than weakened, and an agricultural process establishment that continued to depend on that assumption would be strengthened as well.

The Reform Problem after the FAIR Act Expires

Much still remains undetermined regarding the future of U.S. farm policy. This future is uncertain because it depends upon actions and choices yet to be made by reformers and their opponents, and also because of uncertainty regarding a number of powerful policy-driving factors both within and beyond the agricultural sector. A possibly frustrating conclusion for reform advocates is that a more complete victory than the compromises reached in the 1996 FAIR Act may require not only hard work, but also good fortune. The unplanned farm support payments extended in 1998 together with our characterization of best- and worst-case scenarios for reform in the next farm bill illustrate how many risks and uncertainties the farm policy process still faces in the aftermath of the FAIR Act. Depending on market circumstances, party control of Congress, changing budget prospects, and a variety of international policy developments, the near-term future of U.S. farm policy could at one extreme bring an elimination of almost all remaining budget outlays and market distortions, or at another extreme a backsliding into a revived use of costly and intrusive policy instruments. In the longer term, a strong force for technical change in agriculture is going to continue to drive both the structural modernization process and the policy reform process forward, perhaps at an accelerated rate. But in 2002, these long-term reform pressures could be overwhelmed by more immediate economic and political circumstances.

Considering actual probabilities, neither the extreme best- nor worst-case outcome is the most likely to develop in the near term. For a best-case reform scenario to play out, a nearly unimaginable combination of events is required. In our illustration, commodity prices must regain strength substantially; at the same time, Republicans must retain (and increase) their majority in Congress; budget constraints must be limiting (but not too limiting); and noticeable progress must be made advancing policy reforms and negotiating new market-opening agreements abroad. The absence of any one of these key ingredients in the best-case scenario could be enough to weaken the full-scale reform result. Likewise, for the worst-case reform setback scenario to occur, there must be sustained commodity price weakness. Assuming stronger prices, the leading participants in the next farm bill debate—be they Republicans or Democrats—are likely to conclude that the 1996 decision to end annual ARP authority and decouple payments to farmers was on balance good for U.S. agriculture, and worth sustaining.

The most probable near-term future for U.S. farm policy therefore comes neither from the best- nor the worst-case reform scenario, but instead from some less extreme situation. Such a situation could emerge if renewed strong prices coincide with a Democratic Congress, or with lax budget rules, or with no policy reform in the European Union and no progress on new trade agreements. In any of these cases, the most likely outcome for the next farm bill is not restoration of payments coupled to prices or production, nor restoration of annual ARPs, but a continuation of some payments to export crop producers, possibly a ratcheting up of loan rates, retention of traditional programs for import-competing commodities, and renewal, once again, of permanent farm program legislation. In other words, the most likely outcome would be minimal change from the new equilibrium established under the 1996 FAIR Act.

A number of hybrid low-price scenarios are also imaginable, including low prices with Republican majorities in Congress, or low prices with continued budget discipline. Under these scenarios as well, the most likely outcome would include a retention of the key FAIR Act reforms—planting flexibility, ARP elimination, loan rate caps, and decoupling—much as was the case in 1998. Yet there might also be an increase in direct payments, the creation of new income and revenue insurance programs, and a retention of interventionist programs for import-competing commodities. There would be no elimination of permanent law. This again suggests that the most probable near-term future outcome for U.S. agricultural policy could be a renewal of the FAIR Act compromise—somewhat weakened perhaps, but not reversed. Decoupled cash payments would continue to be made for export crops, and producers of these crops would be protected against adverse market outcomes in various ways, while import-competing commodity programs would once again escape reform. If this emerges as the new policy equilibrium, the farm policy reform problem must be considered unresolved.

Conclusion

Ending Farm Subsidies

IN THIS BOOK we have documented the political difficulty of securing market-oriented, fiscally disciplined agricultural policy reform. Productivity growth and structural change in American agriculture have created a strong need for policy reform, but the political system has been slow to meet that need. Even the 1996 FAIR Act, hailed as the most significant agricultural policy reform in six decades, resulted in more—not less—farm program spending, continued paid land-diversions, essentially unchanged protection of import-competing commodities, and no repeal of the permanent law authorizing intrusive farm price supports and production restraints. In this concluding chapter we summarize the policy-driving factors that have brought the evolution of U.S. farm programs to this point, then we reprise the reform strategies available for taking the next steps forward. We conclude that the approach to policy reform that has worked best up to now—the approach of a cash out—might be usefully extended into several new policy areas, and then converted into a more complete squeeze out in all areas.

The Difficulty of Achieving Farm Policy Reform

Our analysis has confirmed some of the reasons traditionally given to explain why the farm policy reform process is so difficult. The political power of farm organizations has persisted despite declining numbers of farmers, confirming the expectations of various public choice theorists of policy change. These theorists argue that political power comes primarily from organization, and that declining numbers can, up to a point, ease the task of sustaining interest group lobbies. Formation of coalitions internal to and beyond the farm sector has also boosted the political power of farm organizations, consistent with those that have stressed the importance of legislative logrolling. Finally, the political power of farm organizations has persisted, in conformity with the expectation of theorists who stress the importance of policy feedback. The farm policies set in place during the Great Depression have tended to perpetuate themselves, by giving farm organizations new resources, new incentives to engage in lobbying (to protect

226

asset values raised by past successes), and an easier lobbying task (because program preservation requires less political strength than program creation). Once set in place, the New Deal–era farm programs tended to create a process establishment, a nexus of agricultural policy officials and organizations centered around the congressional agriculture committees and the USDA, with an institutional interest in program preservation.

Somewhat more elusive is the argument that farm organizations continue to exercise power over policy outcomes by promoting an idea (a mythology some would say) of traditional agrarian values, one that essentially denies the reality of the technology-driven structural transformation within agriculture. We found that agrarian mythology played little or no role in the 1996 FAIR Act outcome, perhaps because the Democratic Party in Congress—the stronger propagator of that mythology—had by then been replaced in the majority by the Republican Party, which preferred to promote different kinds of ideas about farming, including market orientation and a desired freedom from government regulation and taxation. Yet these ideas promoted by the new Republican majority also played only a limited role in the 1996 FAIR Act outcome, which moved farm policy toward market orientation only for export crops, and only because of the opportunity to capture a windfall in new decoupled payments to farmers. Thus, we have confirmed that both interests and institutions are critical to the pace and direction of policy change in agriculture, but we have not so clearly confirmed the independent importance of ideas. We do not deny that large (third-order) policy changes are possible in agricultural policy; such a change took place in 1933, with the initial legislation of intrusive farm programs under the original AAA. Yet we would prefer to delimit the ideational basis for such changes. The consensus in favor of market-intrusive farm programs was never complete even during the New Deal, just as the consensus to move away from such programs is certainly not complete some seventy years later.

We have also pointed out the limited impact of international negotiations on U.S. farm policy. The 1986–93 Uruguay Round negotiations had some liberalizing impact on agricultural policies in the European Union, but we found little evidence that they materially advanced the cause of policy reform in the United States. The quest for bargaining leverage in this marathon negotiation, and the need in the end to pass implementing legislation, gave U.S. farm groups and farm program supporters in Congress opportunities to extract additional entitlement benefits, first in the guise of getting more subsidies to win a better international deal, then by seeking compensation for the budget spending they falsely claimed to have lost because of GATT. We hold out hopes that future trade negotiations will be able to go beyond the reform accomplishments of the Uruguay Round; perhaps a second follow-on round of multilateral negotiations on agriculture will be able to build on the useful rule changes that were embraced to enlarge market access and reduce export subsidies, all the while locking in some of the subsequent reforms achieved under the FAIR Act. We hold out more hope for this two-stage game approach to securing reform from international negotiations, in contrast to the simultaneous two-level game approach championed at the time of the Uruguay Round.

Beyond this mix of views toward various explanations of agricultural policy continuity and change in the United States, we derive from our analysis several other critical lines of causation. The first of these is an emphasis on fluctuating macroeconomic conditions. Over the long history of U.S. agricultural policy, macroeconomic instability has been detrimental to market-oriented reform. The macroeconomic collapse of the 1930s helped produce the original AAA interventions. A subsequent macroeconomic recovery and boom, during the Second World War, then failed to undo the AAA farm programs; to the contrary, temporarily high commodity prices enabled farm groups to ratchet up loan rates. Loan rates were likewise ratcheted upward under the cover of high inflation in the 1970s, then kept high far too long in the ensuing period of slower inflation and dollar appreciation.

A second systemic factor—exposure to world market customers and competitors—has also been at work. Whenever world market outlets have been available to U.S. agriculture, producers of export crops have been more willing to tolerate market-oriented policy reform, and vice versa. An absence of export opportunities during the Great Depression helps explain the original embrace, under the AAA, of supply controls and high crop loan rates. As long as commercial export opportunities remained limited through the 1950s, supply-control and price-support instruments remained in favor politically. Only with the emergence of larger commercial export opportunities in the 1960s and 1970s were producers of some crops willing to accept (as they had not in 1949) the cash-out reform strategy. Export crop producers began accepting direct cash payments in place of supply controls and high loan rates—in part because they hoped to gain larger foreign market shares through more competitive export pricing, and in part because of their growing awareness that in the context of expanding world markets, unilateral supply controls had become self-defeating.

The availability of world market outlets actually saved U.S. farm policy from what might have otherwise been, during the farm crisis years of the mid-1980s, a massive reversion to supply controls and high price supports. Had potentially larger world markets for U.S. grains not been available when the 1985 farm bill was debated (a potential that the U.S. was forfeiting due to high loan rates), the farm bill written in that year might have embraced the market-intrusive option of mandatory supply controls. The legislation that actually emerged was instead a move toward lower loan rates in order to boost both domestic consumption and exports.

Record cash outlays were used to compensate producers for lower prices under the 1985 farm bill, and the size of these outlays (plus short-term reliance on greater supply controls) tended at the time to mask what was being accomplished. At a critical moment of macroeconomic-induced downturn, when a reversal of market-oriented reforms might have been expected, what emerged instead was continued progress down the earlier established path of a cash out of intrusive price supports. This path would not have been politically feasible without continued growth in world market opportunities for U.S. crops.

World market conditions do not always trump macroeconomic conditions. Despite a farm crisis brought on in the 1920s in part by diminished exports, the farm bloc in Congress was mostly unsuccessful in securing support interventions for the sector. On this occasion (before the institutionalization of farm programs), a relatively strong macroeconomy seems to have superceded world market circumstances as a policy-driving force. Not until macroeconomic conditions deteriorated after 1929 did programmatic support for agriculture emerge as a viable political option.

A third line of explanation that receives special emphasis in our analysis is party control of government, especially Congress. Most analysts of U.S. farm policy stopped emphasizing the party control variable sometime after the mid-1950s, but the diminished impact of this variable was mostly an illusion. Party control didn't seem to matter between 1955 and 1994, only because the Democratic Party controlled the House of Representatives (and often the Senate and the White House as well) without interruption throughout this period. When the Republican Party finally recaptured Congress after 1994, new political space was created to move U.S. farm policy in a more market-oriented direction.

The unexpected 1996 FAIR Act outcome was in part a reflection of momentarily higher crop prices and the CBO budget baseline capture option, but it was just as much a reflection of how the first Republican Congress in four decades decided to exercise that option. With Republicans in charge, annual ARP authority was eliminated to please agribusiness and exporter interests, and cash payments to farmers were completely decoupled. If Democrats had been in charge, higher market prices might instead have resulted in a stronger safety net for export crop producers, rather than an end of ARP authority, capped loan rates, and decoupled payments.

These policy-driving forces working together over the past six decades have generated something of a trifurcated outcome for U.S. agriculture. For import-competing commodities (dairy, sugar, peanuts, tobacco), little or no program reform remains the rule. The import restraints and the market-intrusive programs first established for these commodities during the Great Depression largely remain in place, despite the 1996 FAIR Act. These unreformed commodity markets furnish a relatively small share of national farm cash receipts (about 15 percent), yet regionally they remain a significant part of the U.S. farm sector.

For export crops (feed grains, wheat, cotton, rice), a significant reform has been achieved, along the path of a cash out. For these crops, programs that originally supported farm income—through market-intrusive supply controls and price-support loan rates backed by government stockholding—have been redesigned to support farm income almost exclusively through direct cash payments (the CRP and the EEP remain exceptions). Farm support entitlements for these crops were cashed out slowly over several decades, beginning implicitly in the 1960s, and then explicitly under the terms of the 1973 farm bill. In subsequent reform steps, the payments made to farmers under this cash out were incrementally decoupled, first from crop yields (in the 1985 farm bill), then from planting decisions and market prices (in the 1996 FAIR Act). These export crops make up nearly 25 percent of national farm sales receipts annually, and the cash-out reform that has been achieved deserves to be counted as a significant market-oriented accomplishment—albeit a costly one to taxpayers.

A third category of commodities received little support under the original New Deal–era programs—these commodities include most livestock products, hay, oilseeds (for which loan rates are not often intrusive), and fruits and vegetables (some of which are regulated by domestic marketing orders or continue to receive significant protection at the border from import competition). For these commodities, price supports and market-intrusive taxpayer-financed stockholding schemes were never set up in the first place, and thus never faced the need for adjustment or reform. This nonprogram component of U.S. farming was always significant, and in the 1990s has constituted nearly 60 percent of total national farm sales receipts.

Explaining this trifurcation of U.S. farm policies is not difficult. Most of the nonprogram commodities were biologically unsuited to supply controls (animals cannot be idled, they have to be killed), or they were excluded from intrusive government stockholding measures because they were highly perishable. Programs for import-competing commodities remain unreformed because they have a low opportunity cost in terms of federal budget costs or lost export sales. These programs impose a cost on U.S. consumers, but one built into market prices and therefore not transparent—and the consumers are in any case too wealthy and too numerous to organize for program dismantlement. Support programs for export crops have been cashed out because they developed, beginning in the 1960s, a high opportunity cost. The cash out was politically acceptable to producers because they sensed the long-term loss of world market share they might suffer otherwise. It was politically acceptable to taxpayers because other categories of federal spending expanded even more rapidly (enlarged spending on farm programs thus tended to escape attention) and because even in their original form (especially when large government-owned stocks accumulated), the programs for these crops had never seemed a budget bargain.

The 1996 FAIR Act did not substantially alter this longstanding trichotomy of U.S. farm policy, and under some near-term scenarios it could remain quite durable into the future. For market-oriented reform advocates who are not satisfied with this mix of partial and nonreformed policy outcomes, however, some next steps might hold the promise of achieving further market liberalization and fiscal cost containment.

Reform Strategy Options

Throughout our analysis of the political problem of farm policy reform, we have emphasized four different strategies for achieving market-oriented policies for U.S. agriculture: a cash out, a buyout, a squeeze out, and a cutout. A cash out is a gradual and partial reform option, one that reduces the market intrusiveness of programs over the long run by offering program beneficiaries a continuing stream of cash compensation payments. A buyout is a quick termination of support entitlements, made politically palatable through significant but temporary compensation up front, presumably in the form of a large cash windfall. A squeeze out is an incremental reduction in the generosity of farm programs, managed slowly enough to avoid triggering a backlash from subsidy-dependent farmers, yet significant enough over time to inspire voluntary nonparticipation and reduce program costs and distortions. A cutout is a quick termination of all program support entitlements without compensation.

Our assessment of the multidecade history of farm policy reform efforts clarifies the actual promise of these various hypothetical reform strategies. We confirm the expectation of political theorists that the abrupt cutout approach is likely to fail in the face of strong resistance from program defenders. We reviewed the outright failure of various unilateral cutout proposals, offered by the Nixon administration in 1973, and then by the Reagan administration in 1981 and again in 1985. These proposals were all summarily rejected by Congress. Frustration was also encountered when the Reagan administration tried to secure a cutout of farm programs at home and abroad through the zero option negotiating proposal in the GATT Uruguay Round. The zero option technically offered the possibility of direct cash compensation (making it a buyout, not a straight cutout) but farm groups were not interested. They managed instead to use the zero option as a device for slowing the pace of the international negotiation, and eventually to avoid additional cuts entirely. Finally, we recounted another set of cutout proposals that were put forward in the 1995–96 farm bill debate, by Senator Lugar and by Representatives Schumer and Zimmer. These proposals were mostly ignored by the agricultural policy process establishment, which went forward instead first to defend the farm budget baseline, then to debate the desirability of using a capture of this baseline through decoupled payments or of extending the status quo.

In the few instances in which the option to buy out farm program entitlements has been proposed, it has likewise fallen short. A buyout was discussed by some policy reform advocates in the 1960s, but it was never introduced in Congress. In the dairy sector, a costly program adopted in 1985 to induce individual farmers to suspend production (for five years only) was labeled a "whole herd buyout" but was in fact only a temporary and expensive supply-control measure. Prior to the 1996 FAIR Act, the closest proposal to a serious buyout was the 1985

Boschwitz-Boren bill, a measure that was viewed even by most Republicans at the time as not only too daring, but far too expensive. This buyout proposal failed when the anticipated costs proved too great for budget officials, yet still not high enough to entice farmers.

The 1996 FAIR Act failed to qualify as a clear buyout of traditional farm support programs, even for export crops, because a budget baseline remained in place indefinitely, and because permanent legislation was never repealed. We have presented at least one possible scenario under which the 1996 FAIR Act might successfully evolve into a buyout, yet we classified this reform scenario as not an especially likely one.

The squeeze-out strategy has also been, historically at least, quite difficult to follow. The original squeeze-out attempt launched by the Eisenhower administration in the 1950s ran afoul of a Democratic Congress, and was thwarted as well by productivity growth in the sector so high as to ensure that even substantially lower price supports remained a market-intrusive inducement to overproduction. A different kind of squeeze-out opportunity emerged during the inflationary period of the 1970s, when a simple freeze in nominal support levels would have implied a fall of real price supports to nonintrusive levels. This opportunity for a squeeze out was lost when Congress instead ratcheted nominal support prices upward. Some progress toward an eventual squeeze out via inflation was finally made when the 1985 farm bill imposed a freeze and then small reductions in nominal target price levels. A modest squeeze-out dimension was also built into the 1990 farm bill, when, in response to budget pressure, the number of acres on which payments could be collected was reduced by 15 percent.

The 1996 FAIR Act was not a squeeze out, however. It resulted in more program spending and higher program participation rates than would have been the case under an extension of the 1990 law. We have argued that a more serious squeeze out could be resumed in 2002, if an expansion of the farm program budget baseline is avoided, and if enlargement of new safety net interventions and off-budget benefits is stopped. Continued Republican control of Congress and a consistent application of strict pay-as-you-go budget rules may be key to sustaining this squeeze-out approach. The much lower level of inflation in the general economy in the 1990s has worked somewhat against this approach (by undercutting the option of pushing real entitlement levels downward without having to attack nominal spending levels), as has the emergence of federal budget surpluses, which have relieved the pressure for budget discipline.

Several aspects of the 1996 FAIR Act itself may be working in favor of a squeeze out, at least for export crops. First, the caps on per-unit commodity loan rates imposed under the FAIR Act prevented those rates from moving up automatically in nominal terms in response to temporarily high market prices in 1996 and 1997, thus avoiding market-distorting price incentives, intervention government commodity purchases, or large *mandatory* expenditures when prices fell in 1998. Second, with the discontinuation of ARPs as a policy instrument, it is no longer necessary to make program benefits sufficiently attractive to ensure the participation of large commercial farmers. This opens a potentially interesting option of reducing program costs and squeezing out program participants through a targeting or means-testing of benefits. Farm groups have successfully resisted or found legal grounds to avoid most benefit targeting and means-testing efforts in the past, and they will no doubt continue to resist any such restrictions on farm program eligibility. But the argument that targeting could drive the largest farmers out of participating in annual supply-control programs can no longer be used as a cover for this resistance. In this sense, the transparency of decoupled cashed-out income support payments to farmers may make them more susceptible to a political squeeze out over the long run.

The strategic option that has served reform best, so far, has been the cash out. First suggested as a new approach within the 1949 Brannan Plan, the move toward supporting farm income with cash payments (eventually decoupled cash payments) rather than with market interventions is only a partial step toward reform, but it is better than no step at all. Once income support entitlements have been cashed out and decoupled, they can either be continued indefinitely or they can be subjected to a second-stage squeeze out. When mounting a squeeze out against transparent and totally decoupled outlays, the question only becomes one of budget feasibility and subsidy entitlement.

For all these reasons, the cash out should be valued as an important intermediate reform victory, at least for the supported export crops that make up one important part of agricultural production in the United States. Yet this is a precarious victory. It remains costly to taxpayers, and it leaves the traditional agricultural policy process establishment in place—ever ready to seek expanded benefits whenever circumstances offer the political opportunity, and all the while searching for new programs to deliver, and then manage. Thus, as long as only a cash out is underway for export crops, there will be no end to the policy reform problem in American agriculture. Getting beyond a simple cash out for export crops will be the challenge.

For import-competing commodities, the challenge is simply achieving a cash out. A cash out of these programs might not seem an attractive policy option, given the implication of larger rather than smaller budget outlays in the short run, yet it may be the essential prelude to a squeeze out, and more feasible than either a cutout or a costly buyout. Cash outs are half measures, but they give markets more room to operate, they are politically palatable, and they can always lead to more complete squeeze outs, buyouts, or cutouts later on. The prospect of larger budget outlays in the short term did not prevent the European Union from cashing out its cereals programs under the MacSharry reforms in the 1990s, and budget circumstances in the United States might permit increased outlays at the turn of the century for a legitimate policy reform objective. If combined with an international agreement that liberalizes agricultural trade globally, or at least one that ensures parallel reforms regionally, perhaps a cash out of the U.S. sugar or peanut program will not be such an impossible option for reformers to imagine in the years ahead. Looking even further down the road, the next step might be to decouple this cash out for import-competing crops, just as the 1996 FAIR Act decoupled cash payments for export crops. This step would encourage producers of these crops to undertake more rapid adjustments to international market conditions, perhaps creating more economic and political space for an eventual squeeze out.

Slow-motion half measures such as cash outs and squeeze outs are not as appealing, in the minds of committed reformers, as swift full measures such as buyouts and cutouts. Yet in American politics, the dismantling of entitlement programs that are no longer justified may have to be a gradual process. Such programs can be enacted quickly, but once in operation, they tend to create new institutional and political forces that cannot be changed abruptly. The 1996 FAIR Act deserves to be seen as another significant step in the direction of a successful cash out of at least one category of U.S. farm programs—but by no means is it the last of the steps that are needed. If the FAIR Act cash out can be followed by a squeeze out, and if the cash out—squeeze out strategy can then be extended to the unreformed import-competing commodities as well, perhaps an overdue end to the New Deal–era farm programs can at last be possible. If the endgame for these programs is now underway, it will nonetheless require all the ingenuity and persistence of reform advocates to secure a victory.

Summary of the 1996 FAIR Act

TITLE I: Agricultural Market Transition Act

Income support is no longer related to market prices. Restrictions on acreage and crops planted are substantially reduced. The nonrecourse loan program with marketing loan provisions continues, subject to maximum loan rates. Permanent law of the Agricultural Adjustment Act of 1938 and the Agricultural Act of 1949 is retained but temporarily suspended. A commission is established to make recommendations about the appropriate future role of the federal government in production agriculture.

Income support for feed grains, wheat, cotton, and rice	Farmers who have participated in the support programs in any one of the past five years can enter into seven-year production flexibility contracts (PFCs) for 1996–2002. Total PFC payment levels for each fiscal year are set at $5.6 billion in 1996, $5.4 billion in 1997, $5.8 billion in 1998, $5.6 billion in 1999, $5.1 billion in 2000, $4.1 billion in 2001, and $4.0 billion in 2002. Allocations of the payments are 26.26 percent for wheat, 46.22 percent for corn, 5.11 percent for sorghum, 2.16 percent for barley, 0.15 percent for oats, 11.63 percent for upland cotton, and 8.47 percent for rice. Land eligible for PFCs is equal to a farm's base acreage for 1996 calculated under the previous support programs, plus any returning Conservation Reserve Program (CRP) base and less any CRP enrollment. Program payment yields are frozen at 1995 levels. Sign-up for PFCs is restricted to one period in 1996, but land from expiring CRP contracts can be enrolled later. A per-unit payment rate for each contract commodity will be determined annually by dividing the total annual contract payment level for each commodity by the total of production eligibility.
Planting flexibility and restrictions	Land must be maintained in agricultural use. Participants may plant 100 percent of their total contract acreage to any crop, but planting of fruits and vegetables (excluding mung beans, lentils, and dry peas) is restricted. Unlimited haying and grazing and planting and harvesting

Condensed from U.S. Department of Agriculture, Economic Research Service, *Agricultural Outlook: Special Farm Bill Supplement,* April 1996.

of alfalfa and other forage crops are permitted with no reduction in payments.

Authority for ARPs is eliminated. The 0/85–92 and 50/85–92 programs are also eliminated.

Price support (loan rates)

Nonrecourse loans are extended. Any production of a contract commodity by a producer who has entered into a PFC is eligible for loans. Marketing loan provisions are continued, allowing repayment of loans at less than full principal plus interest when prices are below loan rates. Loan deficiency payments are available for all loan commodities except extra long staple (ELS) cotton. Authority for the Farmer-Owned Reserve (FOR) is suspended.

Feed Grains and Wheat

Loan rates are set at 85 percent of the five-year Olympic moving average of farm prices, subject to a maximum of $1.89 per bushel for corn and $2.58 per bushel for wheat. The secretary of agriculture retains authority to decrease feed grain and wheat loan rates up to 10 percent based on the projected stocks-to-use ratio, but authority for an additional 10 percent discretionary adjustment is repealed. Loan rates for grain sorghum, barley, and oats are based on the feed value relative to corn. Rye is no longer eligible for price support.

Cotton

The loan rate for upland cotton is set at the lesser of 85 percent of the five-year Olympic moving average of spot market prices, or 90 percent of the Northern Europe–based average price, subject to a maximum of $0.5192 per pound and a minimum of $0.50 per pound. Provisions for various adjustment mechanisms and import quotas are maintained but certain reforms are made to the cotton loan program, including elimination of the eight-month cotton loan extension. Total expenditures for upland cotton user marketing certificates (Step 2 payments) cannot exceed $701 million over fiscal years 1995–2002.

Rice

The rice loan rate is set at $6.50 per hundredweight.

Oilseeds and Soybeans

The soybean loan rate is set at not less than 85 percent of the five-year Olympic moving average of farm prices, subject to a maximum of $5.26 per bushel and a minimum of $4.92 per bushel. The loan rates for sunflower seed, canola, rapeseed, safflower, mustard seed, and flaxseed cannot be less than 85 percent of the Olympic moving average of farm prices for sunflower seed, subject to a maximum of $0.093 per pound and a minimum of $0.087 per pound.

Conservation compliance	Participants must continue to maintain conservation plans, including compliance with highly erodible land conservation provisions and wetland conservation provisions (swampbuster) to receive contract payments.
Payment limitations	Individual farmers can receive up to $80,000 per year in total contract payments on three separate farming operations ($40,000 on the first operation and $20,000 each on two additional entities). Limits on marketing loan gains continue at $75,000 on the first farm and $37,500 each on two additional entities.
Insurance	*Crop Insurance* Purchase of crop insurance is no longer required for farm program benefit eligibility if producers waive rights to emergency crop loss assistance. *Revenue Insurance Pilot Program* A revenue insurance pilot program is required for crop years 1997–2000. Research is also authorized through pilot programs to determine whether futures and options contracts can provide protection from financial risks.
Dairy	*Price Support* The minimum support price for milk maintained through government purchases of butter, nonfat dry milk, and cheese is to decline from $10.35 per hundredweight in 1996 to $9.90 in 1999, after which it is to be eliminated. Budget assessments on dairy producers are eliminated immediately. Starting in 2000, a recourse loan program is to be implemented for butter, nonfat dry milk, and cheese at loan rates equivalent to $9.90 per hundredweight. Import tariff-rate quotas (TRQs) are retained with no change. *Federal Milk Marketing Orders* Federal milk marketing orders are to be consolidated from thirty-three into ten to fourteen. Multiple basing points for the pricing of milk are authorized, California may maintain its own fluid milk standards, and the secretary of agriculture may, upon the finding of a compelling public interest in the area, grant the New England region the authority to enter into a dairy compact to

terminate with the implementation of federal order reforms.

Peanuts	*Price Support* The peanut program is revised to operate at "no-net-cost" to taxpayers. The quota support rate for domestic sales is frozen at $610 per ton, reduced from $678 in 1995. *Domestic Quota* The minimum national quota and provisions for carryover of undermarketings are eliminated. Out-of-state nonfarmers cannot hold quotas, but limited sale, lease, and transfer of quotas are permitted across county lines within a state.
Sugar	*Price Support* No-net-cost provisions and its associated TRQ for imports are retained. The raw cane and refined beet sugar loan rate remain fixed at the 1995 levels of $0.18 per pound and $0.229 per pound, respectively. Loans are recourse when the level of the TRQ is at or below 1.5 million short tons (raw value); if the TRQ is raised above that level, loans become nonrecourse. *Marketing Allotments* Authority for domestic marketing allotments is eliminated.

TITLE II: Agricultural Trade

Food aid	The authority for PL 480 and Food for Progress (FFP) agreements is extended.
Food security commodity reserve	The Agricultural Act of 1980 is amended to establish the four-million-ton Food Security Commodity Reserve—expanded to include corn, grain, sorghum, and rice in addition to wheat.
Export credit guarantee (GSM) programs	GSM-102 and GSM-103 are mandated at $5.5 billion annually. Allows credit guarantees for high-value products with at least 90 percent U.S. content (by weight).
Emerging markets program	The CCC is required to make available not less than $1 billion of direct credit or credit guarantees to emerging markets during fiscal years 1996–2002.

The market promotion program (MPP)	Funding for the program is authorized at $90 million annually and the name is changed to the Market Access Program (MAP).
Export subsidies	The Export Enhancement Program (EEP) expenditures are capped at $350 million in fiscal year 1996, $250 million in 1997, $500 million in 1998, $550 million in 1999, $579 million in 2000, and $478 million in 2001 and 2002. The 1996–99 values total $1.6 billion less than the Uruguay Round GATT (UR-GATT) commitments. The Dairy Export Incentive Program (DEIP) is extended to 2002. The secretary of agriculture must authorize subsidies sufficient to export the maximum volume of dairy products allowable subject to UR-GATT limits.
Embargo compensation	Producers are assured of compensation if a future export embargo is imposed on any country for national security or foreign policy reasons, and if no other country with an agricultural economic interest joins the U.S. sanctions within ninety days.

TITLE III: Conservation

Highly erodible land	Conservation compliance provisions are retained. Producers are allowed to modify their practices if the modifications will provide greater erosion control.
Swampbuster	USDA's Natural Resources Conservation Service is designated the lead agency in wetlands delineation (as well as regulation of grazing lands). Existing wetland delineations remain valid unless a producer requests a review.
Conservation reserve program (CRP)	Maximum CRP area is capped at 36.4 million acres. The secretary of agriculture can enroll new land in the CRP to replace expiring acreage. New acreage must meet stricter criteria regarding environment and conservation benefits to be accepted. With sixty days' notice, farmers can remove land enrolled for five years from the CRP prior to contract expiration. Wetlands, highly erodible land, and other environmentally sensitive areas are not eligible for early release.
Wetlands reserve program (WRP)	WRP area is maintained at 975,000 acres, to be split equally among permanent easements, thirty-year easements, and restoration cost-share agreements.

Environmental quality incentives program (EQIP)	EQIP is authorized at $1.3 billion over seven years to assist producers with environmental and conservation improvements, with at least half of the funding for environmental concerns associated with livestock production. The program awards five- to ten-year cost-share or incentive payment contracts.
Other programs	Conservation farm option contracts, National Natural Resources Conservation Foundation (NNRCF), Grazing Lands Conservation Initiative (GLCI), Flood Risk Reduction Program, Wildlife Habitat Incentives Program, and the Farmland Protection Program are established. The secretary of agriculture may designate watersheds or regions of special environmental sensitivity as conservation priority areas eligible for enhanced assistance.
Everglades agricultural area	The U.S. Treasury provides $200 million (not CCC funds) to the secretary of interior to conduct restoration activities, which may include land acquisition, in the Everglades ecosystem. In addition, federal land in Florida worth $100 million may be sold or swapped for land in the Everglades.

TITLE IV: Nutrition Assistance

The Food Stamp Program is reauthorized for two years. The commodity distribution programs and the Temporary Emergency Food Assistance Program (TEFAP) are reauthorized.

TITLE V: Agricultural Promotions

Producer-funded research and promotion programs for canola and rapeseed, kiwifruit, and popcorn are authorized. The existing promotion program for fluid milk is extended.

TITLE VI: Credit

Farm loan programs administered by the USDA Farm Service Agency are reauthorized. Authority to make loans for most nonagricultural purposes is repealed, and new restrictions on emergency loans are invoked. Borrowers with delinquent accounts face tighter rules.

The Farm Credit System (FCS) Reform Act of February 1996 streamlines the regulation of the FCS and reforms the Federal Agricultural Mortgage Corporation. Under the FAIR Act, the secretary of agriculture is required to conduct a study for Congress on rural credit.

TITLE VII: Rural Development

Existing programs are consolidated. The new Rural Community Advancement Program (RCAP) is authorized. The renamed Alternative Agricultural Research and Commercialization Corporation has enhanced abilities to finance new industrial uses for agricultural products, funding for water and waste facility grants is increased to $590 million, and programs for telemedicine and distance learning services are reauthorized. The new Fund for Rural America is established to augment existing resources for agricultural research and rural development. Funding is authorized from the CCC for $50 million in fiscal year 1996, $100 million in fiscal year 1997, and $150 million in fiscal year 1998.

TITLE VIII: Research, Extension, and Education

Federal agricultural research, extension, and education programs are provided with specific authorization for fiscal years 1996 and 1997. Broad authorization for all programs is provided subject to appropriations for fiscal years 1998–2002. A task force is authorized to consider the development and consolidation of federally supported agricultural research facilities, and the National Agricultural Research, Extension, Education, and Economics Advisory Board is established (replaces three separate advisory committees).

References

"Administration Offers New Funds to Dampen Farm Opposition to GATT." 1994. *Inside U.S. Trade*. 23 September, 3.

Alexander, Barbara, and Gary D. Libecap. 1998. "The Importance of Firm Heterogeneity in Policy Design and Support: Why New Deal Agricultural Regulation Survived, While Industrial Policy Failed." Paper presented at the annual meeting of the American Economic Association.

Amstutz, Daniel G. 1986. "Letter to the Editor." *Choices* (fourth quarter): 38.

Anderson, Kym. 1993. "Multilateral Trade Negotiations, European Integration, and Farm Policy Reform." Adelaide, Australia: University of Adelaide, Centre for International Economic Studies.

Anderson, Kym, and Yujiro Hayami. 1986. *The Political Economy of Agricultural Protection*. Sydney: Allen and Unwin.

Ball, Eldon V., Jean-Christophe Bureau, Richard Nehring, and Agapi Somwaru. 1997. "Agricultural Productivity Revisited." *American Journal of Agricultural Economics* 79, no. 4 (November): 1045–63.

Barnard, Charles H., Gerald Whittaker, David Westenbarger, and Mary Ahearn. 1997. "Evidence of Capitalization of Direct Government Payments into U.S. Cropland Values." *American Journal of Agricultural Economics* 79, no. 5 (December): 1642–50.

Batie, Sandra, S., and J. Paxton Marshall. 1989. *A Proposed New Structure for Food and Agricultural Policy*. Information Series 89-1. Blacksburg: Virginia Polytechnic Institute and State University, Virginia Agricultural Experiment Station.

Batie, Sandra S., Leonard Shabman, and Randall Kramer. 1985. "U.S. Agricultural and Natural Resource Policy." Manuscript. Blacksburg: Virginia Polytechnic Institute and State University, Department of Agricultural Economics.

Beech, Douglas E. 1996. "Capitalization of Farm Program Benefits into Asset Values." In *Issues in Agricultural Policy Analysis*, ed. Michael T. Herlihy and C. Edwin Young. ERS/CAD Staff Paper AGES-9610. Washington D.C.: U.S. Department of Agriculture.

Benedict, Murray R. 1953. *Farm Policies of the United States, 1790–1950*. New York: Twentieth Century Fund.

Benson, Ezra Taft. 1960. *Freedom to Farm.* New York: Doubleday.

Black, John D. 1929. *Agricultural Reform in the United States.* New York: McGraw-Hill.

Blandford, David. 1990. "The Costs of Agricultural Protection and the Difference Free Trade Would Make." In *Agricultural Protectionism in the Industrialized World,* ed. Fred H. Sanderson. Washington, D.C.: Resources for the Future.

Bonnen, James T., and William P. Browne. 1989. "Why Is Agricultural Policy So Difficult to Reform?" In *The Political Economy of U.S. Agriculture: Challenges for the 1990s,* ed. Carol S. Kramer. Washington, D.C.: Resources for the Future, National Center for Food and Agricultural Policy.

Brandow, George E. 1977. "Policy for Commercial Agriculture." In *A Survey of Agricultural Economics Literature,* ed. Lee R. Martin. Minneapolis: University of Minnesota Press.

Brinegar, George K., and Stewart Johnson. 1954. "On Letting Go of the Bear's Tail." *Journal of Farm Economics* 36, no. 1 (February): 30–43.

Brooks, Jonathan C., and Colin A. Carter. 1994. *The Political Economy of U.S. Agriculture.* Research Report 94.8. Canberra: Australian Bureau of Agricultural and Resource Economics.

Browne, William P. 1988. *Private Interests, Public Policy, and American Agriculture.* Lawrence: University Press of Kansas.

———. 1995. *Cultivating Congress: Constituents, Issues, and Agricultural Policymaking.* Lawrence: University Press of Kansas.

Browne, William P., et al. 1992. *Sacred Cows and Hot Potatoes: Agrarian Myths in Agricultural Policy.* Boulder: Westview Press.

Bullock, David S. 1992. "Objectives and Constraints of Government Policy: The Countercyclicity of Transfer Payments to Agriculture." *American Journal of Agricultural Economics* 74, no. 3 (August): 617–29.

Center for National Policy (CNP). 1991. "U.S. Agriculture: Myth, Reality and National Policy." *Report on a Project Explaining the Effect of Perceptions About Farming and Rural Life on U.S. Agricultural Policy.* Washington, D.C.: Center for National Policy.

Center for Responsive Politics. 1995. *Down on the Farm: Agricultural Interests and the 1995 Farm Bill.* Washington, D.C.: Center for Responsive Politics.

Clarke, Sally H. 1994. *Regulation and the Revolution in United States Farm Productivity.* Cambridge: Cambridge University Press.

Cochran, Thad. 1995. *Background Statement on the Agricultural Competitiveness Act of 1995.* Released by the Senator's Office, 10 August, 3.

Cochrane, Willard W. 1958. *Farm Prices, Myth and Reality.* Minneapolis: University of Minnesota Press.

———. 1993. *The Development of American Agriculture: A Historical Analysis.* 2d ed. Minneapolis: University of Minnesota Press.

Cochrane, Willard W., and C. Ford Runge. 1992. *Reforming Farm Policy: Toward A National Agenda.* Ames: Iowa State University Press.

Cochrane, Willard W., and Mary E. Ryan. 1976. *American Farm Policy, 1948– 1973.* Minneapolis: University of Minnesota Press.

Coleman, William D., Grace Skogstad, and Michael M. Atkinson. 1997. "Paradigm Shifts and Policy Networks: Cumulative Change in Agriculture." *Journal of Public Policy* 16: 273–301.

Coleman, William D., and Stefan Tangermann. 1997. "Linked Games, International Mediators, and Agricultural Trade." Paper presented at the annual meeting of the International Agricultural Trade Research Consortium.

Congressional Quarterly, Inc. *Congressional Quarterly Almanac.* Various years. Washington, D.C.: CQ Books.

De Gorter, Harry, D. J. Nielson, and Gordon C. Rausser. 1992. "Productive and Predatory Public Policies: Research Expenditures and Producer Subsidies in Agriculture." *American Journal of Agricultural Economics* 74, no. 1 (February): 27–37.

Destler, I. M. 1980. *Making Foreign Economic Policy.* Washington, D.C.: Brookings Institution.

Dixit, Avinash. 1996. "Special Interest Lobbying and Endogenous Commodity Taxation." *Eastern Economic Journal* 22, no. 4 (fall): 375–88.

Dobson, Wendy. 1991. *Economic Policy Coordination: Requiem or Prologue?* Washington, D.C.: Institute for International Economics.

Economist Intelligence Unit (EIU). 1995. "The EIU Guide to World Trade Under the WTO." London: EIU.

Epstein, Susan B., and A. Barry Carr. 1991. "If the Export Enhancement Program were Eliminated." Washington, D.C.: Library of Congress, Congressional Research Service.

Espy, Mike, and Alice M. Rivlan. 1994. Letter to Honorable E. (Kika) de la Garza. Washington, D.C.: Department of Agriculture, Office of the Secretary. 30 September.

Fain, J. R. 1920. "Presidential Address." *Journal of Farm Economics* 2: 4–8.

Fatseas, Nicole. 1996. *The Role of Special Interest Groups in Agricultural Policy: A Case Study of the 1995 Farm Bill.* Master's thesis. Virginia Polytechnic Institute and State University, Blacksburg.

Ferejohn, John A. 1986. "Logrolling in an Institutional Context: A Case Study of Food Stamp Legislation." In *Congress and Policy Change,* ed. Gerald C. Wright, Leroy N. Rieselbach, and Lawrence C. Dodd. New York: Agathon Press.

Finegold, Kenneth. 1982. "From Agrarianism to Adjustment: The Political Origins of New Deal Agricultural Policy." *Politics and Society* 11: 1–26.

Floyd, John E. 1965. "The Effects of Farm Price Supports on the Returns to Land and Labor in Agriculture." *Journal of Political Economy* 73: 148–58.

Food and Agricultural Policy Research Institute (FAPRI). 1992. "Implications of a GATT Agreement for World Commodity Markets, 1993–98: An Analysis of the Dunkel Text on Agriculture." Ames, Iowa: FAPRI.

———. 1995a. "Policy Options for the 1995 Farm Bill." Ames: Iowa State University, FAPRI, April 27.

———. 1995b. "Analysis of the United States House and Senate Agricultural Reconciliation Provisions." Working Paper 15-95. Columbia: University of Missouri, FAPRI, October 26.

———. 1996. "FAPRI 1996 Baseline Briefing Paper." CNFAP 9-96. Columbia: University of Missouri, Center for National Food and Agricultural Policy, May.

Frydenlund, John. 1995. "Freeing America's Farmers." Washington, D.C.: The Heritage Foundation.

"Gains and Losses in Final EU-15 GATT Schedules." 1996. *Agra Europe,* 8 March, E5.

Gardner, B. Delworth. 1995. *Plowing Ground in Washington: The Political Economy of U.S. Agriculture.* San Francisco: Pacific Research Institute for Public Policy.

Gardner, Bruce L. 1983. "Efficient Redistribution Through Commodity Markets." *American Journal of Agricultural Economics* 65, no. 2 (May): 225–34.

———. 1987. "Causes of U.S. Farm Commodity Programs." *Journal of Political Economy* 95: 290–310.

———. 1991. "Changing Economic Perspectives on the Farm Problem." *Journal of Economic Literature* 30, no. 1 (March): 62–101.

———. 1995. "Practical Policy Alternatives for the 1995 Farm Bill." In *Agricultural Policy Reform in the United States,* ed. Daniel A. Sumner. Washington, D.C.: The AEI Press.

———. 1996. "The Political Economy of U.S. Export Subsidies for Wheat." In *The Political Economy of American Trade Policy,* ed. Anne O. Krueger. Chicago: University of Chicago Press.

Goetz, Stephan J., and David L. Debertin. 1996. "Rural Population Declines in the 1980s: Impacts of Farm Structure and Federal Farm Programs." *American Journal of Agricultural Economics* 78, no. 3 (August): 517–29.

Goldstein, Judith. 1993. *Ideas, Interests, and American Trade Policy.* Ithaca: Cornell University Press.

Goldstein, Judith, and Robert O. Keohane, eds. 1993. *Ideas and Foreign Policy: Beliefs, Institutions and Political Change.* Ithaca, N.Y.: Cornell University Press.

Gopinath, Munsimay, and Terry L. Roe. 1997. "Sources of Sectoral Growth in an Economy Wide Context: The Case of U.S. Agriculture." *Journal of Productivity Analysis* 8: 293–310.

Grennes, Thomas, and Barry Krissoff. 1993. "Agricultural Trade in a North American Free Trade Agreement." *The World Economy* 16: 483–502.

Grossman, Gene M., and Elhanan Helpman. 1994. "Protection for Sale." *American Economic Review* 84: 675–708.

———. 1995. "Trade Wars and Trade Talks." *Journal of Political Economy* 103: 675–708.

Hagstrom, Jerry. 1995. "The Farm Team." *National Journal*, 1 July, 1705–9.

———. 1996. "Plowing a New Field: The 1996 Farm Law." *National Journal*. 4 May, 982–85.

Haley, Stephen. 1991. "The Export Enhancement Program: Prospects Under the FACTA of 1990." Baton Rouge: Louisiana State University, Department of Agricultural Economics and Agribusiness.

Hall, Peter A. 1993. "Policy Paradigms, Social Learning and the State: The Case of Economic Policy Making in Britain." *Comparative Politics* 25: 275–97.

Hansen, John Mark. 1991. *Gaining Access: Congress and the Farm Lobby, 1919–1981*. Chicago: University of Chicago Press.

Harrington, David, Gerald Schluter, and Patrick O'Brien. 1986. "Agriculture's Links to the National Economy." Economic Research Service Agriculture Information Bulletin No. 504. Washington, D.C.: U.S. Department of Agriculture.

Hathaway, Dale. 1963. *Government and Agriculture*. New York: Macmillan.

———. 1964. *Problems of Progress in the Agricultural Economy*. Glenview: Scott, Foresman.

———. 1994. "The Treatment of Agriculture in the Uruguay Round: Matching Expectations with Reality." Washington, D.C.: National Center for Food and Agricultural Policy.

Hellman, Ralph. 1995. "After You Left the Roberts / Gingrich Meeting on Friday." E-mail addressed to DEREG, 26 September.

Honma, Masayoshi, and Yujiro Hayami. 1986. "The Determinants of Agricultural Protection Level: An Econometric Analysis." In *The Political Economy of Agricultural Protection*, Kym Anderson and Yujiro Hayami. Sydney: Allen and Unwin.

Ikenberry, John. 1988. "Market Solutions for State Problems: The International and Domestic Politics of American Oil Decontrol." *International Organization* 42: 151–77.

Ingersoll, Bruce. 1996. "Congress Passes New Farm Bill That Dismantles Subsidy Programs after Much Vote Trading." *Wall Street Journal*, 1 April, A16.

International Agricultural Trade Research Consortium (IATRC). 1994. "The Uruguay Round Agreement on Agriculture: An Evaluation." St. Paul: University of Minnesota, Department of Applied Economics.

Johnson, D. Gale. 1947. *Forward Prices for Agriculture*. Chicago: University of Chicago Press.

———. 1973. *World Agriculture in Disarray*. London: Macmillan.

———. 1987. "Commentary." In *U.S. Agriculture and Third World Development: The Critical Linkage*, ed. Randall B. Purcell and Elizabeth Morrison. Boulder: Lynne Rienner.

———. 1991. *World Agriculture in Disarray* (Second Edition). New York: St. Martin's Press.

———. 1997. "Agriculture and the Wealth of Nations." *American Economic Review* 87: 1–12.

Johnson, D. Gale, Kenzo Hemmi, and Pierre Lardinois. 1985. *Agricultural Policy and Trade: A Report to the Trilateral Commission*. New York: New York University Press.

Johnson, Martin, Louis Mahe, and Terry Roe. 1993. "Trade Compromises Between the European Community and the United States." *Journal of Policy Modeling* 15: 199–222.

Jones, Ronald. 1971. "A Three-Factor Model in Theory, Trade, and History." In *Trade, Balance of Payments, and Growth: Papers in International Economics in Honor of Charles P. Kindleberger*, ed. J. N. Bhagwati et al. Amsterdam: North-Holland.

Josling, Timothy E. 1998. *Agricultural Trade Policy: Completing the Reform*. Washington, D.C.: Institute for International Economics.

Josling, Timothy E., Stefan Tangermann, and T. K. Warley. 1996. *Agriculture in the GATT*. New York: St. Martin's Press.

Kilman, Scott. 1994. "The Outlook: Some Farmers Favor Ending Crop Subsidies." *Wall Street Journal*. 21 November, 31.

———. 1998. "Crop Regulation Is Put to the Test in New Rural Crisis." *Wall Street Journal*, 9 November, 1.

Koester, Ulrich, and Ernst-August Nuppenau. 1987. "The Income Efficiency of Government Expenditure on Agricultural Policy." *Intereconomics* (March–April): 74–75.

Koester, Ulrich, and Stefan Tangermann. 1990. "The European Community." In *Agricultural Protectionism in the Industrialized World*, ed. Fred H. Sanderson. Washington, D.C.: Resources for the Future.

Kuhn, Thomas S. 1962. *The Structure of Scientific Revolutions*. Chicago: University of Chicago Press.

Lipsey, Robert E. 1994. "U. S. Foreign Trade and the Balance of Payments, 1800–

1913." Working Paper 4710. Cambridge: National Bureau of Economic Research.

Lugar, R. G. 1994. "Draft Questions for Comprehensive Senate Agriculture Committee Hearings on the 1995 Farm Bill." Senate Committee on Agriculture, Nutrition and Forestry, Washington, D.C.

Malmgren, Harald B. 1972. *International Economic Peacekeeping in Phase II*. New York: Quadrangle Books.

Manfredi, Eileen M. 1995. "CBO Testimony." Statement made before the Committee on Agriculture, Nutrition, and Forestry, March 16. Washington D.C.: Congressional Budget Office.

Maraniss, David, and Michael Weisskopf. 1995. "Aggies and the Road Gang Crunch the Numbers." *The Washington Post*. 26 May, A1, A20.

McConnell, Grant. 1969. *The Decline of Agrarian Democracy*. New York: Atheneum.

McLeod, Michael R. 1995. "Interview with Chairman Pat Roberts of the House Agriculture Committee." *Agricultural Law Letter*, January–February, 1, 11–12.

Melichar, Emanuel. 1984. "A Financial Perspective on Agriculture." *Federal Reserve Bulletin* (January): 1–13.

Moyer, H. Wayne, and Timothy E. Josling. 1990. *Agricultural Policy Reform: Politics and Process in the EC and USA*. New York: Harvester Wheatsheaf.

National Center for Food and Agricultural Policy (NCFAP). 1995. "Report of the Working Group on Price and Income Stability." 1995 Farm Bill Working Group Paper Series. Washington, D.C.: National Center for Food and Agricultural Policy.

Olson, Mancur, Jr. 1965. *The Logic of Collective Action*. Cambridge: Harvard University Press.

———. 1985. "Space, Agriculture and Organization." *American Journal of Agricultural Economics* 67, no. 5 (December): 928–37.

Orden, David. 1990. "International Capital Markets and Structural Adjustment in U.S. Agriculture. *American Journal of Agricultural Economics* 72, no. 3 (August): 749–54.

———. 1996. "Agricultural Interest Groups and the North American Free Trade Agreement." In *The Political Economy of American Trade Policy*, ed. Anne O. Krueger. Chicago: University of Chicago Press.

Orden, David, Robert Paarlberg, and Terry Roe. 1996a. "Can Farm Policy Be Reformed: Challenge of the Freedom to Farm Act." *Choices* (first quarter): 4–7, 39–40.

———. 1996b. "A Farm Bill for Booming Commodity Markets." *Choices* (second quarter): 13–16.

Organization for Economic Cooperation and Development (OECD). 1995. *Agricultural Policies and Trade in OECD Countries, 1994.* Paris: OECD.

Paarlberg, Don. 1964. *American Farm Policy.* New York: John Wiley & Sons.

Paarlberg, Robert L. 1985. *Food Trade and Foreign Policy.* Ithaca, N.Y.: Cornell University Press.

———. 1988. *Fixing Farm Trade.* Cambridge: Ballinger.

———. 1995. "Does the GATT Agreement Promote Export Subsidies?" *Choices* 10: 8–12.

———. 1997. "Agricultural Policy and the Uruguay Round: Synergistic Linkages in a Two-Level Game?" *International Organization* 51: 413–44.

Paarlberg, Robert, and David Orden. 1996. "Explaining U.S. Farm Policy in 1996 and Beyond: Changes of Party Control and Changing Market Conditions." *American Journal of Agricultural Economics* 78, no. 5 (December): 1305–13.

Patterson, Lee Ann. 1997. "Agricultural Policy Reform in the European Community: A Three-Level Game Analysis." *International Organization* 51: 135–66.

Penny, T. J. 1994. "The New Political Realities." In *Farm and Food Realities for the Twenty-First Century: Symposia Proceedings.* Washington, D.C.: National Center for Food and Agricultural Policy.

Pianin, Eric, and Guy Gugliotta. 1995. "Farm, Tax Cut Plans Leave GOP Shy of Budget Votes." *Washington Post.* 25 October, A7.

Pierson, Paul. 1994. *Dismantling the Welfare State? Reagan, Thatcher, and the Politics of Retrenchment.* Cambridge: Cambridge University Press.

Putnam, Robert D. 1988. "Diplomacy and Domestic Politics: The Logic of Two-Level Games." *International Organization* 42: 427–60.

Rapp, David. 1988. *How the U.S. Got into Agriculture and Why It Can't Get Out.* Washington, D.C.: Congressional Quarterly, Inc.

Rausser, Gordon C. 1982. "Political Economy Markets: PERTs and PESTs in Food and Agriculture." *American Journal of Agricultural Economics* 64, no. 5 (December): 821–33.

———. 1992. "Predatory Versus Productive Government: The Case of U.S. Agricultural Policies." *Journal of Economic Perspectives* 6: 133–58.

Roberts, Pat. 1995. "Opening Statement at the Public Forum on the 1995 Farm Bill Hosted by Agriculture Secretary Dan Glickman." Washington, D.C.: USDA, 31 October.

Runge, C. Ford, John A. Schnittker, and Timothy J. Penny. 1995. "Ending Agricultural Entitlements: How to Fix Farm Policy." Paper prepared for the Progressive Policy Institute, Washington, D.C.

Ruttan, Vernon W. 1984. "Social Science Knowledge and Institutional Change." *American Journal of Agricultural Economics* 66, no. 5 (December): 549–59.

Sachs, Jeffrey D., and Andrew Warner. 1995. "Economic Reform and the Process of Global Integration." *Brookings Papers on Economic Activity:* 1–118.

Sanderson, Fred H. 1994. "Agriculture and Multilateralism." Paper presented at a conference sponsored by the Institute for Agriculture and Trade Policy, Bretton Woods, N.H.

Schertz, Lyle P., and Otto C. Doering. 1999. *The Making of the 1996 Farm Act.* Ames: Iowa State University Press.

Schoppa, Leonard J. 1993. "Two-Level Games and Bargaining Outcomes: Why *Gaiatsu* Succeeds in Japan in Some Cases but Not Others." *International Organization* 47: 353–86.

Schleich, Joachim. 1997. *Essays on the Political Economy of Domestic and Trade Policies in the Presence of Production and Consumption Externalities.* Ph.D. diss., Virginia Polytechnic Institute and State University, Blacksburg.

Schleich, Joachim. 1999. "Environmental Quality with Endogenous Domestic and Trade Policies." *European Journal of Political Economy* 15: 53–71.

Schmitt, Eric. 1996. "House-Senate Committee Agrees on Overhaul of Farm Programs." *New York Times.* 22 March, A1.

Schuh, G. Edward. 1976. "The New Macroeconomics of Agriculture." *American Journal of Agricultural Economics* 58, no. 5 (December): 802–11.

Schultz, Theodore W. 1945. *Agriculture in an Unstable Economy.* New York: McGraw-Hill.

Shepsle, K. A., and B. R. Weingast. 1994. "Positive Theories of Congressional Institutions," *Legislative Studies Quarterly* 19, no. 2 (May): 149–79.

Shoemaker, Robbin, Margot Anderson, and James Hrubovak. 1989. *U.S. Farm Programs and Agricultural Resources.* AR-16. Washington D.C.: U.S. Department of Agriculture.

Sparks Companies, Inc. (McLean, Va.). *SCI Policy Report.* Daily newsletter.

———. *SCI Washington Report: 1995 Farm Bill.* Twenty-three occasional reports.

Spillman, W. J. 1927. *Balancing the Farm Output.* New York: Orange Judd.

Stigler, George J. (1988). *Chicago Studies in Political Economy.* Chicago: University of Chicago Press.

Stinson, Thomas F., Jay Coggins, and Cyrus Ramezani. 1998. "Was FAIR Fair to U.S. Corn Growers?" Presented at the Annual Meeting of the American Agricultural Economics Association.

Stuart, Kimberly, and C. Ford Runge. 1997. "Agricultural Policy Reform in the United States." *Australian Journal of Agricultural Economics* 41: 117–36.

Sumner, Daniel A., ed. 1995. *Agricultural Policy Reform in the United States.* Washington, D.C.: AEI Press.

Swinbank, Alan, and Carolyn Tanner. 1996. *Farm Policy and Trade Conflict: The Uruguay Round and CAP Reform.* Ann Arbor: University of Michigan Press.

Swinnen, Johan F. M. 1994. "A Positive Theory of Agricultural Protection." *American Journal of Agricultural Economics* 76, no. 1 (February): 1–13.

Swinnen, Johan F. M., and Frans A. van der Zee. 1993. "The Political Economy of Agricultural Policies: A Survey." *European Review of Agricultural Economics* 20: 261–90.

Thompson, Robert L. 1990. "The Food Security Act of 1985 as the Basis for Future Farm Legislation." In *Agricultural Policies in a New Decade*, ed. Kristen Allen. Washington D.C.: National Center for Food and Agriculture Policy.

Thurman, Walter N. 1995. *Assessing the Environmental Impact of Farm Policies.* Washington, D.C.: AEI Press.

Tweeten, Luther. 1989. *Farm Policy Analysis.* Boulder: Westview Press.

———. 1995. Testimony on "Farm Programs: Are Americans Getting What They Pay For?" Senate Committee on Agriculture, Nutrition and Forestry. Washington D.C.: March 9.

———. 1998. "Agricultural Policy at the End of the 21st Century," in *Increasing Understanding of Farm Problems and Policies.* Chicago: The Farm Foundation.

Tweeten, Luther, and Carl Zulauf. 1997. "Public Policy for Agriculture After Commodity Programs." *Review of Agricultural Economics* 19, no. 2: 263–80.

Tyers, Rod, and Kym Anderson. 1992. *Disarray in World Food Markets.* Cambridge: Cambridge University Press.

U.S. Department of Agriculture (USDA). 1987. "Who Gets Those Farm Program Payments?" *Farmline* 8, no. 1 (December–January).

———. 1989. *Western Europe Agriculture and Trade Report.* Washington, D.C.: U.S. Government Printing Office.

———. 1992. "U.S.-EC Oilseed Dispute Eases." *Agricultural Outlook.* AO-192: 18–22.

———. 1994. *Effects of the Uruguay Rround Agreement on U.S. Agricultural Commodities.* Washington, D.C.: USDA Office of Economics and the Economic Research Service.

———. 1995. *The 1995 Farm Bill: Guidance of the Administration.* Washington D.C.: USDA.

———. 1996. "A Close-Up of Changes in Farm Organization." *Agricultural Outlook* AO-227: 2–4.

———. 1998. *Agricultural Baseline Projections to 2007.* Report WAOB-98-1. Washington D.C.: USDA.

U.S. General Accounting Office (GAO). 1994. "General Agreement on Tariffs and Trade: Agricultural Department's Projected Benefits Are Subject to Some Uncertainty." Washington, D.C.: GAO Report to the Chairman, Committee on Agriculture, House of Representatives.

U.S. Statutes at Large. 1996. Vol. 110, pp. 888–1197. *Federal Agriculture Improvement and Reform Act of 1996.*

Van der Sluis, Evert, and Willis L. Peterson. 1994. "Do Cropland Diversion Programs Harm Rural Communities?" *Minnesota Agricultural Economist.* St. Paul: University of Minnesota, Department of Applied Economics.

Warren, George F. 1919. "Some After-the-War Problems in Agriculture." *Journal of Farm Economics* 1: 12–23.

———. 1928. "Which Does Agriculture Need—Readjustment or Legislation?" *Journal of Farm Economics* 10: 1–115.

Warren, George F., Jr. 1998. "The Spectacular Increases in Crop Yields in the United States in the Twentieth Century." *Weed Technology* 12. In press.

White House. 1995. "Press Release on Budget Veto." 6 December.

Wittman, Donald. 1995. *The Myth of Democratic Failure.* Chicago: University of Chicago Press.

Womach, Jasper. 1998. "Compensating Farmers for the Tobacco Settlement." CRS Report 98-133-ENR. Washington D.C.: Congressional Research Service.

World Trade Organization (WTO). 1994. *The Results of the Uruguay Round of Multilateral Trade Negotiations: The Legal Texts.* Geneva: The World Trade Organization.

Wright, B. D. 1995. "Goals and Realities for Farm Policy." In *Agricultural Policy Reform in the United States,* ed. D. A. Sumner. Washington, D.C.: AEI Press.

"Yeutter Vows Personal Involvement in Working Out Final Farm Bill." 1990. *Inside U.S. Trade,* 17 August, 20.

Young, C. Edwin, and Dennis A. Shields. 1996. "Provisions of the 1996 Farm Bill." *Agricultural Outlook.* Special Supplement (April).

Young, C. Edwin, and Paul C. Westcott. 1996. The 1996 U.S. Farm Act Increases Market Orientation." Economic Research Service Bulletin 726. Washington D.C.: U.S. Department of Agriculture.

Name Index